Eusebius of Caesarea (*c.* 260–339 CE) is (
intellectuals whose writings survive fror
made lasting and wide-ranging contributi _____ ___..._., ...ug
and apologetics to biblical commentary and Christian oratory.
He was a master of many of the literary and scholarly traditions of
the Greek heritage. Yet he left none of these traditions unaltered
as he made brilliant and original experiments in the many genres
he explored.   .

Aaron P. Johnson offers a lively introduction to Eusebius' chief
oeuvre while also discussing recent scholarship on this foundational
early Christian writer. Placing Eusebius in the context of his
age, the author provides a full account of his life, including the
period when Eusebius controversially sought to assist the heretic
Arius. He then discusses the major writings: apologetic treatises;
the pedagogical and exegetical works; the historical texts; the
anti-Marcellan theological discourses; and expositions directly
connected to the Emperor Constantine.

AARON P. JOHNSON is Assistant Professor of Humanities and
Classics at Lee University, Cleveland, Tennessee. He is the author
of *Ethnicity and Argument in Eusebius' Praeparatio Evangelica*
(2006) and of *Religion and Identity in Porphyry of Tyre: The Limits
of Hellenism in Late Antiquity* (2013).

Aaron Johnson is one of the best among the new wave of scholars who are giving us an entirely new way of looking at Eusebius of Caesarea. His book is far more than an introduction: it is a powerful, original and authoritative presentation of one of the most important contributors to the intellectual development of Christianity. Drawing on his impressive command of pagan philosophy, late antique culture and Christian theology, Johnson shows just how crucial Eusebius' works were and why, both in his own day and for future generations including our own.

—Averil Cameron, DBE, FBA, Professor of Late Antique and Byzantine History, University of Oxford, formerly Warden of Keble College

In his new book, Aaron Johnson explores the many facets of the amazing scholar–theologian, Eusebius of Caesarea – apologist, exegete, historian, theologian and encomiast. With his fresh and uncluttered approach, Johnson demonstrates how different facets of the bishop relate to each other, and builds up a credible picture of Eusebius that will surprise many.

—Andrew Louth, FBA, Professor Emeritus of Patristic and Byzantine Studies, Durham University, and Visiting Professor of Eastern Orthodox Theology, Vrije Universiteit, Amsterdam

UNDERSTANDING CLASSICS

EDITOR: RICHARD STONEMAN (UNIVERSITY OF EXETER)

When the great Roman poets of the Augustan Age – Ovid, Virgil and Horace – composed their odes, love poetry and lyrical verse, could they have imagined that their works would one day form a cornerstone of Western civilization, or serve as the basis of study for generations of schoolchildren learning Latin? Could Aeschylus or Euripides have envisaged the remarkable popularity of contemporary stagings of their tragedies? The legacy and continuing resonance of Homer's *Iliad* and *Odyssey* – Greek poetical epics written many millennia ago – again testify to the capacity of the classics to cross the divide of thousands of years and speak powerfully and relevantly to audiences quite different from those to which they were originally addressed.

Understanding Classics is a specially commissioned series which aims to introduce the outstanding authors and thinkers of antiquity to a wide audience of appreciative modern readers, whether undergraduate students of classics, literature, philosophy and ancient history or generalists interested in the classical world. Each volume – written by leading figures internationally – will examine the historical significance of the writer or writers in question; their social, political and cultural contexts; their use of language, literature and mythology; extracts from their major works; and their reception in later European literature, art, music and culture. *Understanding Classics* will build a library of readable, authoritative introductions offering fresh and elegant surveys of the greatest literatures, philosophies and poetries of the ancient world.

UNDERSTANDING CLASSICS

Aristophanes and Greek Comedy	JEFFREY S. RUSTEN *Cornell University*
Augustine	DENNIS E. TROUT *Tufts University*
Cicero	GESINE MANUWALD *University College London*
Euripides	ISABELLE TORRANCE *University of Notre Dame*
Eusebius	AARON P. JOHNSON *Lee University, Tennessee*
Homer	JONATHAN S. BURGESS *University of Toronto*
Latin Love Poetry	DENISE MCCOSKEY & ZARA TORLONE *Miami University, Ohio*
Martial	LINDSAY WATSON & PATRICIA WATSON *University of Sydney*
Ovid	CAROLE E. NEWLANDS *University of Wisconsin, Madison*
Pindar	RICHARD STONEMAN *University of Exeter*
Plutarch	MARK BECK *University of North Carolina, Chapel Hill*
The Poets of Alexandria	SUSAN A. STEPHENS *Stanford University*
Roman Comedy	DAVID CHRISTENSON *University of Arizona*
Sappho	PAGE DUBOIS *University of California, Berkeley*
Seneca	CHRISTOPHER STAR *Middlebury College*
Sophocles	STEPHEN ESPOSITO *Boston University*
Tacitus	VICTORIA EMMA PAGÁN *University of Florida*
Virgil	ALISON KEITH *University of Toronto*

EUSEBIUS

Aaron P. Johnson

UNDERSTANDING CLASSICS SERIES EDITOR:
RICHARD STONEMAN

LONDON · NEW YORK

Published in 2014 by I.B.Tauris & Co Ltd
6 Salem Road, London W2 4BU
175 Fifth Avenue, New York NY 10010
www.ibtauris.com

Distributed in the United States and Canada Exclusively by Palgrave Macmillan
175 Fifth Avenue, New York NY 10010

ISBN: 978 1 78076 555 6 (HB)
         978 1 78076 556 3 (PB)

A full CIP record for this book is available from the British Library
A full CIP record is available from the Library of Congress

Library of Congress Catalog Card Number: available

Text design, typesetting and eBook versions by Tetragon, London

Printed and bound in Great Britain by T.J. International, Padstow, Cornwall

CONTENTS

For b.e. (...with affection)

Preface

EUSEBIUS OF CAESAREA IS ONE of the most important intellectuals whose writings survive from Late Antiquity. His texts made deep and wide-ranging contributions in a number of fields of enquiry, from history-writing and apologetics to biblical commentary and Christian oratory. He was a master of many of the literary and scholarly traditions of the Greek heritage. Yet he left none of these traditions unaltered as he made brilliant and original experiments in the many genres he explored. The following pages seek to trace some of the most salient features of Eusebius' corpus as literary works. The issues of his reliability as a historian and scholar, with which much of Eusebian scholarship has been preoccupied, are here for the most part bracketed.

While the present book aims to introduce the general reader to his works, it does not avoid the attempt to push the scholarly conversation in new, hopefully beneficial, directions. In particular, in an attempt to extend several of the more fruitful trajectories in recent work on Eusebius, my discussion draws upon the following convictions. The first is that Eusebius was not a 'court theologian', and that it is severely misleading to see his writings as representative of an official imperial platform. Secondly, not only is it erroneous to identify him as being 'Arian' or a 'modified Arian' at any point in his life (including the brief period when he sought to assist Arius – even while, it is often forgotten, advising him to submit to his bishop at Alexandria), it is also misleading to see the Arian conflict as determinative of Eusebius' long-standing theological expressions. Thirdly, Eusebius was an original and creative thinker and writer who also aimed to pass on the traditions of the Church and of the ancient Hebrews. Modern exclamations of his unoriginality are themselves banal and do little to aid our appreciation of his diverse scholarly and literary contributions. Fourthly, Eusebius' incisive use of quotation in many of his works deserves continued study as a literary and pedagogical phenomenon in its own right, not just in terms of his accuracy or fidelity to the sources quoted. Fifthly, the historical and biographical works must be examined as literature; analysis of their accuracy or omission of historical fact, while important for the historian, must not displace a literary approach to these works as an end in itself. Finally, Eusebius' intellectual project was, at its most fundamental and pervasive levels, the envisioning of his Late Antique world in terms of the Bible, especially the Hebrew Scriptures (or Christian Old Testament). The Scriptures provided the fund of metaphors, words, characters, ideas, principles and narrative patterns by which to make sense of the world, nations, individuals and events of the fourth-century Mediterranean and beyond.

The sequence of the book is generally chronological, without always following such an order strictly (in any case, several works cannot be dated with precision). The first chapter, which introduces the age in which Eusebius was formed and offers an account of what we can know about his life and compositional activity, is followed by chapters on the major clusters of his writings: the apologetic treatises (Chapter 2); his pedagogical and exegetical works (Chapter 3); the historical texts (Chapter 4); the anti-Marcellan theological treatises (Chapter 5); and the writings directly connected to Constantine (Chapter 6). It is hoped that the reader is not under the impression that any of these categories can be neatly circumscribed. His late theological writings elaborated doctrinal concerns that we discover in his earliest works. His historiographical vision was pervasive and may be found expressed in his apologetic texts, commentaries and orations. A deep and meticulous conversation with the biblical writings informs every work that survives from his pen. At the same time, his wide-ranging dialogue with the philosophical culture of his own day and the Greek literary and intellectual traditions of the past is exhibited pervasively throughout his corpus.

This is an introduction to the texts of Eusebius, not to the scholarship on Eusebius. I have, therefore, sought to limit bibliographical references only to the most necessary texts. Especially in the case of the great number of important, provocative and often excellent works of scholarship in non-English languages that are rapidly extending our knowledge of the problems and possibilities of various approaches to Eusebius' corpus, this constraint has admittedly been painfully felt. I hope this book is received as a part of the ongoing conversation about Eusebius' works, not as the final word on the many issues that have arisen in that conversation over the course of the last century.

Acknowledgements

I HAVE ACCRUED SEVERAL DEBTS while working on the present volume. First, I am grateful to Richard Stoneman for the invitation to write the book and for his recognition of the importance of including an introduction to Eusebius in a series on 'Understanding the Classics'. Noel Lenski, as always, gave much needed advice and encouragement. Students of my Eusebius seminar provided a myriad of ideas and questions on a great many aspects of Eusebius; Kevin Lawrence, in particular, read and discussed portions of the Greek text of the *Commentary on the Psalms* with me. Skip Jenkins furnished opportunities to discuss Eusebius' theology in his graduate seminar on fourth-century theology. I am grateful to Paul Conn for allotting a Lee University President's Grant for continuing my work on Eusebius. Andrew Clay, David DeVore and Mark DelCogliano read individual chapters, while Jared Wielfaert read the entire manuscript, and gave astute advice on improving the presentation and argument. Remaining errors and shortcomings are due to my own recalcitrance or limitations. Randy Wood, Bob Barnett, Jared Wielfaert and Alan Wheeler provided encouragement and laughter at every stage. My wife and children, as always, have been my support. Without them, reading and writing would give me little pleasure.

I

CONTEXTS, LIFE
AND WORKS

UNLIKE THE SCATTERED BUILDING BLOCKS that now extend
from the beach into the Mediterranean Sea on the northern coast of the
modern state of Israel, the city of Caesarea in the third and fourth centuries
was a bustling metropolis of intense economic and Roman administrative
affairs that provided a space for intellectual and religious diversity. What
had once been a military fortress in the Hellenistic period was urbanized
and renamed Caesarea by Herod the Great in 22 BCE and had become one
of the most important cities of Roman Palestine by the time of Eusebius
(*c.* 260–339 CE). Syrian and Roman paganism flourished alongside strong
Jewish, Christian and Samaritan communities in this vibrant and richly
complex city, which formed a centre of power for strong men wielding
administrative, ecclesiastical or rabbinic authority.[1] At the same time, the
years of Eusebius' life saw his city and the larger Mediterranean world of
which it was a part pulled nearly to the breaking point by the dynamic inter-
play of centrifugal political, religious, social and economic forces. Roughly
a decade before his birth, the first systematic, Empire-wide persecution of
Christians sought to placate the gods by forcing the adherents of the rival

deity to offer sacrifice, in an attempt to ameliorate the troubled period now known as the 'Third Century Crisis'. Ever since the *Historia Augusta*, written in the fourth century and popularized inimitably in the modern period by Gibbon, the age has been represented as one of brutality, revolt, war, poverty, famine and plague.

Though based on the identification of very real problems, such a characterization nonetheless masks a more variegated range of economic and social factors throughout the Roman Empire and often occludes the flourishing of intellectual activity during this period. Eusebius was both the inheritor and the purveyor of intellectual and literary discourses of vast importance in the making of Late Antique thought.[2] It was in the contexts of crisis, persecution and the shocking shift in imperial religious policy under Constantine that Eusebius' literary habits and intellectual proclivities would be formed and find fresh and innovative expression as he began to rethink and reapply established genres in new ventures of thought and writing. Part of the reason that this period was able to provide the crucible in which Eusebius' thinking was shaped is that the 'Third Century Crisis' was arguably something of a misnomer – at least in some important respects.

Recent investigations have tempered the bleak image of the discord and disorder of the third century with a more nuanced account.[3] Economic troubles were not uniform, but varied in degree and duration by region. In the midst of foreign invasion, some cities grew, public figures advertised their importance in inscriptions, philosophers crossed the Empire in search of learning, and Christianity produced some of its greatest thinkers and saints. Gallienus, an emperor during Eusebius' early years, provides an instructive picture. After ruling jointly with his father Valerian from 253 to 260, he was unable to rescue or avenge him when the latter was captured by the Persian sovereign, Shapur I, and treated with humiliation as a human footstool until being flayed alive so that his skin could be stuffed and made into a trophy. According to an unflattering biography of the next century, Gallienus' reign was spent battling down usurpers, inadvertently allowing numerous northern barbarian groups to invade Asia, the Balkans and Italy, and engaging in unbridled vice and luxury. At the same time, the account admits that Gallienus was an accomplished orator and poet.[4] Another biography of the early fourth century offers a kinder picture: the emperor and his wife favoured philosophers and valued (at least in principle) the leisured pursuit of truth and virtue. None other than Plotinus, the 'father of Neoplatonism', would conduct his cosmopolitan school of intellectually and spiritually serious philosophers in Gallienus' Rome and earn the admiration of the emperor. This image combines with visual representations (such as statues and coins) of a holy emperor with an otherworldly look in his eyes.[5] Christians, too, felt his holiness when he favourably responded to Christian concerns over property confiscated during the persecution by his father.[6]

It was during Gallienus' reign that Caesarea would fall under the control of the short-lived but significant Palmyrene Empire.[7] When it became clear that the emperor was unprepared to redeem the captured Valerian, a chieftain of Palmyra in the region north-east of Caesarea named Odenathus stepped in to preserve Roman stability and interests in the East and keep Persia at bay. In spite of overtures by Odenathus and then, after his death, by his powerful wife Zenobia, Romans saw the Palmyrene control of the area as an illegitimate seizure of power, which was allowable only so long as Rome was too weak to deal with the two. Gallienus' successor, the emperor Aurelian, a devotee of Sol Invictus and the most successful of the emperors of the Third Century Crisis, would eventually defeat Zenobia and lead her in a triumphal procession through the streets of Rome. Though a woman, she fought like a man.[8]

Aurelian died a few short years after his triumph over Zenobia and was followed by a series of less successful, militarily beleaguered emperors who met violent deaths one by one at the hands of the next claimant to the throne. None of them made any recognizable impression on Eusebius until Diocletian, the man now credited with ending the Third Century Crisis, whom our author would later recall seeing when he visited Palestine.[9] Following the assassination of his predecessor, an act in which he was likely involved, Diocletian made the brilliant move of electing first one and then two more fellow emperors. The creation of this Tetrarchy ('rule of four'), consisting of two senior emperors bearing the title of Augustus and two junior emperors with the title of Caesar, provided legitimate imperial rulers across the span of the Empire from the British Isles to the Persian frontier. Along with a sustained attempt to stabilize the economy and reduce inflation, Diocletian made clear and active overtures towards attaining the divine goodwill. He and his junior emperor in the East, Galerius, claimed the patronage of Jupiter; the two emperors in the West, Maximian Augustus and his Caesar Constantius I, claimed Hercules as their divine protector. The coinage and sculptural representations of the Tetrarchy advertise an image of unity among the emperors and closeness to the gods.

As had occurred already in the reigns of earlier third-century emperors, the renewed *pax deorum* ('peace' or 'pact' with the gods) entailed a suppression of those elements within the Empire that threatened the working relationship between the Romans and their gods.[10] According to contemporaneous sources (Lactantius, a Christian rhetorician at the court of Diocletian, and Eusebius himself), persecution of Christians was fanned into flame by certain catalysts, such as when a Christian covertly made the sign of the cross during the sacrificial procedures at the court of Diocletian, or an oracle of Apollo complained that the Christians were a threat to his work, or pagan intellectuals presented anti-Christian arguments at Diocletian's court in Nicomedia.[11] While there may have been other motivations behind his persecution of Christians, and while we should not forget that the Empire never had the capacity to act as a police state and relied heavily on local men of power (what has been named a 'minimalist' view of imperial administration), or that sacrifice mandates may not have had Christians as their sole target,[12] the so-called Great Persecution (303–11, with resurgences up until 324) is still imagined today as a war of an oppressive state against Christianity alone. This impression remains largely shaped by Eusebius' narratives in the brief memorial of the *Martyrs of Palestine*, significant portions of the *Ecclesiastical History* and the first part of the *Life of Constantine*. The persecution came in phases: first the purge of Christians from the army and upper levels of the administration, then the seizure of Church property, and finally the imprisonment, torture and execution of ecclesiastical leaders and other Christians.[13] It persisted with varying levels of intensity through the retirement of the first two senior emperors (in 305) and intermittently until the last of the second generation of Tetrarchs, Constantine, the son

4

of Constantius, became sole ruler of the Roman Empire and put a stop to persecution once and for all.

We should be careful not to gloss over the unevenness of the persecution itself or of the persecuting policies. Physical brutality and bloody suppression broke out apparently only in certain parts of the Empire: especially the Near East, Asia Minor, Egypt and North Africa. In the West, Constantius limited himself to the closure of a few token churches.[14] If we trust Eusebius' account, he even protected Christians in his court and praised their stalwart courage.[15] Meanwhile, the son of another Tetrarch, Maxentius, restored Church property confiscated during the persecution after he had usurped control of Italy and North Africa.[16] Persecution was most heated in other areas of the Empire, in particular in close proximity to the emperors Diocletian, Galerius and Maximinus Daia (a Caesar of the next generation of Tetrarchs). Yet we are told that Diocletian's heart was not in the persecution (he had fallen under the sway of Galerius, who had become immensely popular and powerful due to a triumph over the Persians[17]), and even Galerius and Maximinus Daia – both known as the most virulent of persecuting emperors – renounced their policies of persecution before their deaths. It may be that their religious policies were exploratory moves groping at a solution to the impasse at which they found themselves. On the one hand, persecution may have been perceived as no longer effective in maintaining the peace and stability of the Empire. Though still a small minority, the Christians represented an itch the emperors could not adequately scratch. Or rather, the more they scratched the more chafed and raw the body of empire felt. Neither the emperors nor the elite inhabitants of the Empire were always or equally supportive of the religious assumptions or of the precise ways in which those assumptions should be implemented. Furthermore, Christians were finding new tactics for surviving the persecuting edicts. If the encyclical of Peter of Alexandria is any indication, rich Christians were allowed options other than confession, torture and death. One could force one's slave to suffer in one's stead (a confession by proxy), pay for an exemption or, if one wanted to impress fellow Christians as a brave witness, pay for a bogus torture session.[18] Persecution was not having its desired effect of aligning dissident elements, who stood as 'security threats' to the Empire, with Roman society.

On the other hand, the abandonment of persecuting policies by both Galerius and Maximinus Daia may have been less an honest admission of failure or wrong-headedness and more a strategic manipulation of their subjects' responsiveness to empire. The edict of toleration that has been entitled 'Galerius' palinode' was probably a successful move that rendered innocuous certain troubling tendencies that had manifested themselves during the persecution.[19] Christianity had been conceived and practised by many as a political alternative to the Empire, even while remaining within it. An incident that occurred in Caesarea in 303 reminds us that theological difference and spirituality were not neatly circumscribed domains: theology became (or already was) a political matter. At a governor's tribunal, a Christian named Procopius stepped forward and quoted Homer: 'The rule of many is not good, let there be one king.'[20] On a theological level his statement was a criticism of polytheism. But taken on a political level, it conveyed a deep criticism of the Tetrarchic form of government. His tongue was cut out before he was tortured and executed. By a singular shift in conception, Galerius and later Maximinus Daia sought through belated toleration to undercut such polarizing tendencies among Christians. No longer was Christianity deemed religiously other or bad for empire. On the contrary, it was reframed as a vital part of the imperial–religious complex.

The emperors' attempts at a conceptual shift in Christianity's role within the Empire were only partly successful. In times of tension, rival emperors after Galerius would choose to identify their political struggles as the conflict between rival gods.[21] Such a practice suggests a reversion to the traditional polarizing framework. When Licinius, the last emperor to fall before the advance of Constantine, adopted this strategy, his eventual defeat marked its definitive end (at least until Julian the Apostate in the 360s). Nonetheless, the experimentation in relativizing Christianity symbolized in Galerius' palinode remains a significant feature of the administrative processes that temper any singular approach to the problem of imperial religious ideology in the early fourth century.

The remarks offered here, insofar as they can be substantiated by closer analysis (in this book and elsewhere), produce a first step towards unsettling the established narrative of the reign of Constantine.[22] That narrative runs something like this: being born the son of Constantius, he was kept under the vigilant eye of the Tetrarchs Diocletian and Galerius in the East (in order to prevent a dynastic principle replacing the meritocracy of the Tetrarchs' government),[23] until he was able to finagle an agreement out of a drunken Galerius to join his father in Britain; Constantine hamstrung the horses of the imperial post as he hastened across the expanse of the Empire to avoid recriminations by the emperor when he sobered up; soon after arrival in Britain, his father died and he immediately found himself hailed Augustus (that is, a senior-ranking emperor) by the troops; after successfully stabilizing the frontiers in the north-west, he marched against the usurper Maxentius in Rome in an attempt to prove his own legitimacy as a Tetrarch; while Maxentius consulted the pagan Sibylline books, Constantine received divine admonition at midday (and again at night) instructing him to conquer in the sign of Chi-Rho (the first two letters of the Greek name for Christ); the sign was duly painted on his soldiers' shields and victory was achieved; this 'conversion' was followed by an edict of toleration (the so-called 'Edict of Milan', proclaimed jointly with another of the Tetrarchs, Licinius),[24] the commencement of church-building projects (most notably in Rome and later in the Holy Land) and involvement in the affairs of the Church (most notably in the hosting of the councils of Arles in 314 and Nicaea in 325, dealing with the Donatist schism and the Arian controversy, respectively); illness curtailed an attempt by Constantine to rescue persecuted Christians in the Persian Empire, and he was baptized before his death in 337; his burial place was to be 13th alongside the 12 Apostles in a huge mausoleum in his new capital city of Constantinople. Significant to this narrative is its unproblematic understanding of a conversion that represented a crucial turning point, an event setting Constantine apart as a Christian ruler who would begin to model a monarchic rule on earth imitative of the monarchic rule in heaven (that is, monotheism).

Such a narrative depends fundamentally upon an uncritical reading of the writings of Lactantius (who became tutor of Constantine's eldest son, Crispus, after serving as a rhetor under Diocletian) and Eusebius himself. One tendency of modern historians has been to distrust these accounts. The judgement of Jacob Burckhardt was severe: Eusebius was 'the first thoroughly dishonest historian'.[25] More recent historians have been gentler, but have often determined to begin their investigations of Constantine's reign with other sources before letting Eusebius speak.[26] The issue will be considered in later chapters on Eusebius' historical and biographical works. For the moment, we may accept that Constantine's conversion need not have been a singular dramatic event at one point in his life, but was a process of learning to tell his narrative and the role of the divine in his life over a series of years. Like a patient on an analyst's couch, Constantine probably told and retold his story to bishops and other Christians, learning to relate it in a way that was deemed appropriate and even therapeutic. Both Lactantius and Eusebius seem to offer snapshots of a retelling, which, in turn, are grafted onto their own narrations.[27] The actions of the emperor (such as building both churches and pagan temples, continuing to use pagan iconography while belatedly adopting the Chi-Rho monogram on coinage, or holding Church councils while closing only a limited number of pagan sites), combined with his own words, rhetorically overwrought though they may be (in his edicts, letters and orations), illumine the presence of narrative layers draped around his person like the jewel-encrusted regalia he wore at the Council of Nicaea. Part of Constantine's genius may have been his ability to create supple stories to answer the hopes and visions of rival constituencies in his complex Empire.

By the time of Constantine's death, it seemed that a sea change in the position of the Church in the Roman world had occurred. The representation of the reign of Constantine as the definitive Christian triumph over a dying paganism may, however, overstate the case. Resolute pagan senators in both Rome and Constantinople advocated religious tolerance, maintained meticulously their ancient heritage and perpetuated pagan rituals in the following generations.[28] Pagan intellectuals would dismiss the newly formulated theologies and spirituality of Christians, while practising rigorous immersion in philosophical texts combined with a gentle asceticism and a revivified spiritual vibrancy.[29] Furthermore, Christianity was not quickly or easily made coterminous with empire. What many today have labelled 'Constantinianization' – that is, the dual processes of imperial involvement in the affairs of the Church and the rise of an allegedly over-comfortable, mediocre or dysfunctional Christendom which replaced the radical religion of the early Christians – simplifies the diverse complexity of Christian communities and individuals before, during and after the reign of Constantine. Complacency had been a complaint levelled against groups of Christians since apostolic times, while the involvement of zealous emperors in ecclesiastical matters was often dampened by the austere firmness of bishops and holy men (beginning already under Constantine and continuing into the Byzantine Empire).[30] The label neglects the rugged independence exhibited by many Christians and overstates the case for direct imperial control of what was otherwise still something of a rogue Church. Constantine's reign did have significant impact on Christianity: a new fund of monetary and political resources became available to bishops, a diversification of the channels of social authority occurred, the visual, architectural presence of the Church began to stand out starkly against the urban landscape, and a new catalyst for violence arose. But the impact was variable according to local factors and personalities. In our attempt to assess Eusebius' literary and conceptual work we must be sensitive to the power of his carefully crafted representations, his construction of a Constantinian revolution and the fissures that exist between his portrayal and the polyphony of other voices and visions of Late Antiquity. Constantine's reign was somewhat different from the shaded image of Eusebius' portrait.

Following Constantine's death, a swift purge of all other viable candidates for the purple (except for two) left his three sons heirs to the Empire.[31] The Empire was divided among the three: Constantine II received the western regions, Constans the middle and Constantius II the eastern regions. Within a little over a decade, Constantius II would be the only surviving emperor. He would be compelled successively to elevate to the rank of Caesar the only two remaining relatives of Constantine: first Gallus, the son of Constantine's half-brother Julius Constantius (351–4), then, following Gallus' execution on probably trumped-up charges of conspiracy, the younger brother, Julian.[32] Julian would reveal himself as a pagan when he obtained sole rule (360–3) and would thereby earn himself the nickname 'the Apostate'. Eusebius, however, had died roughly 20 years earlier (c.339), when the young Julian was still reeling from the bloodbath that overtook his family at the hands of his cousins, Constantine's sons.[33]

Eusebius' depiction of the reign of Constantine's sons as a joyous time of peace under a 'trinity' of divinely graced rulers was, therefore, a rich and brilliant but deceptively thin veneer lying lightly over the more jagged realities. The fact, furthermore, that some elite, well-placed pagans (such as the Constantinopolitan senator Themistius) preferred life under the mild rule of Christian emperors to the polarizing world of Julian exhibits a continued vitality of paganism for which Eusebius' vision did not allow. But complaints of Eusebius' being the first 'thoroughly dishonest' historian will only predispose us to neglect his overwhelming contribution to the history of thought. We must, rather, be struck by the depth and tenacity of his vision's hold on a world that was not so easily tamed and his industry in crafting a new conception of a new age. As we shall see, his writings provided a comprehensive interpretation of his world through the words and world provided by Scripture, held in a creative counterpoise with the words and worlds of the classical heritage.

Intellectual Culture

The third and early fourth centuries were pivotal to the history of thought in the medieval West and the Byzantine East. Two fundamental nodes of creative energy lay in the areas of culture and metaphysics. From the beginning to the end of our period a breathtaking series of cultural engagements was performed by itinerant intellectuals. Already in the half-century before Eusebius' birth in the 260s, the Roman Near East had become a switchboard of philosophical currents transmitted from further east to the Mediterranean world. The centres of gravity lay not so much in Rome or Athens, though these belatedly received infusions of scholarly and intellectual energy from the East. It was, rather, Syrian Edessa, Apamea and Antioch and Alexandria in Egypt that pullulated with the production of knowledge, research and learned cross-cultural dialogue in what William Adler has aptly named an 'eastern sophistic'.[34] The politically involved yet philosophically and scientifically serious pair of easterners, Bardaisan and Julius Africanus, hosted embassies from India, exchanged books, collated magical knowledge (including an ancient equivalent of chemical warfare) and produced comparative ethnographic accounts, before moving (separately) to Rome where their vast learning was diffused into the imperial West.[35]

Despite the fact that both of these men were Christian (though their orthodoxy was deemed suspect by later generations), they typify the movement of ideas across empires, cultures and languages that would persist throughout the third century and into Late Antiquity.[36] It is a scholarly mistake to study pagan philosophers and other literati as though they pursued their literary, philosophical and religious labours untouched by the Christian thinkers who shared their world. As Peter Brown perceptively remarked: 'compared with the vast and menacing stretches of their own countryside and the new horizons of the barbarian world, a hair's breadth separated pagan and Christian members of the intelligentsia.'[37] Of course, some intellectuals sought to heighten the difference and fortify the boundaries of identity separating Christians from religious traditionalists and barbarians from Greeks. Diogenes Laertius exhibited an overt Hellenocentrism when he criticized those who found barbarian influences in Greek philosophy, claiming that the first philosophers were well-born Greeks and had no need to borrow an alien wisdom from outsiders. Philostratus bolstered claims to Greek superiority in both his *Lives of Sophists* and his *Life of Apollonius of Tyana*. Yet Philostratus had been involved in a literary circle around the empress Julia Domna, the powerful daughter of a Syrian priest whose grand-nephew, Elagabalus, later became both a priest of Baal and emperor of the Roman world. With a cosmopolitan range, she fostered a coterie of both pagan and Christian intellectuals in ways that would be imitated by other women of her family (including Julia Mamaea, who would host the great Origen himself.)[38]

The most important circles of scholarly philosophers of the third century, however, splintered off from a shadowy figure named Ammonius Saccas, a man claimed by both Christians and pagans as a philosophical authority and holy man. After studying with the Brahmans in India, Ammonius returned to his native Alexandria where he taught three of the most notable thinkers of Late Antiquity: Longinus, Plotinus and Origen. The fact that scholars today have posited the existence of two Origens, one a pagan and one a Christian (and even two different men with the name of Ammonius, again, one pagan, the other Christian), based on different sources describing Origen as studying with either pagans or Christians, only shows how deep is our own modern proclivity for categorizing too neatly the lives and identities of Christians as distinct from pagans.[39] In spite of sometimes rhetorically vitriolic debate, our evidence instead indicates close contact between Christians and pagans, who studied in promiscuous fellowship under the same teachers, shared strikingly similar values and often sought answers to the same ontological and theological questions within broadly resonant conceptual frames of reference. These three thinkers, together with Porphyry of Tyre, who was the student first of Longinus and then of Plotinus, were the most significant for creating the intellectual culture that formed Eusebius, and so we shall pause over each of them in turn.[40]

Eusebius was still a youth when Longinus joined Zenobia's Palmyrene court. Though we have a letter from Longinus to his former student Porphyry (who was living in Sicily at the time) inviting him to come to the East, we cannot ascertain the precise reasons for Longinus' move from Athens to the court of the eastern queen.[41] His execution soon after Aurelian's victory (in 273) indicates that he was a person of some significance at the court and not merely a disinterested scholar who happened to be in Zenobia's realms for other reasons.[42] His significance for appreciating Eusebius' life and works is twofold: he was the teacher of one of the most important pagan interlocutors for the Christian bishop (Porphyry) and he was the purveyor of a large cache of philosophical works to the East, which may have ended up in the library of Caesarea.[43]

Before his ill-starred decision to move east and accept Zenobia's patronage, Longinus had been a Middle Platonist philosopher and rhetor who guided a school of learned men in Athens.[44] Though we cannot with any firmness attach the well-known treatise *On the Sublime* to him (though some still do), precious indications of Longinus' literary acuity and philosophical seriousness survive from his student, Porphyry, who later moved to Rome to study under Plotinus. We discover that Longinus had brought together an energetic circle of erudite students. They investigated problematic words and passages in Homer's poetry, detected plagiarism of varying degrees in authors of the classical and Hellenistic periods, gathered knowledge of other peoples and their religious and cultural ways of life and commented on the texts of Plato. The philological and exegetical training instilled in Longinus' school would soon haunt the Christians when Porphyry turned the learning he acquired there onto the Christian Scriptures in his infamous *Against the Christians*. This would be a source of some consternation to Eusebius, who composed a response, *Against Porphyry* (none of which survives[45]), and quoted, alluded to or borrowed from a number of the works of the philosopher in many of his own writings, from the *Chronicon* to the *Ecclesiastical History*, *Preparation for the Gospel* and *Proof of the Gospel*.

Longinus is important, however, for more reasons than educating the most notorious anti-Christian before the modern age. He also brought with him to Zenobia's court a personal library containing a wealth of philosophical material, especially of Plato's corpus and the writings of Middle Platonist thinkers whose works and thought have only partly survived to the present. It has been suggested that Longinus' library made it into the hands of the Christians at Caesarea following its liquidation by the victorious Aurelian. As our single most important Christian source for Middle Platonism, Eusebius may have been the unintended heir of Longinus. If so, we are confronted with a rather crisp irony that, in many ways, epitomizes the age: the wisdom and learning, accumulated painstakingly by the great savant from Athens, was transmitted to Late Antiquity by the mutually hostile and alienated pair, Porphyry and Eusebius. If Eusebius was present at the beating of Porphyry by Christians in Caesarea (as a late report tells us), the irony would be all the more pointed.[46]

Even if Porphyry was not actively involved in the fomenting of persecution, some of his works might have been grist for the persecutors' mill.[47] Other works of the philosopher exhibit an intellectually serious, theologically acute and spiritually robust paganism.[48] Far from being on the wane, paganism in its various manifestations was scarcely a dead religion waiting to be brushed aside by the vivacious strength of Christianity. Not only were popular forms of pagan religion holding powerful sway at both the civic and imperial levels during the years of persecution, but a rarefied paganism conveyed a ponderous gravity and motivated a meticulous searching for truth at the scientific, philosophical and mystical levels in the theological systems of Porphyry and his one-time student Iamblichus. In spite of significant points of departure in emphasis and in formulation, both have received the not always helpful label of Neoplatonist. Whatever we take Neoplatonism to mean, any reader of Porphyry and Iamblichus must admit the necessity of reading them in conversation with Plotinus, one of the most significant philosophers from antiquity.

Plotinus, who may have studied under Ammonius Saccas before Longinus did, was a native of Egypt who moved from Lycopolis to Alexandria to study philosophy but then went to Persia in the entourage of an emperor, Gordian III (238–44), whose death may have come at the hands of his own troops rather than the Persians. Plotinus' motives for joining the short-lived Roman campaign may have been to fulfil a quest for learning eastern wisdom in imitation of Ammonius. After a gap in our knowledge of his whereabouts, the philosopher turns up in Rome where he started a school of a cosmopolitan texture. Students from across the Empire audited his seminars, where he pronounced on texts of Plato and Aristotle, counselled those pupils who struggled psychologically, provided financial guidance for others and sought mystical union with 'the One', a goal that was at the heart of his metaphysical and spiritual system. Yet, given that Plotinus died in loneliness at a former student's estate in Campania, one wonders whether his school was as popular as some of his students make out or recognized by his contemporaries at Rome as being the centre for the birth of what we now call Neoplatonism. He was attacked by Greek sophists, was denied the imperial resources to found a philosophical community (a Platonopolis), wrote (and probably spoke) in a broken Greek, was nearly deemed an incoherent and second-rate thinker by contemporaries (before receiving Porphyry's better-edited versions of his treatises), and saw his most promising students leave for other parts of the Empire before his painful death from gout (Porphyry was in Sicily at the time, while another prominent student named Amelius had moved to Apamea in Syria).[49] It may be that Plotinus' greatness was a post-mortem promotion by Porphyry, who possessed adequate editorial skills to revise his teacher's lectures (a task he had commenced before the latter's death, but which seems not to have been completed until 30 years later). Porphyry did more than correct infelicities in the Greek expression of the lectures; he also organized them according to a systematic, Pythagoreanizing structure in six books of nine essays each (hence the title *Enneads*, or 'nines') and added a biography, the *Life of Plotinus*, which was as much self-advertisement as promotion of his teacher's spiritual and pedagogical abilities.

Plotinus' metaphysical breakthrough represents the second node (beside cross-cultural exchanges) of intellectual energy of the third century. Reflection on the One that was 'beyond being' in Plato's thought led Plotinus to posit the One as an ineffable and utterly transcendent principle of which nothing could be predicated. In an ongoing procession arising from the sheer generosity and plenitude of the One, reality spilled out into lower, ever more diverse levels. The cascading ontological stream that opened below it contained Intellect and its thoughts ('intelligibles'), then the World Soul, and then individual souls who became implicated in the chaotic multiplicity of matter. Ascetic ways of life and a relentless chastening of the body's wayward impulses were necessitated by the philosopher's call to seek the higher levels of being. One could thus achieve intellectual escape from the material bonds that held the soul in the confusion of existence even while remaining in the body. Union with the Intellect and even, in a manner of speaking, standing on intellectual tiptoes and achieving union with the One was an aim sought through rigorous and austere contemplation. What his disciple Porphyry was able to attain only once, namely unity with the One, Plotinus experienced four times.[50]

It is difficult to determine the degree to which Plotinus' system and its mystical tenor were expressions of Ammonius' philosophy. If so, they manifested themselves little in Longinus' thought (so far as we can tell). Therefore, given the paucity of evidence to the contrary, Plotinus is credited with being the instigator of this creative mixture of metaphysics, theology and mysticism that has come to be known as Neoplatonism. It lay behind Porphyry's philosophical engagement with issues as diverse as animal sacrifice, religious iconography and divination. It also lay behind the divergent tendencies of Iamblichus, who developed a sacramental formulation of Neoplatonic ontology. In his *On the Mysteries*, this Syrian student of Porphyry emphasized the Platonic notion of 'participation' of lower entities in the higher levels of reality that were their sources. An ontological 'sympathy' bound together things of our physical world (bodies, stones, statues or magical symbols) to visible or invisible divine beings (stars and other gods).[51] The proper use and philosophical understanding of ritual became essential to his system. Theurgy (or 'doing the work of a god') became the province of the wise philosopher who required means external to his or her intellect to effect the salvation of the soul. Whereas Plotinus and Porphyry deemed the intellect sufficient in achieving its own salvation, understood as escape from the bonds of the material world, Iamblichus declared the necessity of divine grace through ritual acts that functioned in a sacramental way. We have little evidence to indicate that Eusebius even knew of Iamblichus or his thought, yet it remained an important element of fourth-century philosophy that was felt by the likes of Augustine and Pseudo-Dionysius.[52]

Christian thinkers were equally at the centre of the intellectual developments of the period. Unless a claim made by Eusebius is mistaken, the same Ammonius who was the teacher of Plotinus also had Origen as a student, and, unless Porphyry has chosen to speak of two Origens in his writings while refusing to distinguish them for the sake of later readers, then Origen too shared in the same Alexandrian scholastic context as Plotinus. Origen's impact on early Christianity and on Eusebius in particular cannot be overstated. He possessed the rare virtue of combining original and exploratory thought with meticulous research. His *On First Principles* may rightly be considered the first systematic theology of early Christianity. Organized around the central issues of the divine (Book 1), creation (Book 2), the relation of humanity to God (Book 3) and the Scriptures (Book 4), Origen's work formulated a comprehensive account of reality that rivalled and showed the marks of a conversation with the philosophical systematizations being developed in middle and Neoplatonic circles. In particular, Origen's elaboration of the doctrine of the Logos as creator, providential administrator and mediator would find strong echoes in Eusebius' theology.

Origen's contributions to the study of the Bible were likewise deeply important for the development of Christian biblical thinking in general and to Eusebius in particular. In addition to the production of numerous commentaries and homilies on many books of the Bible, Origen's most innovative and painstaking project was the Hexapla, a six-column version of the entire Old Testament. The first column contained phrases or verses in Hebrew script. This was followed in the second column by a transliteration into Greek, apparently in order to allow a Greek speaker to pronounce the Hebrew without having to learn the language or even the alphabet. The remaining columns contained the four main translations: the Septuagint (the 'LXX', or 'Seventy', to denote the 70, or 72, translators who allegedly made the translation under the patronage of Ptolemy II Philadelphus in the third century BCE), and those by Aquila, Symmachus and Theodotion. If further Greek translations were available to Origen, as in the case of the Psalms, he included them in additional columns.[53]

The result was a highly useful scholarly (and potentially polemical) tool for appreciating (or excluding) the range of possible renderings of the Hebrew original. While Origen may have intended the work as a step towards appreciating the value of learning Hebrew or the benefit of considering other interpretive options, this reference work may have aided the neglect of the Hebrew and the arbitrary adoption of whichever rendering fit one's argument against Jews or other Christians. The copying of the work would have been quite expensive and time-consuming, and, besides, the entire work would not have lent itself to easy use as a quick reference tool. At a time marked by the rise of smaller and more transportable textual forms of Scripture, the Hexapla, though it required composition in codex rather than scroll form, would still have been an unwieldy tome (or collection of tomes) to carry or consult. No complete version survives from antiquity. Eusebius himself remains the most important witness to the Hexapla, since he describes it in his *History*, while in his biblical commentaries he frequently made reference to the other translators' renderings and even the original Hebrew itself (always in transliteration, of course) – though it is difficult to assess the extent of his knowledge of the language.[54]

In many respects, Eusebius continued the intellectual project(s) of Origen.[55] He sought to expound the sacred texts historically, lexically and allegorically (see Chapter 2). He developed a theology and cosmology with the Logos at its centre (see Chapter 5). Like Origen, who had composed an apologetic work that combined point-by-point criticism and more general thematic arguments against a little-known critic named Celsus, Eusebius would likewise develop and greatly expand the apologetic tendencies in Origen (see Chapter 3). One of his preliminary steps in this regard was taken under the guidance of the single most significant figure in the preservation of Origen's literary heritage, Pamphilus. Together with his teacher, Eusebius composed an *Apology for Origen* before Pamphilus was martyred in 310.[56] In this joint work, many of the later features of Eusebius' corpus appear, from theological concerns to his quotational method of apologetics. Through Pamphilus' mediation, Origen had found an heir to preserve, modify and extend his intellectual project.

Origen lived during a time of 'crisis' in the Empire. He was imprisoned under the persecution promulgated by the emperor Decius, which had been promoted as a religious response to that crisis. Yet the third century was marked by a rich intellectual vitality and stands as one of the most significant phases in the intellectual history of those cultures linked to the Mediterranean (namely, the Western and Eastern Roman Empire, as well as the Late Antique Egyptian, Syrian, Armenian and Arabic east). Glinting with the likes of Origen and Plotinus – as well as other remarkable scholars and visionaries, such as Mani, Bardaisan, Cyprian and Porphyry – the third century is nothing short of dazzling in its brilliance of thought and creative genius. These individuals would provide the variegated conceptual world that shaped Eusebius, from whom he would learn so much, and against whom he would react with percipient intensity.

Life and Works

In spite of Eusebius' voluminous output and presence at some of the most memorable events of the age, especially the Great Persecution and the Council of Nicaea, we know little about the specific details of his life. For a man who was so quick to write about others, he is only too taciturn about himself. We presume, but cannot be certain, that he was born in the early 260s or thereabouts at Caesarea. We know that he was closely attached to his teacher, Pamphilus, even correcting biblical manuscripts at his side while the latter was imprisoned at the mines of Phaeno before his martyrdom. He seems to have spent some time in Egypt since he testifies to being present at the executions of some martyrs in the Thebaid.[57] Two works can be securely dated to the period of persecution: the *Chronicon* and the *General Elementary Introduction*. According to a complex but highly convincing argument (based on the detection of the correction of the dates of entries at the death of Constantius I), Richard Burgess has shown that any edition of the *Chronicon* cannot be dated to before 306.[58] Because the badly damaged beginning of the surviving portion of the *Introduction* (which went under the subtitle of *Prophetic Selections*) names the *Chronicon* as already written, it too cannot be assigned an earlier date. Because it describes persecution as ongoing and intense, it probably should be dated to the period of Galerius' persecution (*c*.310), though it could date to the peak of persecution under Maximinus Daia (313).[59]

Following a tenure of indefinite length as a presbyter (presumably of Caesarea),[60] Eusebius became bishop of Caesarea possibly as early as 313, a position he held until his death sometime around 339. He began composing his monumental double apologetic work, the *Preparation for the Gospel* and the *Proof of the Gospel*, sometime after the defeat of Maximinus Daia, since he refers to Licinius' trial and execution of Maximinus' henchmen at Antioch.[61] Because of theological language in these two texts that seems inappropriate to a post-Nicene context, especially the appearance of the phrase 'second God' as a label for the Son, the second person of the coeternal consubstantial Trinity (according to the Nicene Creed), and because they make no explicit reference to Constantine or the Council, they are almost universally considered to have been completed before 325. While an appeal to language is inconclusive[62] and the appeal to the emperor or his council is only an argument from silence,[63] the fact that the *Proof* makes allusion to ongoing persecution (which must, therefore, be that of Licinius)[64] lends weight to a date of completion before late 324.

The *Theophany*, which has clear parallels with the *Preparation* and the *Proof*, seems to be an abbreviated adaptation of those works (though for different audiences and different ends; see Chapter 3). The evidence for the date of its composition is likewise imprecise. A reference to the cult at Baalbek (or Heliopolis) as still functioning places the treatise before Constantine's suppression of that cult, though Eusebius' own discussion in the later *Life of Constantine* provides little by which we might specify the date of that occurrence except to place it after Nicaea (325).[65] Likewise, the treatise must date to a time before the construction of the Church of the Holy Sepulchre in Jerusalem (335), since the *Theophany* refers to the site without any mention of a church there.[66] As the author of an oration on that church, it seems unlikely that he would have mentioned the site, but not the newly constructed edifice there, after its dedication. On the other hand, the work can be dated after the persecutors Galerius and Maximinus Daia had successively issued recantations of their persecuting policies, thus sometime after 314.[67] If it does, indeed, base itself on the *Preparation* and *Proof* (rather than being their precursor, which seems unlikely),[68] the *Theophany* must have been written in the 320s or early 330s. We can be no more precise.

There has been wide divergence of scholarly opinion on the date of the *Ecclesiastical History*, stemming from the attempt to posit various editions based on the changing times through which Eusebius lived and his change of perspective throughout these transitions. Burgess' dating of the *Chronicon* to no earlier than 306 again has direct relevance, since, like the *Introduction*, the *History* names the *Chronicon* in its prologue.[69] Thus, earlier arguments for a pre-persecution (that is, pre-303) edition comprising Books 1–7 are no longer tenable.[70] The supposition propounded in some studies that Eusebius made supplemental additions to earlier books (especially the prologue of Book 1), as well as adding additional books to the now ten-book *History*, should be rejected as depending on unverifiable hypotheses about the author's attitude or concerns at precise moments in his life. Any sound dating of the *History* must place it after the 306 (or later) composition of the *Chronicon*.

Various arguments remain favouring either two or three editions, composed between the first half of the second decade of the fourth century and 326 (when Crispus, Constantine's first son, was executed, and his name removed from two passages in the tenth book). Each argument for multiple editions arises from an attempt to make sense of clearly identifiable patterns in the manuscript witnesses to the *History*, combined with varying assumptions about Eusebius' shifting perspective on events. It has not yet been recognized that all the phenomena can be adequately explained by positing a single edition dating to 324. Further considerations promoting a single-edition thesis will be offered in Chapter 4.

In the years before Nicaea, Eusebius also delivered an oration at the inaugural ceremonies of a church building in Tyre (in c.314 or c.316). The oration is quoted in full as the fourth chapter of Book 10 of the History. It describes the defeat of persecuting emperors by Christ, the 'tyrant-slayer', and refers to the 'supreme rulers' as trampling down pagan religion.[71] Because the plural 'supreme rulers' is used, it has been supposed that the date of delivery must have been at a time when Constantine and Licinius were on amicable terms. The precise nature of their relationship and, in particular, a date for their first conflict (the Battle of Cibalae) is not agreed on by all historians. What is missed in the controversy, however, is that the vague reference in the oration need have no relation to Licinius at all and hence have no bearing on determining the date of the imperial falling-out (or vice versa). The generalizing plural is common in panegyrical rhetoric[72] and could refer to Constantine alone, or in combination with his son(s), as readily as to Constantine and Licinius. The building probably could not be constructed, nor the oration delivered, during the repression of Christians in the latter years of Licinius' reign. A date between 314 and 320 is permissible; greater precision is impossible.

Before Nicaea Eusebius also came into contact with Arius (c.318 or c.322[73]), initially defending what he thought was his position (without adopting it entirely), and was put on a sort of theological probation in the spring of 325 at a synod held at Antioch.[74] He was present at the Council of Nicaea and may have given an opening address to the bishops gathered there (though, if true, this would have been quite odd – unless Constantine was dismissing his probationary status), and subsequently agreed to the Creed, justifying this move by explaining his interpretation of some of its key elements – in particular the catchword *homoousios*.[75] Since *homoousios* (a word probably chosen because of Arius' earlier explicit denunciation of it) only belatedly entered orthodox discourse in a significant way roughly 20 years after Nicaea, Eusebius' failure to use the term in his theological works is no indication of the sincerity of his acceptance of the Creed.[76] That he was not happy with some of the personalities at Nicaea, on the other hand, is clear from his participation in the removal of Eustathius from his see at Antioch in 327 – Eustathius' name was second only to that of Ossius of Cordova on the list of signatories of the document issued by the earlier 325 synod at Antioch, which had placed Eusebius on the docket for scrutiny at Nicaea.[77]

Between the Council of Nicaea and the death of Constantine, he received a request from the emperor to have copies made of the Scriptures for the Church in Constantinople, a request he claims to have fulfilled. It also seems to be in the decade following Nicaea that he composed two great biblical commentaries, on the Psalms and on Isaiah, apparently in their entirety. Because the latter work alludes to the imperial men genuflecting in church and the imperial destruction of idols,[78] and because it seems to show what Michael Hollerich aptly called a greater 'theological caution' in its avoidance of subordinationist descriptions of the relationship of the Son to the Father, the *Commentary on Isaiah* seems naturally to date to a period after 325. The *Commentary on the Psalms*, on the other hand, designates the Son as a 'second Lord' whose ontological and theological status was 'after the God over all'. The occurrence of such language has prompted some scholars to posit an earlier, pre-Nicene edition of the commentary. Two considerations should be kept in mind, however: first, while it may date to the pre-Nicene period, we now only seem to possess the post-Nicene version of the commentary; and second, as noted already in regard to the *Proof*, it may be inappropriate to suppose that Eusebius changed his language so quickly following Nicaea, especially when expounding texts that would lose their prophetic application to Christ altogether if a dual-Lord interpretation were avoided. In any case, claiming that the double occurrence of the word 'Lord' in Psalm 109, for instance, designated two distinct persons, the 'God over all' and a 'second Lord' need not presume a subordinationist doctrine in such a way as to be incompatible with Nicaea (the phrase 'second God' is, after all, avoided entirely). Furthermore, the language of two Lords seems to be limited to only two discussions in the otherwise massive *Commentary on the Psalms*.[79]

On the other hand, a theologically circumspect tone does seem to emerge in the Isaiah commentary that is lacking in the Psalms commentary. For instance, a line from Isaiah 48 that had received a short chapter of discussion in the earlier *Proof* for its double occurrence of the word 'Lord' was so loosely quoted in the *Commentary on Isaiah* that the word was given only once and no attempt was then made to find a 'second Lord' meaning for the verse. Such an elision certainly does seem to evince a firm avoidance of what had earlier been of some concern to Eusebius. Thus, while precision is impossible we are probably safe to take the *Commentary on the Psalms* as earlier than the Isaiah commentary. Further confirmation of this relative chronology is the mention of emperors (or at least, members of the imperial administration) genuflecting in church and their despoiling of idols from pagans in the *Commentary on Isaiah*, whereas the Psalms commentary briefly mentions only the practice of Holy Sepulchre pilgrimage, which seems impossible before Constantine's patronage of the site, but is not as striking as the other commentary's mention of imperial church attendance.

Just over a decade after Nicaea, Eusebius delivered a panegyric oration, the *Tricennial Oration*, honouring the emperor's 30-year anniversary in 336. In addition, he may have delivered a speech he had composed the year before at the dedication of the Church of the Holy Sepulchre in Jerusalem.[80] His travels first to Tyre (where an initial synod was conducted), then to Jerusalem and finally to Constantinople in 335–6 were closely tied to his involvement in ecclesiastical disputes regarding first Athanasius and then Marcellus.[81] The issue surrounding Athanasius involved the fiery bishop's behaviour, not theology, and we have little evidence of Eusebius' precise assessment of the man.[82] The case of Marcellus, on the other hand, was deeply doctrinal and we are fortunate to have two highly significant treatises laying out Eusebius' critique of Marcellus' theological position.

His *Against Marcellus* and *Ecclesiastical Theology* were both composed in the immediate aftermath of Marcellus' deposition following the synod at Constantinople in 336.[83] The ending of the *Against Marcellus* declares Eusebius' intention to answer those who supposed that Marcellus had been wronged by the bishops gathered there.[84] No doubt it would have carried the additional force of justifying his own prominent role in the anti-Marcellan movement. The *Ecclesiastical Theology* was clearly written after the *Against Marcellus*, since its dedicatory epistle (addressed to Flacillus of Antioch) as well as its prologue explicitly name that work and claim that the present one, comprising three books to reflect the blessed Trinity, would go beyond the mere quotation of damaging passages from Marcellus' work to offer a thorough refutation of his views from Scripture.[85] It seems likely that its composition was completed before the emperor's death (in 337), though we cannot be certain.[86]

The *Life of Constantine*, whose attribution to our author was once seriously doubted, was composed shortly following the death of its subject and the deaths of the other competitors for the throne at the hands of the three sons of Constantine. Its prologue claims that Constantius II, Constantine II and Constans reigned as a trinity on earth modelled on the Trinity in heaven. Eusebius finished it sometime before his own death two years later (*c.*339),[87] and thus before he could see the dissolution of this trinity when Constantine II attacked but was killed by Constans (in 340).[88]

At the time of his death, Eusebius had left an extensive corpus of writings that contained contributions in a number of areas of intellectual enquiry and made substantial exploratory efforts in several genres. Pedagogical manuals and commentaries stand alongside encomiastic orations, various innovative historical works and apologetic treatises. Even if the literary aesthetic that fostered large-scale use of quotation is not to our taste, Eusebius possessed a literary vision that was at once careful and creative.[89] The following chapters seek to trace some of the rich texture and dynamic movement of the products of that vision especially as they might play off earlier literary discourses, even if in tenuous or broken refractions. After all, Eusebius was no idle imitator of his predecessors.

II

DEFENDING
THE FAITH

A SIGNIFICANT PORTION OF EUSEBIUS' literary output consists of apologetic writings, though apologetic tendencies can be found in a wider range of his works. He composed a massive *Against Porphyry* in 25 volumes (now entirely lost), the apologetic 'diptych' of the 15-book *Preparation for the Gospel* and its sister the 20-book *Proof of the Gospel* (roughly half of which survives), the shorter, five-book *Theophany* and the even briefer *Oration on Christ's Sepulchre* (discussed in Chapter 6).[1] It is difficult to date the *Against Porphyry* and *Theophany*, but the consensus has been that the former is the earliest of the apologetic works, that the diptych was composed later, and that the *Theophany* was produced later still, as something of an abbreviated version of that diptych, forming a more manageable treatise than the massive double work (five books instead of the 35 that make up the *Preparation* and *Proof*). In each of these works, Eusebius had precise aims, and particular problems that he sought to address. In spite of a good deal of overlap between the *Theophany* and the *Preparation* and *Proof*, these works are not merely echoes of each other or simple variations on a theme. Both as literature in a general sense and as apologetic treatises, they made important contributions to the literary culture of the fourth century.

The Preparation for the Gospel *as Apologetic*

The *Preparation for the Gospel* strikes modern students with the oddity of what appear to be its quotational excesses and lack of creative or original thought. One commentator has quipped: 'The reader lays [it] aside [...] not without a sense of relief.'[2] Even if read against the backdrop of the widespread quotational tendencies in earlier apologetic literature (which began among pagans of the classical period with Isocrates' *Antidosis* and continued through the Christian apologies of Origen and Lactantius), Eusebius comes across as a bookish curmudgeon whose many hours in the library have caused him to lose all sense of proportion and literary tact. The 15 books of the *Preparation* took a good thing too far: since 71 per cent of its pages are direct quotation it would appear to have reduced its stature as an intellectual product to a mere anthology and its usefulness has seemed to many to be limited to its preservation of sources that would otherwise be lost to us. Eusebius has thus been seen as a second-rate thinker, whose display of erudition fails because of what are alleged to be loosely connected and poorly ordered sequences of quotations, which comprise inappropriately lengthy fragments from source texts.

Such a reaction to the *Preparation* is, however, too severe and exhibits a failure to appreciate the ways in which it participated in a broader cultural shift in aesthetic sensibilities, which valued the juxtaposition of traditional units of previous art or literature into new composite wholes evincing what has been called elsewhere a 'cumulative aesthetic'. Like the constructors of the Arch of Constantine at Rome, which was composed of panels from the times of Trajan, Hadrian, Marcus Aurelius and Constantine, Eusebius sought to produce in the *Preparation* (as well as many other texts) a monumental work of accumulation and contrast of varied older units, and so created a text containing a collage of quotations from other sources within its pages.[3] This is an important context, but it is not, however, the only means of gaining a better appreciation of Eusebius' work. Beyond this aesthetic milieu, the *Preparation* placed itself within other ancient discursive contexts that deepen our understanding of its quotational prolixity. The work is a fascinating literary experiment of a character at once creative, wide-ranging, judicious and thoughtful.

Two further approaches offer themselves as beneficial in properly accounting for this apologetic treatise. The first will receive greater attention in the next chapter and it suffices only to state it briefly here: the *Preparation* was conceived as an educational textbook for part of a larger pedagogical project. Its extensive use of quotation can only partly be explained by the use of quotation in earlier apologetic writings. Since Eusebius had openly stated that it was to be an 'introduction' (*eisagōgē*) for students,[4] comparison with other such introductory textbooks produced by philosophical teachers is thus the proper context within which to understand the work. Just as an introduction might quote the base text and then provide directives on the proper interpretation of the quoted material, so the *Preparation* contained lengthy quotations with Eusebius' commentary on how a Christian should understand such texts. This does not mean that the *Preparation* was not also intended as apologetic (he himself calls it an apologia) – but it was an apologetic couched within a pedagogical programme.[5] The treatise would thus form an integral component, along with the works to be discussed in the next chapter, of a wide-ranging and powerful curriculum for Christian students. The *Preparation* taught the apprentice reader how to approach the literature of the Greek heritage, while those other works targeted the literature of the ancient Hebrews.

The second approach seeks to identify the larger lines of argument that unite the work into a coherent whole. Such an investigation moves beyond a representation of the work as a composite of awkwardly stitched together quotations that make up crudely conjoined sections addressing a disparate range of polemical issues.[6] The fact that Eusebius continues to remind his reader of the arrangement of the whole, at the very least should prohibit any characterization of the *Preparation* as a disjointed series of arguments. Instead, the work constructs a wide-ranging, world-historical metanarrative, which, through its very telling, stands as its own apologetic argument. In particular, the metanarrative of the *Preparation* comprises the interwoven narratives of ethnic descent of the greatest nations of Eusebius' world, especially the Greeks, whom he saw as his primary antagonists.

In a programmatic passage in the preface he lays out a two-pronged accusation against the Christians by two imaginary critics, one from each of the two primary sources of opposition, the Greeks and the Jews, in a way Eusebius deemed would be most fitting for establishing the framework and major components of the apologetic argument to follow.

> What then may the strangeness in us be, and what the newfangled manner of our life? And how can men fail to be in every way impious and atheistical, who have apostatized from those ancestral gods by whom every nation and every state is sustained? [...] And what forgiveness shall they be thought to deserve, who have turned away from those who from the earliest time, among all Greeks and barbarians, both in cities and in the country, are recognized as gods with all kinds of sacrifices, and initiations, and mysteries by all alike, kings, lawgivers and philosophers, and have chosen all that is impious and atheistical among the doctrines of men? And to what kind of punishments would they not justly be subjected, who deserting the customs of their forefathers have become zealots for the foreign mythologies of the Jews, which are of evil report among all men? [...] Nay, [they do] not even adhere to the God who is honoured among the Jews according to their customary rites, but cut out for themselves a new kind of track in a pathless desert, that keeps neither the ways of the Greeks nor those of the Jews.[7]

This accusation of double apostasy on the part of Christians highlighted the contours of what non-Christian critics considered a problematic identity. Christians had rejected their ancestral (Greek) traditions, on the one hand, but then had misappropriated the Jewish Scriptures, renouncing (the Jewish interpretation of) the Law of Moses, on the other. Though many have thought this passage derives from or summarizes Porphyry's infamous *Against the Christians*, there is little reason to believe that Eusebius is thinking of that treatise (to which he had elsewhere responded in 25 books, according to Jerome).[8] Both edges of the double-apostasy theme had, in any case, been raised in various ways by earlier anti-Christian polemicists (especially Celsus, but also Diognetus) and were likewise representative of many discussions in Christian texts. Porphyry may, in fact, represent a shift away from the widespread anxiety over apostasy from ancestral traditions (rather, *apostasis* and its cognate forms bear a positive valence in works such as Porphyry's *On Abstinence from Eating Meat*).[9] His persistent elevation of and focus upon the austere life of the true philosopher left little room for the ethnocentric assumptions lying behind the pagan defence of Greek superiority over Christianity's 'barbarian' allegiances (namely, its bestowal of authoritative status upon the Hebrew Scriptures and worship of the Jewish Jesus as divine). Instead, Porphyry held the Jews in a consistently high regard in his other works, citing both Josephus and Genesis favourably. In spite of Adolf von Harnack's collection of many 'fragments' of Porphyry's *Against the Christians* under the rubric of 'Criticism of the Old Testament', one is hard-pressed to find criticism of the Hebrew writings as such (as opposed to Christian interpretations of those writings) in the material that can firmly be attributed to Porphyry.[10]

If the passage from Eusebius' preface belongs to Porphyry, we must admit that the latter not only allowed himself to diverge from his basic cultural and philosophical tendencies for the sake of his religious polemic but also that he then merely repeated and affirmed the basic components of popular discomfort towards Christianity felt by many pagans, from Celsus in an earlier century to Maximinus Daia only a few years before the composition of the *Preparation*. The problematic status of the Christians resided for these pagans in issues of racial and cultural identity. Especially following the conquests of Alexander the Great (though already present before), the precise relationship and cultural status of the various nations (*ethnē*) who had been brought so swiftly into confrontation and comparison with each other had become a matter of great import. Works of a historical, scientific, philosophical and literary nature continually maintained or shifted ethnic conceptions along an axis of particularism at one end and universalism on the other. Ethnographic data (of varying value by modern standards) was compiled, classified and exploited.

Representatives of barbarian peoples defended the greater antiquity and cultural achievements of their ancestors against rival claims to ethnic superiority. If the Greeks were no more than children beside their cultural elders and had only belatedly come to share in the contributions made to world history by the grand and ancient civilizations of Egypt, Syria or elsewhere, then their assertions to be the legitimate purveyors of high culture (*paideia*) rang hollow. If, on the other hand, the Greeks had only gathered scattered bits of wisdom, art or learning from the barbarian nations in order to improve upon them – in order to perform cultural or philosophical tasks that inferior races were unable or too confused by superstition or irrationality to pursue – then a Hellenocentric smugness could be maintained. The Greeks, in a manner of speaking, would have to help those who could not help themselves – as Plutarch in the second century made explicit when alleging the need to narrate an Egyptian myth in a proper philosophical way in order to salvage its truths from the barbarian, native forms of telling it.[11]

Even if one sought to avoid the sharper cultural engagements or abrasive formulations of racial or cultural superiority, the fundamental pull of piety (*eusebeia*) remained deeply rooted. Unlike later notions of individualized religiousness, classical conceptions of piety tightly linked together devotedness to the gods with filial fidelity to one's fathers and one's fatherland. Rejection of the constellation of practices and cult acts, which had served so well to rivet a community's relationship with the gods and each other and held the weight of a venerable antiquity, was deemed a grave error that brought serious, even catastrophic, consequences. Both civic and imperial religion, with their heavy layers of historical narratives, calendrical structures, ritual acts and sacred spaces, were held by an encumbering inertia.

And so, even if one was not pulled into the contestation between Greeks and barbarians over ethnic superiority, there remained an acute anxiety when faced with a person who overtly and even ostentatiously turned aside from the traditions and the gods of their forefathers. A quiet neglect might receive admonition, but at least was less dangerous than outright apostasy. It was not only Christ's death that was 'foolishness' to the Greeks (1 Corinthians 1:18–23). Beyond the apparent absurdity of worshipping a victim of crucifixion, Christians had allowed adherence to Christ to supplant their ancestral allegiances and ethnic identities. We need not believe that all early Christians were equally radical in their withdrawal from such identities to recognize the strength of the rhetorical representation, whether articulated by critics or believers, and its unsettling discursive power within conceptual frameworks in which piety, race and history were integral components. It is precisely within this racial, religious and cultural problematic that Eusebius chose to situate his apologetic project.

Porphyry may not have shared the concerns over popular piety or public religious expressions. There remained nonetheless an assumption lying behind the double-apostasy theme in Eusebius' preface that Porphyry would have shared. All interlocutors, whether the pagan traditionalists, otherworldly philosophers like Porphyry, or Christian intellectuals like Eusebius, held a historiographical notion that posited an original truth which had become fragmented over generations of progressive moral decline and rising sophistry.[12] The narrative assumption that the history of ideas conveyed a decline from ancient wisdom to present-day confusion found expression in Porphyry's accounts of eating habits (from primitive vegetarianism to contemporary gluttonous meat diets) in the *On Abstinence* as well as in Eusebius' *Preparation*. Indeed, the latter developed a sophisticated response to pagan accusations of double apostasy by constructing a narrative argument that simultaneously addressed the criticism that Christians required a blind and unthinking faith in their adherents and hence the supposition that they were ignorant of Greek philosophy and letters; the presumption that Christianity's withdrawal from ancestral ways was foolish and impious; the related notion that the gods of the nations and city-states were the true benefactors of humanity; the bias against barbarian peoples, in particular the ancient Hebrews; and lastly the twin ideas that posited Christianity's misappropriation of the Jewish Scriptures against the legitimacy of Jewish interpretations of those Scriptures. A complex narrative of decline undergirded Eusebius' answer to the sets of accusations of both the Greeks and the Jews.[13]

Against the Greeks

The narrative of the *Preparation* can be briefly stated. Among the most ancient nations of the world the original forms of religious life involved the worship of the stars and other heavenly phenomena. There were not yet any myths, animal sacrifices or visual iconography in this purer form of polytheism.[14] Only to the ancient Hebrews was knowledge of God granted through visions and oracles – what later Christian thinkers would label 'special revelation'. In the Hebrews alone were true rationality and piety embodied, so that they sagely looked past the visible luminaries to their Creator, recognizing the rational necessity of positing a divine administrator behind the order displayed in the regular movements of the heavens.[15] In contrast, the other nations, typified most extensively by the Phoenicians and Egyptians, fell away from their primitive astral religion and began to worship humans who had gained high esteem for their benefactions to civilization (such as the introduction of agricultural arts) or who were notorious for their great power and unforgettable deeds (such as sacrificing their children in an attempt to stop famine).[16] In spite of the several accounts of rulers, inventors, founders and benefactors in this narrative, Eusebius persistently reminded the reader of the great flow of history away from astral polytheism to greater levels of moral and spiritual confusion with the introduction of an ever greater number of deities whose sordid lives and ignorance of the one true God vitiated their accomplishments and discoveries.

Absent from the earliest periods of history and its culture heroes were, significantly, the Greeks.[17] Repeated asseverations of their lateness and ignorance highlighted a lack that was fundamental to Greek identity. Chronological investigations combined with the study of the histories of barbarian peoples proved the belatedness and inadequacy at the very origins of the Greeks whose *paideia* had been so touted for generations by their own historians and thinkers.[18] Their primal lack had instead forced the ancient Greeks to steal the historical narratives of more ancient nations, in particular the Phoenicians and Egyptians, misunderstand them, and reformulate them as their own myths – only later to feel embarrassment at the immoral and irrational elements in those tales and so seek to allegorize them.[19]

The nadir of national, especially Greek, decline was reached, according to Eusebius' narrative, when wicked daemons attached themselves to the cultic confusion prompted by the worship of humans and the proliferation of stories and cult acts memorializing them. Hovering like flies around the blood and smoke of animal sacrifices, daemons encouraged the slaughter, theological confusion and immorality through oracles that (mis)informed the human consultants about the nature of the divine world and the sorts of worship required to receive the desired responses from the divine.[20] The conception of fate that lay behind the giving and receiving of oracles was faulty on philosophical and moral grounds.[21] Not only did fatalism inadequately account for secondary forms of causation to all actions, but it denied the Providence of God, which both governed the universe according to rational laws and granted humans the dignity and responsibility of free will.

In this narrative of decline, a single individual sought (albeit unsuccessfully) to break away from the progressively more irrational and corrupt movements of the history of nations, and that was Plato.[22] In spite of Eusebius' (only partly persuasive) assurances that he was hesitant to malign the great philosophical master, the *Preparation* sought to show that Plato's efforts to resist the increase in Greek inferiority and ignorance remained only a hiccup in cultural and theological fragmentation. His own writings contained the bad intermingled with the good,[23] and his followers quickly reduced his great system to fractured and incoherent splinters in their inter- and intra-scholastic debates. Books 14 and 15 of the *Preparation* are replete with an incessant and lavish layering of quotations exhibiting the discord among the generations of both Presocratic and post-Platonic philosophers.

Framed within the clear contours of the decline of nations, this hiccup of Plato in the Greek history of ideas represents one of the fascinating achievements of the *Preparation*. Books 11–13 provide the reader with the most sustained and forthright comparison of Plato's philosophy and biblical thought in all antiquity. In order to prove that Plato took all the good elements of his thought from the Hebrew Scriptures, Eusebius sets passages of the two literary corpora side by side for nearly 200 pages. Two salient features of this comparison strike the reader. The first is that the quotations are not limited to passages of Plato alone but include Plato's latter-day interpreters, such as Numenius, Atticus, Porphyry and Plotinus. This inclusion of later Platonists should not surprise. Given the scholastic contexts of both Eusebius' writing and the broader reading of Plato's texts in the third and fourth centuries (as we shall see in the next chapter), the incorporation of learned commentators on Plato would have lent a good deal of credibility to Eusebius' claims. The modern reader is tempted to raise a sceptical eyebrow and wonder if Eusebius thought his audience gullible enough to believe that Platonic passages of varying thematic closeness to the Bible indicated borrowing or even outright translation by the Greek philosopher from Hebrew wellsprings. The apologist had, in fact, gradually moved from general assertions that Plato and the Bible possessed similar ideas to declarations of borrowing, and finally statements that Plato was 'all but translating' the words of Moses into Greek.[24] Modern suspicions may only obscure the power of this portion of the *Preparation*. An earlier genera-tion of Christian intellectuals had already found the great Neopythagorean Numenius remarking that Plato was only a 'Moses speaking Attic Greek',[25] and many thinkers within imperial Platonism were open to the benefits of eastern wisdom and imagined philosophers of their own and earlier times sojourning among barbarian nations as far away as India. Eusebius' appeal to Platonic commentators of eastern origin and barbarian sympathies, such as Numenius the Syrian, Plotinus the Egyptian and Porphyry the Phoenician, could well have formed a persuasive confirmation of Plato's travels and intellectual dependencies.[26]

Secondly, Eusebius' quotations from Plato and his commentators loom large in terms of their sheer size in comparison with the biblical passages beside them. Some of the latter quotations extend to several lines or nearly a paragraph, but they are often much shorter, consisting of a single short sentence or phrase. Several times Eusebius dispenses with direct quotation from the Scriptures altogether and merely provides a brief summary of a passage. Quotations from Plato or his successors, by contrast, may run for several pages, interspersed with only the briefest of notes where Eusebius has opted to omit some material.[27] This disparity in the amount of quoted texts from the two sources highlights the status of the biblical texts as 'classics' for Christian readers. In the same way that Aulus Gellius in *Attic Nights* (itself a quotation-heavy work, which the author had labelled a 'literary storehouse') limited his quotations from the authoritative Virgil to short snippets since longer quotations of the great poet would have been unnecessary to his well-educated audience, but quoted at length from sources that were less ready to hand or obscure to his audience, Eusebius' short biblical quotations and long Platonic excerpts indicate a proposed audience of those already steeped in the Scriptures who were less well versed in Plato.[28]

Another possible explanation for this quotational phenomenon in the biblical–Platonic comparisons might lie in the author's ostentatious impulse to exhibit the thoroughness of his own learning in philosophical matters. After all, a complaint of pagans had been the intellectual inadequacies of 'the faithful'. The barrage of massive quotations from the great Plato himself, attended by his later imperial-age commentators, would have overwhelmed the supercilious pagan who dismissed Christians as unlearned. Whatever Eusebius' exact motives in adopting the citational methods, the *Preparation* marks an exquisite literary manifestation of the 'cumulative aesthetic' mentioned above. Eusebius' readers likely shared the taste developed in the fourth century for the composite, for pastiche, for bricolage.

Plan(s) of Attack

The broad outlines of Eusebius' apologetic argument in terms of a narrative of national decline are firm. Several complexities remain, however, which trouble the reader and caution against simplistic readings of the work as though it were aimed at a single target. For instance, he waits until the opening of Book 4 to alert his reader to the fact that since the ninth chapter of Book 1 he has been marshalling an argument that seeks to exhibit the weaknesses of two of the great branches of a pagan tripartite theology:

> Due order bids me to refute the third form of polytheistic error [...] For
> since they divide their whole system of theology under three general

heads, the mythical treated by the poets in tragedy, and the physical
which has been invented by the philosophers, and that which is enforced
by the laws and observed in each city and country; and since two of
these parts have been already explained by us in the preceding books,
namely the historical, which they call mythical, and that which has
transcended the mythical, and which they call physical, or speculative
[...] this present book [will examine] what they call political [theology].[29]

It is striking that he postpones this announcement until he has worked
through two-thirds of the system. On several earlier occasions he offers clear
markers of where the reader is in the overall argument of the *Preparation*. The
physical–allegorical approach was a much later development, he avers, which
followed the earlier branch of theology (namely the worship of humans as
gods, whom the Greeks had misunderstood as being mere myths).[30] He does
not, however, alert the reader to its importance within a great systematic
tripartite theology (probably of Stoic origin). It can scarcely have been an
afterthought. Considerations of the structure and interrelations of the books
of the *Preparation* (to which we shall turn in a moment) caution us against
readily adopting the view that the argument grew and shifted in Eusebius'
mind as he was writing the work. There is inadequate reason to suppose that
the apologist tackled his argument in an ad hoc or disconnected way – as
strange as his approach may seem to the modern reader. If he was not an
absent-minded or forgetful writer and if, furthermore, the overall structure
of the *Preparation* bears strong indications of a well-ordered and carefully
connected argument, why did he delay the explicit naming of the tripartite
theology until so late in the argument?

The most plausible and attractive answer to this question lies in his
privileging of the historicizing approach to pagan religion. In a fundamental
way, all contemporary pagan religious phenomena were rooted in the lives
of particular historical figures who were the forefathers of their nations.
Though these forefathers may have only practised forms of astral religion,
the worship they received from later generations of descendants lay at the
heart of paganism. The belated Greek misconstrual of these figures and
their histories as myths, followed by the embarrassed attempt to allegorize

their shameful actions and immoral characters, was rooted in confusion, ignorance and contradictory claims. To commence his apologetic argument with an explicit announcement of the tripartite theology would have allowed the rubrics of both 'the mythical' and 'the physical' a validity that Eusebius denied them. Both theological categories arose from what Eusebius supposed to be a series of gross misunderstandings and misrepresentations of the history of nations.

The postponed appeal to the notion of a tripartite theology at the beginning of Book 4, on the other hand, provided Eusebius with the opportunity both to highlight his awareness of the grand theological systems of the philosophers and to target oracular religion in particular. Under the rubric of 'political theology', Eusebius was able to combine a cluster of issues important to him. Continued soreness at the roles played by many eastern Mediterranean civic personnel in the last wave of the Great Persecution under Maximinus Daia – in particular the damage done by forged oracles calling for suppression of Christianity – found expression in the severe castigation of oracles as the workings of deceptive, self-aggrandizing humans in cooperation with wicked daemons. This argument gave occasion to utilize the odd compilation of oracles by Porphyry, who was at once one of the most renowned of contemporary philosophers, the foremost enemy of Christianity and an 'advocate of daemons'.[31] The material from Porphyry, especially oracles that admitted to lying to their human consultants due to the daemons' inability to make accurate astrological readings, provided a compelling reason to turn in Book 6 to the significant doctrine of fate. Notions of fate and traditional civic religion might otherwise only be loosely connected in the reader's mind; oracular cult, under the administration of civic magistrates, became a linchpin in the argument of Books 5 and 6.

This argument was appropriate to his overall schema of the decline of nations. It also made sense within the tripartite theological system advocated by many philosophers (even while criticizing that system). Eusebius doubled the persuasive cachet of his argument, however, by appealing to another pagan system as well. Whereas the Stoics could offer a tripartite systematic theology, Platonists had developed a hierarchical theological system that posited (in a top-down ontological flow) the One (or 'the God over all'), the gods, daemons (both good and bad) and heroes. Eusebius introduced this structure not many chapters after his explication of the tripartite theology.[32] Since Platonists located the daemons in a sublunar location, and since furthermore these lower realms were marked by wickedness and moral ambiguity, Eusebius found the philosophers to be mistaken in their attempts to salvage the daemonic category as possessing some who were 'good daemons'. Instead, the philosophers had committed a theological error.

Important for our present concerns is the way in which the apologist invokes some of the central theological systems of his day but without allowing his argument to become merely a response to those systems. Each is introduced only when addressing one of its primary components: the political branch of the Stoic tripartite theology, and the daemonic category of the Platonic theological hierarchy. Both of these remain couched within Eusebius' own historicizing argument of national decline. Political theology was merely that branch that treated the contemporary expressions of cults rooted in the historical landscape of the ancient worship of humans. Daemons, furthermore, were diligently working through the oracles to bring about theological confusion and moral depravity. They had capitalized on the ancient worship of ancestors and manipulated such practices for their own ends. Eusebius' narrative argument thus claimed to understand rightly the components of the philosophers' theological systems and to trump their attempts at rationally accounting for pagan religious phenomena.

The various organizational schemata invoked in the first half of the *Preparation* are not the only difficulties that demand consideration. We must now turn to the problem of the general plan of the work as a whole. There is good reason to presume that Eusebius had a fairly firm idea of the direction his argument would take when he commenced the *Preparation*. His synopsis of the Greek and Jewish criticisms in the second chapter of Book 1, which would form the overarching layout of his apologetic diptych in both the *Preparation* and *Proof*, is followed towards the end of the preface by a more precise enumeration of the areas his argument would traverse. There, he states that he will provide an investigation of, in order: pagan cosmological ideas; the first and most ancient superstition of humanity (that is, astral religion); Phoenician matters; Egyptian matters; the Greek 'mythical delusion'; physical (that is, allegorical) philosophy; oracles; the 'serious doctrines of the noble philosophy' of the Greeks; and finally an account of the teachings of the Hebrews.[33] Several books confirm or elaborate upon the basic structure set out here. Yet once we enter the great Platonic–biblical comparison beginning in Book 11, there is reason to wonder if there has not been some change of plan in the structure of the apologetic project. Paul Kalligas thus suggested that Eusebius suddenly acquired the books of Longinus' library, which contained much of the Platonic corpus.[34] Striking upon this philosophical gold mine became the catalyst for Eusebius' alteration of and addition to the comparative material that fills the last five books of the *Preparation*.

The possibility is intriguing. Longinus (the teacher of Porphyry in Athens, whose letter inviting the latter to move east with him to Phoenicia survives in quotation in Porphyry's *Life of Plotinus*[35]) was executed in the early 270s, soon after the defeat of Zenobia, the queen of the eastern Mediterranean who had offered patronage to him (see Chapter 1). The 40 years up to the time when Eusebius began composition of the *Preparation* – sometime after 314 – would be sufficient for Longinus' library to have fallen into any number of other hands before coming into the possession of Christians at Caesarea. It is possible that the defeat of Maximinus Daia in 313 by Licinius, accompanied by the executions of many of his key supporters in the East,[36] could have made available to Eusebius (or a well-placed friend) Longinus' library if it had been under the care of one of those supporters.

An element of the *Preparation* that lends itself to Kalligas' thesis is the precise range of texts that Eusebius quoted. Probably most important are the quotations from two treatises by Plotinus, which have been the source of serious scholarly conversation in attempts to determine which editions of these works was at the library at Caesarea.[37] One possibility is an edition made by Eustochius, the disciple who was with Plotinus at his death and who is recorded as having made an edition of at least one of his master's treatises. A second is Porphyry's well-known edition of the treatises in the *Enneads*. A third is a copy circulated by Amelius, who is known to have distributed some copies of Plotinus' treatises and importantly to have moved to the East after studying under Plotinus.[38] Because Eusebius uses the titles assigned to Plotinus' essays by Porphyry as well as the fact that he quotes elsewhere from the writings of both Amelius and Porphyry himself, it seems that the second possibility is the most likely. Indeed, we possess a letter by Longinus requesting that Porphyry send him treatises of Plotinus.[39]

These considerations certainly lend support to Kalligas' contention that Eusebius had access to Longinus' library. But at the same time the range and placement of Eusebius' quotations from Porphyry's writings lead us to question the supposition that Eusebius acquired Longinus' books only after completing the first half of the *Preparation*. The first half of Eusebius' work contains important works by Porphyry, including *Against the Christians*, *Philosophy from Oracles*, *On Images*, *Letter to Anebo*, and *On Abstinence from Eating Meat*. In addition, quotations from Philo of Byblos and Plutarch, both of whom were important sources in Porphyry's own writings, appear in this section. It is possible, but not entirely likely, that Eusebius acquired a pagan's library containing these sorts of works without much Plato. Yet it is more probable that if Eusebius acquired the works of Plato from what was originally Longinus' collection (as Kalligas argues) he would have also obtained the works of Porphyry, Plotinus and other Platonists at the same time. Furthermore, the possibility cannot be dismissed that the library at Caesarea already contained many or even all of the works of Plato that Eusebius quotes. Origen, the one-time fellow student of both Longinus and Plotinus, had ended his career in Caesarea.[40] The absence in Origen of extended quotations of Plato such as we find in the *Preparation* does not negate the possibility that he possessed much of Plato's corpus and left it for his Christian heirs there.

Even if Eusebius did not acquire Longinus' collection in the middle of composing his *Preparation*, Kalligas nonetheless struck upon the very real difficulty of the clear difference in layout between Books 11–15 and all that precedes them, as well as the problem of finding the argument of these last books expressed in earlier synopses Eusebius had provided for his reader, such as the one noted above from the end of the preface.[41] Are the long block quotations of Plato and his followers meant to align with the 'serious doctrines of the noble philosophy' of the Greeks, mentioned in the preface? Or was that phrase only an appellation for the notions of fate criticized in Book 6, which does, after all, follow the discussion of oracles (in Book 5) and precede a discussion of the doctrines of the Hebrews (in Books 7–9, or even 10), as the synopsis had proposed? If this is the case, then the last books of the *Preparation* do indeed seem to be an unintended appendage of rather immense proportions. Its composition would thus begin to resemble that of Augustine's *City of God* a century later, the magnitude and structure of which only developed in the North African bishop's mind after he commenced the first books addressed to Marcellinus.

On the other hand, it might be best to take the reference to the Hebrew teachings in the synopsis as signifying the entire book of the *Proof* (rather than the *Preparation*, Books 7–9). Then, the 'serious doctrines' of the Greeks would plausibly indicate the treatment of Plato and other philosophers in the second half of the *Preparation*. The discussion of the Hebrews beginning in Book 7 would thus only be a preliminary sketch of the more extensive discussions of the *Proof*, while at the same time functioning as a necessary component of the investigation of the serious doctrines of the Greeks, since Eusebius needed an adequate historical and theological account of the Hebrews that he could declare to be the source of all the good elements he would find in Plato's writings. Indeed, there is a certain natural (and explicit) connectedness between each of the intermediate books that separate the first half of the *Preparation* (namely Books 1–6) from the section on Plato and post-Platonic philosophy (Books 11–15). Book 8 continues the investigation of Hebrew doctrines begun in Book 7, and ends by announcing that whereas it has relied on native sources (such as Philo of Alexandria, Aristeas, Aristobulus and Josephus) he would necessarily turn to 'outside' sources on the Jews in the following book. Book 9 fulfils this role by quoting from numerous Greek accounts about the Jews. The proof that the Greeks did know of the Jews, and were thus dishonest when they denied their importance or the antiquity of their forefathers, contains consequently a crucial step towards the argument of Book 10, which offers preliminary discussion of the plausibility that the Greeks would have stolen from the Hebrews. Book 10, far from being an end in itself, is an integral step towards Books 11–15; it clearly looks forward to the great Platonic–biblical comparison of the following books and presents itself as an essential stage in the argument before the presentation of that comparison. If the comparison was prompted by the sudden acquisition of a large part of Plato's corpus, then Eusebius had a significant enough mastery over his argument to situate his exciting discovery within the several layers of set-up that comprise Books 7–10.

Aside from the limited feasibility of seeing the 'serious doctrines' of the Greeks as applying to the doctrine of fate in Book 6, there is a firm coherency to the entirety of Books 7–15 of the *Preparation* that, in turn, fits squarely within his overall design of defending the Christian apostasy from the ways of their forefathers. The *Preparation* performed a wide-ranging and incisive assault against the first prong of the double-apostasy accusation: Christians were legitimized in their withdrawal from ancestral traditions and identities since the Greeks, following the Egyptians and Phoenicians, embodied a particularly low point within a world-historical narrative of decline. That decline was only interrupted briefly by the Greek adoption of many of the wise practices and teachings of the ancient Hebrews, who alone had pursued the 'God over all' with true piety and rationality.

Caveat Lector

Interpretation of the *Preparation* has often been preceded by two faulty assumptions that must be cleared away so as to avoid misrepresenting its precise position within ancient apologetic discourses and the history of religion more generally. The first involves the very conception that the title often evokes. *Proparaskeuē Evangelikē* (*Praeparatio evangelica*) is frequently rendered 'Preparation for the Gospel' (as Gifford entitled the single English translation of the work and as I have rendered it, though with some discomfort, throughout this chapter). Lying behind this title, for many readers, is the well-known early Christian notion that Greek philosophy was a preparation among the Greeks for the coming of Christ and His Gospel. Just as Moses' Law had been a preparation for the Jews, alerting them to the seriousness of sin and the need for atonement, so Greek philosophy (especially Plato's) heralded certain necessary preliminaries for their reception of the Gospel, such as the doctrine of one unchanging God, the importance of following reason (*logos*) and the immortality of the soul. The historic roles of Moses and Plato were thus thought to share in a common providential movement, so that Plato was only 'Moses speaking Attic Greek'. Both Justin Martyr and Clement of Alexandria had put forth this historiographical conception of a preparation for the Gospel, and it has too frequently been supposed that Eusebius followed suit.

The historiographical vision of the relationship between ancient nations was, however, quite different in the *Preparation*. As already stated above, Eusebius took great pains to exhibit the lateness of the Greeks and their dependency upon other nations. No element of ancient cultural and religious history had been identified as a Greek contribution. Their myths and poetry were confused misappropriations of the histories of more ancient peoples. Their philosophical developments had only been infused with wisdom and rationality when Plato borrowed from, or translated, the more ancient wisdom of the Hebrews. Eusebius emphasized both the partial nature of Plato's adoption of Hebrew wisdom and the immediate fragmentation of even those good components of Hebrew teaching by Plato's successors. In this presentation it is the Hebrews, in fact, who have provided a *praeparatio Platonica*. The numerous comparisons between Plato and the Bible served the purpose of proving this relation of dependency of the Greeks upon Hebrews. Because the Greeks so quickly spoiled the good Hebrew borrowings of Plato, it became impossible, in Eusebius' historical narrative, for the Greeks to provide anything like a preparation for the Gospel. The only preparation for the Gospel for Eusebius, insofar as this was understood in historical terms, were the lives and teachings of the ancient Hebrew holy men, which had been misunderstood by both Jews and Greeks (albeit in different ways and to different degrees).

The title of the *Preparation*, however, does not serve to evoke a historiographical conception at all. Instead, it functions as a marker of its literary relationship to its sister work the *Proof*. The work was a preparation for the higher-level proof of another text.[42] It is a pedagogical not a historiographical label. We misrepresent Eusebius' narrative argument and overarching historical vision when we import the earlier notions of a 'preparation for the Gospel' from Clement and others.

The second misconception about Eusebius' work resides in the frequent, even natural, supposition that the targets of his polemic represent a 'religion' and that Eusebius represents one of the principal figures in the invention of a category of 'religion' distinct from the other categories of culture or race.[43] Whereas ancient religious phenomena were (almost) always rooted within (or at least, conceived to be rooted within) the communal dynamics of family, race, city and nation, Christianity, it has been supposed, marked a universalist and individualist departure from such identities. Conversion to Christianity involved the adoption of an identity that transcended differences of ethnicity. A passage from the *Proof* that seems to support this modern representation of religious history states:

> Now let us consider the nature of Hellenism [*Hellēnismos*] and Judaism [*Ioudaismos*], and inquire under which banner we should find the holy men who lived before Moses, whose godliness and holiness is attested by Moses himself. Judaism would be correctly defined as the polity constituted according to the Law of Moses [...] Hellenism you might summarily describe as the worship of many gods according to the ancestral religions of all nations.[44]

Later he concludes:

> Christianity [*Christianismos*] would therefore be not a form of Hellenism nor of Judaism, but something between the two, the most ancient organization for holiness, and the most venerable philosophy, only lately codified as the law for all mankind in the whole world.[45]

The adoption of the *-ismos* endings for the ethnonyms of Greeks, Jews and Christians (*Hellēnismos, Ioudaismos, Christianismos*) certainly lends itself to an emphasis on the religious doctrine and practice of these peoples. Yet, even here, indications of broader ethnic identities are presented: the worship of many gods that was typical of the Greeks was a continuation of the piety of national forefathers, and Judaism was embodied in a historical polity (*politeia*) instituted by the legislator of a particular people. Furthermore, throughout Eusebius' apologetic corpus the full range of ethnic conceptions and identity markers necessarily comes into play. In fact, without the other components of ethnicity, such as language, land, shared history, common ancestors and communal way of life and thought, Eusebius' argument would dissolve. The *Preparation* involves much more than the staking out of one religious position against its alternatives. The superiority of the one rests in the greater antiquity of its forefathers and their greater rationality and moral uprightness in contrast to the forefathers of other nations. The Greeks remain a distinct people whose collective history was marked by particular relations of dependence upon other nations.

Since the Greeks exhibited so thoroughly the extreme depravity, irrationality and fragmentation of polytheistic forms of thinking and living for a nation's history and character, they provided an apt root for the -*ismos* label. The polytheistic nations could have been aggregated under a collective label drawn from any of them – 'Egyptianism', 'Phoenicianism', and so on. Hellenism was preferred, however, since the Greeks possessed many characteristics that were more appropriate for Eusebius' polemic and that were lacking or less central to the other identities. Not only did the Greeks furnish an image of lateness and confusion, but they had resided for centuries as the positive pole of the Greek–barbarian dichotomy (a dichotomy which was refracted, importantly, in the New Testament)[46] and their claims to cultural and racial superiority had been perpetuated in the Roman era by well-known and admired Hellenocentrist thinkers like Dionysius of Halicarnassus, Plutarch, Celsus and Diogenes Laertius.[47] Furthermore, by choosing the Greeks as the source of the collective appellation of Hellenism for all polytheistic nations, Eusebius opened up the fruitful possibility of engaging with Greek philosophy. His arguments of dependency and discord could converge in that area. The philosophers belonging to this identity provided precious examples of the theft of barbarian wisdom as well as the disordered misunderstanding of that wisdom once adopted.

As contemporary scholarship continues to worry about the precise signification of the Latin label 'pagan' we unduly simplify and schematize Late Antique conceptualizations by assuming that 'Hellene' became a clearly delimited label for a religious position of paganism.[48] Religion certainly mattered in Eusebius' identification of his opponents – but it mattered in ways that were inextricably entangled with the conceptual clusters that made up an ethnic identity (an *ethnos* or *genos*). Language, history, ancestors, laws and national character were deeply connected to a people's religious ideas and behaviour. Eusebius' criticism of those ideas and behaviour sought to attack them in all their ethnic embeddedness. Religion was not extracted from ethnic and cultural identities in the *Preparation*, as well as in the other works by our author – indeed, as we shall see in the case of the *Ecclesiastical History*, the Christians were clearly identified as an *ethnos* themselves. We misrepresent the conceptual worlds of Eusebius and other Late Antique Christians by inappropriately identifying their language of ancestral piety and worship with our modern category of religion.[49] We furthermore neglect the ethnic and historiographical richness of the *Preparation*'s mode of argumentation, which was sweeping in its historical scope and incisive in its articulation of ethnic identities.

The Theophany

Whereas the 'preparation' for the *Proof* in the title of that work was thus embedded within a pedagogical project of teaching Christianity and, in particular, Christian reading skills, the *Theophany* might be deemed a more strictly apologetic undertaking. Its five books comprise all of the central claims of his other apologetic works: monotheism instead of polytheism, Logos theology, the nature and necessity of the Incarnation, the discord of the philosophers, and the deleterious effects of daemons on human history and religious expressions. Its argument follows an arc from a description of the universal scope of the Logos as the creator of all and the singular image of the 'God over all' (Book 1), through an exposition of the moral and theological confusion of humans when they failed to live according to their rationality, that is, the seeds of the Logos implanted in them (Book 2), and then to a case for the need for the Incarnation, and the results and proofs of the truth of the Incarnation (Books 3–5).

Though it is often considered an abridgement of the diptych of the *Preparation* and *Proof*,[50] the *Theophany* follows a different arrangement of its component parts, possesses a more lively tone and contains distinctive features that produce a unique and fresh apologetic piece. Indeed, it is in some sense more like the later *Oration on Christ's Sepulchre* than Eusebius' earlier contributions to the apologetic genre. Like that later oration, the *Theophany* grapples with a problem already dealt with in the *Proof*: the need for and nature of the ultimate theophanic encounter of God with humanity in the Incarnation. His exposition relies upon material drawn both from the *Proof* and the *Preparation*, creatively reconfigured to centre around the person of Jesus Christ as the Incarnation of the Logos.

Indications of the audience and relative date for the piece are sparse. When he does address his readers he seems to presume that they are pagans. For instance: 'your mind is not so entirely darkened, that you cannot think within yourself.'[51] Otherwise, we are given no explicit claims about the audience or how Eusebius may have considered the treatise to function within a particular social or religious context. Importantly, however, we can catch a glimpse of Eusebius' reworking of many of the most significant building blocks of his argument in the earlier apologetic–pedagogical diptych into a new apologetic edifice. Whereas the *Preparation's* earlier expositions of the impact of daemonic effects on human history (such as false or inept oracles, the notion of fate or the rise of human sacrifice) placed them within an argument that sought to assert the rightness of the Christian rejection of the ways of their forefathers, the development of the *Theophany* places them within an argument on the necessity of the Incarnation. Humanity had failed to submit itself to the guidance of reason (*logos*), which had been implanted by the Logos. The emphasis on the miraculous establishment and spread of a church from all nations or the destruction and scattering of the Jews no longer functions to exhibit the truth of the Christian appropriation of the Hebrew Scriptures and prophecies. Instead, the *Theophany* connects these to the prophecies uttered by Christ.[52] The fulfilment of these prophecies, then, stands as proof of the truth of the incarnational claims about Christ – He was no deceiver or magician, but the Logos made manifest in human history.

A shift, therefore, in the very basis upon which the argument rested – from the Hebrew Scriptures as the authoritative frame of reference for the *General Elementary Introduction*, *Preparation* and *Proof*, and of course the biblical commentaries, to the New Testament, particularly the Gospels, in the *Theophany* – is certainly one of the most distinguishing features of the latter work. Of course, the earlier works were not averse to quoting the New Testament, nor was the *Theophany* devoid of quotations from the Hebrew Scriptures. There is, however, a preponderance of New Testament quotations as the foundation for his argument in the *Theophany* (especially Books 3–5, naturally, since the first two books aim at describing the cosmological and historical background for the Incarnation). The fact that all the earlier treatises addressed themselves to Christian students does prompt the suspicion that in the *Theophany*, which explicitly targets pagans, the author has opted for biblical texts that record historically, rather than prophetically, the character and life of Christ – an apologetic strategy that he considered particularly powerful for this specific audience.

Significantly, the components of his argument were not new: as already noted, Eusebius' earlier works had already developed claims about the decline in human history, the necessity of the Incarnation, the providential work of the Logos before, during and after the Incarnation, the miraculous spread of Christianity to all nations under the sun, the divine identity of Christ (against critics who thought Him a liar or magician), and so on. All of these recur in the *Theophany*, frequently with identical language to that of the earlier works, but without any marked reliance upon the Hebrew Scriptures. One might suppose, however, that an apologetic strategy that started with the Hebrews would have been amenable to the cultural and philosophical values of Late Antique pagans. At least since the developments of the late Stoa and Middle Platonism, and in the work of many earlier thinkers, barbarian wisdom and the most primal antiquity were prized as containing a purer and more rational life than that of later generations. The Hebrew Scriptures would seem the most important approach to defend the faith and answer critics – especially those who complained of the newness of Christianity and the humble origins of the first disciples. Yet Eusebius availed himself of this ancient barbarian wisdom only in those works of a hybrid, apologetic–pedagogical nature, while practising a mode of scriptural restraint in his externally oriented *Theophany*. Arguments for historical and philosophical plausibility, which could garner support for the Christ of the Gospels as the figure of Hebrew prophecy, withdrew to the margins.

The later *Oration on Christ's Sepulchre* abbreviated the argument of the *Theophany* and placed it within a unique and limited context, namely the commemoration of Christ's death and Resurrection in the newly constructed Church of the Holy Sepulchre. In a work post-dating that oration, Eusebius obliquely mentioned his engagements with pagans. Just as in Isaiah, which preached against the worship of idols,

> you will find the one God declaring a turning away from polytheistic error, so also in dialogues with the superstitious Greeks we are accustomed to dispense the teaching about Christ at just the right time, and to bring forth refutations of their idolatrous error and show that there is one God with apodeictic speeches.[53]

It is unfortunate that we do not have more from Eusebius' dialogue with the Greeks. Yet the *Preparation* and the *Theophany* are monuments to Eusebius' great learning and perceptive marshalling of creative and powerful apologetic techniques. His reading was broad, his quotational tactics incisive, and his vision was of a world-historical depth. These works were formulations of a larger project of shaping the Late Antique Christian mind. It is to those other works that were specifically aimed at training the Christian mind, which sought to develop a curriculum for Christian intellectuals, that we will turn in the next chapter.

III

WRITING THE
CURRICULUM

THROUGHOUT MUCH of early Christian literature and Eusebius' writings in particular, Christians were identified as a school of true philosophy. In works as diverse as the *Ecclesiastical History* or *Preparation for the Gospel*, a guiding assumption was that Christian corporate identity followed simultaneously the contours of both an ethnic and a scholastic conception (see Chapters 2 and 4). Christians were a nation towards which members of all nations would naturally draw if the eyes of their souls became illumined by true reason (or the Word). At the same time, the succession of bishops matters within the *History* in the same way that the succession of scholarchs was important for the perceived integrity and legitimacy of a philosophical school in antiquity. Similarly, many of the holy exemplars of this nation of philosophers were depicted in the *History* as teachers whose daily lives and interactions with their followers carried out the same sort of work as a school of philosophy.

Eusebius clearly valued the metaphor of Christianity as a school and admired the scholarly and pedagogical activities of the rational and holy leaders of this school within its various civic contexts across the Empire.

Unfortunately, we possess no explicit descriptions of Eusebius' own teaching activities within some sort of school at Caesarea. Fortunately, however, significant indications of Eusebius' role as a teacher present themselves in his exegetical writings, many of which are precisely the sorts of texts developed as pedagogical tools in the philosophical schools. These included introductory handbooks, question-and-answer treatises, reference manuals and commentaries, as well as the *Preparation*, which offered exegesis of pagan texts. Following some brief observations on the teaching of texts in philosophical schools of the imperial era, a survey of the distinctive features of Eusebius' educational works will highlight the textually concrete ways in which the identification of Christians as a philosophical school bore implications for the production of texts for the purposes of reading the core writings on which the school's identity was based.

Contexts: Philosophical Schools and Their Texts

Contrary to the sometimes trite caricature of philosophy under the Roman Empire as marked by intellectual stagnation, schools of philosophy in the three centuries before Eusebius performed creative and diligent work in expounding and elaborating the written thought of the founder, whether this was Plato, Aristotle or Epicurus (while Zeno among the Stoics seems something of an exception). Exploratory thinking remained to a significant degree wilfully tethered to the thought of the master. While a philosophical school was often institutionally undeveloped or distended (geographically or temporally) there was a remarkable concern to restrain movement away from the textual and conceptual foundation of the founder.[1] A modern disdain for such frameworks of authority has until recently hindered an appreciation of the intellectual and spiritual richness of imperial-era philosophy.[2]

Philosophy was a distinctively bookish affair: the written memorials of ancient sages were treasuries of a primal wisdom that had been lost and forgotten by later generations. This was not all, for the writings of Plato or another philosophical master were not always perceived as transparent expressions of the truth. Plato's surviving corpus was only the so-called 'exoteric' body of his thought, which was allowable for a broader audience; the secret truths of an esoteric wisdom were known only to an inner circle of serious disciples who passed on his deeper teachings orally. The teacher of philosophy was, therefore, a teacher of texts and a master reader surrounded by apprentices learning how to read well. Much was involved in undertaking such a course of study, for, in the first place, it comprised more than the mere cognition of propositions about the nature of reality. A concern of many introductory books was the ability and character of the would-be student. The teacher needed discernment in order to determine when an interested individual was properly suited for engagement with the master texts. Then, at least according to one handbook for the study of Plato, the teacher must ascertain which dialogue would make an appropriate starting point for the particular student.[3] Other curricular directives were more stable in their proposed order of reading.[4]

In spite of being one of the highest levels of study in ancient education, the reading process in a philosophical school may have begun with the most basic of practices, namely the determination of the text.[5] Commentaries sometimes pause over potential variants in the text, the syntax of a sentence or the implications of what might at first appear to be extraneous material in the passage at hand. Insofar as commentaries seem to arise from school reading practices, they encapsulate the activity performed in the shared study of teacher and student. But commentaries were not only the result of reading sessions: they were also part of the sessions themselves. Porphyry's account of the regular activity of Plotinus' seminar at Rome is probably typical of most Platonic schools: the philosophical master, surrounded by a coterie of students, would have various commentaries read on a given passage before offering his own brief (and, according to Porphyry, brilliant) remarks on the proper interpretation.[6]

Many schools were likely comprised of various levels of student, from mere 'auditors' (*akroatai*) to the most 'serious' (*zēlōtai*), as are recorded in the case of Plotinus. It is difficult, however, to know who precisely made up the student audience during the close reading of texts with commentaries. It may well have been that only the serious students were allowed to remain for such readings, whereas general lectures were open to a wider gathering. If so, the extant introductions to Plato may indicate differing levels of student, offering on the one hand a general overarching account of the basic contours of Plato's system of philosophy, and on the other a more precise cataloguing of the kinds of dialogue and the order in which they should be read.

The teacher's role as master reader bore the greatest significance for the transmission of true wisdom. Divergence from the right reading of a school's foundational canon of texts could result in the loss of the truth. Commentaries thus expounded both the textual details required for proper interpretation and the points at which rival readings had faltered in understanding 'the mind' of the text (the *nous*, or *dianoia*, or the *nooumenon* of a passage) by misconstruing its precise wording (*lexis*). Even as defenders of the 'divine Homer' clinched their allegories of the epic poems through attention to the smallest points in the given text, so also readers of the 'divine Plato' learned to attend to small details in the Platonic dialogues. The authoritative status given to Plato's works could rival that of an inspired revelation, as a quip by the philosopher Proclus reveals: if he were to choose only two books out of all ancient literature to survive, he would choose the *Chaldean Oracles* and Plato's *Timaeus*.[7]

Platonists did not limit their composition of pedagogical manuals or commentary literature to Plato's corpus, inspired though it may have been considered to be. Introductions and commentaries survive from Late Antique Platonists on Aristotle, Euclid, Ptolemy and others. Platonist schools were central locations for the production of books about books.[8] In their own educational manuals and biblical commentaries, Christians were, therefore, performing interpretive moves and creating contexts for reading in ways parallel to this broader philosophical scholastic phenomenon. As we shall see, Eusebius too enacted the same associations of a philosophical scholastic environment in several of his own works.

The General Elementary Introduction

Just as we know almost nothing about the first half of Eusebius' life, one of Eusebius' earliest surviving works is missing all but the barest hints of the first five of ten original books. He composed the *General Elementary Introduction* at some point during the Great Persecution and before he became bishop of Caesarea. The extant Books 6–9 of this introduction to Christian theology have been printed in the modern period under the title *Prophetic Selections*, which was Eusebius' own subtitle for those books. In spite of its great importance for appreciating his literary career and the possible institutional contexts for his work, the extant portion of this treatise has yet to receive a critical edition or translation into any modern language. Its four books survive in a single codex whose first pages and an intermediate section are badly damaged. Yet its current state, as well as the relative lack of modern interest in the work, should not mislead the student of Eusebius into presuming its unimportance in developing a proper picture of Christian literature at Late Antique Caesarea.[9]

The damaged first page hints at what had come before and specifies a dual audience comprising both those who have just recently converted to the faith and those who are more advanced in sacred studies. The preceding (now lost) five books addressed 'testimonies' about aspects of the life of Christ, which Eusebius had 'confirmed with clear, faithful and true proofs and syllogisms, and finally using quite short testimonies from those divine Scriptures believed in by both Jews and ourselves'.[10] Contrary to most modern characterizations, those first books were not directly aimed at unconverted pagans in an apologetic move, but were probably aimed at the same dual audience as the latter surviving books and seem only to have limited the amount of Old Testament scriptural references made.[11] The testimonies about the life of Christ may have come from the Gospels themselves as well as other sources such as Josephus, Hegesippus, Africanus and others (such as we find in the *History*). The shift being delineated in the broken first sentences is towards a sustained focus on the Christian Old Testament, that is, the Hebrew Scriptures.

For centuries, modern students have been methodically swayed by a powerful metanarrative of Christian origins, which propounds a vision of the Christians as a uniquely bookish people extending and ossifying the Jewish concern with sacred texts, and so becoming a religion of the book. Early Christians and their Jewish forebears had felt the overwhelming gravity of written words that contained the *ipsissima verba* of God, the divine revelation preserved within a textual form. It is true that early Christians were deeply bookish creatures, and Eusebius one of the most bookish of them, but a broader context is necessary. It was not the peculiar mark of a 'religion' to perform such industrious and painstaking work over a corpus of ancient texts. As already remarked, philosophers of the Roman Mediterranean were rather bookish as well, grounded as they were in deep and sustained textual engagements. Even the sacred writings of the Jews, known by many pagans for the religious eccentricities of their ethnic identity, had become the focus of attention among Greek (at least Greek-speaking) philosophers. Quotations from the writings of Moses appear in the work of imperial-era philosophers such as Numenius and Porphyry.[12] Making the Hebrew Scriptures the object of serious study was thus not necessarily a 'religious' activity, somehow distinct from or inferior to the work of philosophy – and furthermore, the highly 'religious' component of much ancient philosophy (the concern with the afterlife and salvation of the soul, the centrality of theology for metaphysics, the practice of spiritual exercises, the esoteric tone and language of the mysteries within the pursuit of philosophy) should prevent any hasty assumption of a distinction between the conceptual categories of philosophy and religion in antiquity.[13]

Eusebius' *Introduction* was not unlike other philosophical introductions (or even those belonging to what we now might consider other academic disciplines such as mathematics or medicine). Indeed, the philosophical life receives explicit attention both here and throughout Eusebius' other text-based writings, such as the *Proof of the Gospel* and the biblical commentaries (to which we shall turn below). The concern of Eusebius and other Christians with the biblical writings was resonant of the philosopher's work, as well as the philosopher's identity. Just as philosophers' schools pored over the master texts (as well as those of rivals), so the *Introduction* indicates a school of Christian seekers after truth, even if the concrete nature and contours of such a school now elude us. Just as philosophers conceived of philosophy as a way of life, not merely a set of doctrinal propositions, and puzzled over the nature, in particular the immortality, of the soul, so Eusebius' conception of the philosophical task exhibited a firm awareness that it was a way of life, lived in accordance with reason (the *logos*) and displayed in poignant clarity through the fearlessness in the face of death of those truest of philosophers, the Christian martyrs.

The following remarks from the preface of the *Introduction*'s ninth book (that is, the fourth book of the *Prophetic Selections*), which was dedicated to the prophet Isaiah, are instructive:

> What would someone think when they saw rustic men [that is, the Prophets] simply dressed, some goatherds and shepherds, coming into the midst of all the nation, and speaking something as if from the mouth of God, and shouting out 'Thus says the Lord', giving public speeches to kings and all the people with an undaunted bearing, showing a superhuman wisdom, which is still even now conveyed in their prophecies, philosophizing a thousand other ineffable things through riddles and parables, passing on to the people in the Hebrew language an ethical and dogmatic teaching, and furthermore exhibiting a life corresponding to their words, and conversing freely to all, refuting the impious to their faces, so as even to be plotted against by them to the point of death, with a strong and noble bearing being presented by the true Word? How, keeping these things reasonably in mind, could anyone not confess that all these things have happened in their situation in accordance with a most truly divine inspiration? For this reason also they were honoured with good reason by sensible people and their words [though] unwritten were preserved by sacred scribes, and still, even now, the whole nation believes that the prophets have come from God; this also is most clearly shown by our discussion about Christ, in which we prove [that] all his economy has happened, and his teachings and the calling out of all nations, which happened through him, were precisely foreknown and foretold so many thousands of years beforehand by those inspired men.[14]

Eusebius here evinces the close interconnection of philosophy, piety and text. The Scriptures contain the teachings of truth and record the lives and proclamation of ancient holy men. The latter-day followers of the prophets were Christians whose bravery in the face of persecution and free speech before hostile judges exhibited a philosophy that was expressive of the truths in the ancient texts in which they were schooled. As Eusebius had written earlier,

> Among us there is a crowd of those who entirely lack a formal education, exhibiting such a virtuous, philosophic way of life [*emphilosophon politeian*], which one cannot easily find even among those trained in philology and boasting in their care of books.[15]

This was a philosophy that went to the heart of the love of wisdom: not merely a love of the talk about wisdom but the life embodying the philosopher's highest aspirations.

In spite of Eusebius' praise for the illiterate Christian philosopher, whether man, woman or child, who exemplified the love of wisdom and the true belief in the immortality of the soul, the care for the educated person's soul centred on the scupulous reading of the ancient Hebrew texts. Such an authoritative collection of writings required a proper introduction by a master reader, namely Eusebius himself, who skilfully culled the most useful passages like flowers from 'meadows of the Word' so as to be 'serviceable for comprehending the truly beneficial and healthful orthodoxy'.[16] Each of the extant books of the treatise provides 'selections' (*eklogai*) of quotations from the Hebrew Scriptures, ranging from a single sentence to several lines, followed by (and often introduced by) Eusebius' comments elucidating the proper interpretation.

The first extant book (that is, the sixth book of the original *Introduction*) traces the activity of the Logos (the Son of God, Christ before the Incarnation) in the lives of the Hebrew patriarchs as recorded in the so-called historic books (from Genesis to Judges, then the Kings, Chronicles and finally Ezra). This book only partly follows the rubric of *Prophetic Selections* since only some of its interpretive work involves identifying passages deemed to be prophecies of Christ's Incarnation. An instance of this prophetic reading is offered in response to a verse from the third book of Kings (or 1 Kings in most modern English versions):

> And now, Lord God of Israel, let your word be trusted, which you spoke
> to your child David my father: if God would truly dwell with men on
> the earth, if the heaven of heaven were not sufficient for you [...][17]

Things similar to these are also said by Solomon in the second book of Chronicles in his prayer to God.[18] After quoting the verse, Eusebius remarks: 'Clearly, therefore, here also God is prophesied as being about to dwell with men on the earth; He has fulfilled this very thing in our times in the present coming of Christ, when God the Word became incarnate and spent time with the human race.'[19]

While many modern readers might consider that Eusebius is finding prophecies where there are none in any proper sense, we are confronted with what the *Introduction* takes as its central aim: the development of a distinctively Christian interpretive approach to writings that had been argued not to belong to Christianity at all. His reading of the Scriptures of the Jews was an emphatically Christocentric, or rather Logocentric, one since it sought to find the pre-incarnate workings of the Word (Logos) which had later 'become flesh and dwelt among us' (according to the Gospel of John). As such, this first book of the *Prophetic Selections* identified more than merely those verses that could be construed as prophetic of Christ; it also expounded upon passages where the Logos appeared in theophanic manifestations to the patriarchs or ancient Israelites.

Of the three strangers who had appeared to Abraham at Mamre in Genesis, one had been distinguished for being addressed as 'the Lord' and had answered Abraham's questions as though he were God Himself. When Sodom and Gomorrah were destroyed, which had been the business of the three visitors to Abraham, the scriptural text had even gone so far as to state that 'The Lord rained down from heaven brimstone and fire from the Lord' (Genesis 19:23). The double use of 'the Lord' was no mere repetition of the name of a single person for Eusebius, but an indication of the existence of a second Lord. Textual clues such as this became the integral 'proofs' for the *Introduction*'s argument that the theophanies of Genesis and other books were not manifestations of the transcendent 'God over all', but rather revelations of the Son, the highest God's Word

(Logos) who remained active throughout history especially to humans who nurtured the rational (*logikon*) part of their soul. As we shall see below, Eusebius' exegesis of these theophanies of the Word did more than merely help Christian students find a way to read the ancient writings through the lens of a later historical event (the Incarnation of Christ); it also provided carefully nuanced interpretive distinctions that were useful for maintaining a critical stance towards the Jews while nonetheless claiming their Scriptures as authoritative.

The other extant books of the *Introduction* turned to the non-historical books of the Old Testament. The seventh book (the second of the *Prophetic Selections*) discovered numerous verses containing a prophetic referent in the future life, suffering and Resurrection of Christ. References to King David as the 'anointed one' (*christos*) in many Psalms provided an easy textual peg on which to hang prophetic readings of the coming of Christ, who was, furthermore, the promised 'Son of David'. Unfortunately, we seem to be missing a large section of this book (though not through physical damage to the manuscript), which fell between Chapters 13 and 14 and would have covered the material between Psalms 21 and 131.[20] The *Introduction*'s eighth book (covering those books of the Old Testament known as the wisdom literature and all the Prophets except Isaiah) and ninth book (dedicated to Isaiah alone) likewise search out prophetic proclamations of the coming of Christ. His suffering, death and Resurrection are, the book claims, foretold in these selections of prophecies. It also argues that some passages declare Christ's second coming or final judgement.

The eighth book is apparently unique in its inclusion of non-biblical sources in support of Eusebius' interpretations. An otherwise lost passage from Arius Didymus' *Physics* describing the way in which panthers (as was believed) lure prey through their sweet odour provided Eusebius with important legitimation of his allegorical–prophetic reading of Hosea's utterance, 'I am like a panther to Ephraim, and like a lion to the house of Judah' (Hosea 5:14). Whereas an anti-Christian accusation of apparently Jewish origins had asserted Jesus' birth from an illegitimate union between Mary and a Roman soldier named Pantera, Didymus' quasi-scientific observation furnished a strikingly powerful allegory of the 'fragrance of the divine Word'.[21]

Christ's connection to a certain panther was not to a Roman soldier of a similar name but to the symbolic aromatic likeness to the animal and thus to the declarations of the ancient prophet, if properly interpreted. In addition to Didymus, the precise determination of Daniel's obscure and confusing prophecies of various numbers of sevens is explored by including a lengthy quotation of the chronographer Julius Africanus, followed by Eusebius' own chronological elaborations, which would be confirmed by brief quotations from the Jewish historian Josephus.[22] By appealing to such weighty authorities on chronography and history, Eusebius could confirm his own interpretation of Daniel while displaying his own erudition. Even though he snubs Africanus for 'filching the years between Cyrus and Artaxerxes' resulting in a 'rather forced' interpretation of the prophet,[23] Eusebius nonetheless admired Africanus' learning and, through the lengthy quotation, prepared in the reader a sense of legitimacy for his own chronological approach to the prophetic text.

The ninth book (that is, the fourth and final book of the *Prophetic Selections*) addresses itself to the prophetic material in Isaiah. While the major themes of the *Introduction* (namely, prophetic material respecting the life and work of Christ and the emergence of the Church gathered from all nations as a displacement of the Jews) find equal emphasis in the ninth book, some relatively new features arise. For the first time, Eusebius makes clear allusions to Origen and his commentary on Isaiah. 'The lover of learning,' Eusebius declares, 'will know what sort of meaning each of the things said literally has when he reads that marvellous man's [Origen's] exegetical works on these passages.' And: 'it is possible to know this [meaning] precisely from the commentaries on these passages by the holy man [Origen].' Second, a heightened emphasis on the displacement of the Jews as the chosen people of God emerges, accompanied by a reference to Eusebius' personal engagement with 'one of the circumcision'.[24]

A further feature, already present in earlier books but more prominent in the ninth, is Eusebius' use of biblical cross-references both to provoke and to confirm an interpretation of a particular passage.[25] Of course, most chapters seek to highlight an episode from the life of Christ as represented in the Gospels that seems to match the words of Isaiah's prophecies. But this is only one way in which verses from Isaiah are shown to interact with the rest of Scripture. Interpretations of the meaning of the references to Mount Libanos in the text of Isaiah are given through consideration of similar references in the prophecies of Ezekiel.[26] This appeal to the latter – notwithstanding the fact that he was a different prophet altogether – allows the astute reader to 'solve' the difficult interpretive problems of Isaiah. Similarly, a prophecy in Isaiah is explained by reference to the titles of Psalms, and, following a tactic of Origen before him, Eusebius uses Leviticus to support the interpretation of a term from a verse in Isaiah apparently prophesying Christ's birth as 'virgin' (rather than 'young girl').[27] Even the Wisdom of Solomon, a work Eusebius elsewhere recognizes as not universally accepted as authoritative, receives notice as containing a parallel to a line of Isaiah.[28]

One of the more pervasive instances of such biblical cross-referencing occurs in the first chapter, which is otherwise of interest for its non-linear approach to the text of Isaiah: beginning with Isaiah 2:1–4, Eusebius proceeds to verses from Matthew, Acts of the Apostles, then moves back to Isaiah 1:8, before quoting in turn other verses from Isaiah 1 and 2, Psalms, Galatians, Isaiah 2 (again), and finally Isaiah 65:1. Sometimes, it is a single word or phrase that prompts the cross-reference (for instance, the passages from Psalms, like Isaiah 2:1, use the phrase 'the mountain of the Lord'). Others are connected more loosely: for instance, the initial passage from Isaiah had prophesied a 'judgement in the midst of the nations and a refutation of a great people' (2:4); apparently the later quotation of the words of Jesus from Matthew ('Your house is left desolate') is an instance of that refutation against the Jews, while a sentence from Acts (loosely quoted) shows God's 'pouring out' grace on all nations. Alternatively, Eusebius' elaboration of the fulfilment of a prophecy in one part of Isaiah prompts consideration of another prophecy from much later in Isaiah whose close connection lies only in its historical fulfilment at the time of Christ rather than in the time of its delivery.[29]

Such proof-texting of passages from various places in different authors would scarcely withstand modern critical scrutiny (even those from the book of Isaiah are now considered to be from different prophetic authors living at different times[30]). Eusebius has, however, adopted a common interpretive technique of Late Antiquity, while adding a twist. Ancient readers of Homer had found a useful tactic for overcoming difficulties in the Homeric texts by drawing upon other passages from elsewhere in the work of that poet. In other words, Homer was to be interpreted by Homer.[31] The technique could be applied to other authors as well.

Eusebius took this same idea but applied it not to the corpus of a single author but to the entire collection of sacred Scriptures. The assumption that Scripture must be interpreted by Scripture became a thoroughgoing principle throughout Eusebius' works. It not only provided a means of finding suitable interpretations of the otherwise opaque words of prophets, it was also a creative and endlessly productive mode of developing a richly interwoven biblical vision of the past, present and future. Eusebius' project in the *Introduction* was to tie together the threads of the diverse range of scriptural texts into (the proper) patterns of meaning and thereby form a single tangled skein of formerly unconnected words. Beyond reading the Hebrew Scriptures through a Christocentric or Logocentric lens, the *Introduction* bound together passages within the corpus of the Hebrew Scriptures themselves into cross-referential knots such as was demanded by a broader Late Antique literary aesthetic as well as by a theology of prophetic revelation of a Word incessantly speaking in a myriad of disparate words.

Pedagogy and Proof

Without more than the *Prophetic Selections* portion of the *Introduction* it is difficult to know precisely how it was situated within a larger course of study. As already noted, the missing first five books seem to have addressed themselves only to the life of Christ and made only a limited appeal to the Hebrew Scriptures to supplement their claims.[32] The *Prophetic Selections* filled this need and so opened its range of vision to the Word's work before the Incarnation, both in theophanic manifestations and in prophetic oracles signifying His future coming and its effects. Such a course of study, if taken in isolation, left important problems unresolved. Why should students trained in the Greek language and literature, who may have been 'Hellenized' in their cultural affiliations and conceptual framework, consider Christianity a viable intellectual option at all? Why turn one's attention away from the glories of Greece and the exhilarating ideas of Greek philosophers? What could drive a student to adopt the ancient writings of barbarians, which had been translated into awkward and confusing Greek in the Septuagint, and become a follower of a barbarian teacher, who may have been only a charlatan or magician? If our surviving apologies from the first four centuries are representative, these were deeply felt and troubling difficulties for early Christians and their critics.

We have no indication that these problems were broached in the first half of the *Introduction*, but the survival of most of a second attempt at developing a curriculum for the faithful is felicitous. Roughly five years after completing the *Introduction*, following the defeat of the worst of the persecuting emperors and Eusebius' elevation to the bishopric of Caesarea, he began work on a massive two-part project that was at once apologetic and pedagogical. The *Preparation* (discussed in Chapter 2) answered the question of why a 'lover of truth' would reject the Greeks in favour of a barbarian wisdom. Strikingly, it claimed for itself the status not only of a defence of the faith (*apologia*) but also an introduction (*eisagōgē*), though of an apparently different nature from that of the *Introduction*.[33] The *Preparation* was an introduction for Christian students who needed training in how to read the Greeks from a distinctively Christian standpoint. This introduction was also, however, a 'preparation' for the higher study of the Hebrew Scriptures themselves from a distinctively Christian standpoint. This higher study was presented within the *Proof*.[34]

Like the *Prophetic Selections* of the earlier *Introduction*, the *Proof* provided the reader with a training in what questions to ask and what features to look for when approaching the ancient writings of the Hebrews. Indeed, there is a good deal of overlap between the two works in the passages discussed and the interpretive positions defended.[35] Two highly salient differences, however, must not be ignored. First, the *Proof* contextualizes its pedagogy of Scripture-reading within a larger polemical framework. The opening books of the *Proof* make a lengthy argument against the Jews, claiming that their forms of worship were limited both temporally and geographically.

This was a claim of no little import, since even if the Christian rejection of the Greeks was deemed valid their simultaneous acceptance of the Jewish writings and rejection of Jewish customs seemed an incoherent move, a helplessly confused and partial conversion.[36]

Eusebius' bold claim was that Christians understood the sacred texts of the Jews better than the Jews themselves. To begin with, the ordinances of Moses' Law could not be practised in any literal sense even by all Jews. Scattered around the Mediterranean world and beyond, the Jews could not possibly have made the annual (or more frequent) visits to the single holy place allowed by the Hebrew Scriptures at Jerusalem.[37] Moses himself had recognized its limitations and had foretold: 'A prophet shall the Lord your God raise up to you from your brethren, like unto me.'[38] He had further recorded that one would come who would rule over the nations and possess an exalted kingdom.[39] Eusebius' conclusion was simple: It is 'quite plain from his own words that he was quite well aware of the failure of the Law he had laid down to apply to all nations, and that another prophet would be necessary for the fulfilment of the oracles given to Abraham'.[40]

The holy men of Hebrew antiquity had not even followed the Law. Eusebius had made a forceful argument in the *Preparation* that Moses' Law was something of a middling form of piety for those descendants of the ancient Hebrews who had become corrupted by polytheism and immorality during their sojourn in Egypt. It was only during this period that they could properly be named Jews; before this, the Hebrews had worshipped God with pure thoughts and rational forms of piety.[41] They had sought God with the clear eyes of the mind and had no need for outward acts of religion such as circumcision or temple rituals. While the *Introduction* had expressed a distinction between the higher religion of the ancient pre-Mosaic Hebrews and the 'fleshly' concerns of the Jews who followed the surface meaning of Moses' Law, the sister works of the *Preparation* and *Proof* made a full-scale theological and historical construction demarcating Hebrew from Jewish identity. Such identity distinctions were key for a Christian understanding of the Scriptures, as well as a proper appreciation of the role of Christ, who was seen from this vantage as a new legislator like Moses, fulfilling Moses' Law while nonetheless reinstating the way of life of the ancient Hebrews.

Christ's legislation thus recalled a true piety that refused geographic, ethnic or temporal limits. His teachings had now spread to all nations.[42]

> Considerations of country, race or locality, or anything else are not to affect them in any way at all. The law and life of our Saviour Jesus Christ shows itself to be such, being a renewal of the ancient pre-Mosaic piety, in which Abraham, the friend of God, and his forefathers are shown to have organized their lives. And if you cared to compare the life of Christians and the worship introduced among all nations by Christ with the lives of the men who with Abraham are witnessed to by Scripture as holy and righteous, you would find one and the same ideal.[43]

The universal spread to all nations of this ancient wisdom embodied in Christ's teachings stood, Eusebius argued, as the fulfilment of ancient oracles enshrined in the Jews' own writings. The entirety of Book 2 of the *Proof* collects prophecies from the Hebrew Scriptures that made reference to blessing or salvation coming to the nations from a member of the Jewish nation. If 'those of the circumcision' (an appellation drawn from the Apostle Paul that repeatedly marked the fleshiness deemed to inhere in Jewish identity every time it was used) criticized Christians as having no legitimate share in the Hebrew Scriptures and despised them as foreigners, Eusebius would respond with an argument based on their own writings. He sought to

> array against them the proofs from the prophecies about the nations, making it clear how full they are of predictions of good and salvation for all nations, and how in no other way did they assert that their promises to the nations could be fulfilled only by the coming of the Christ.[44]

The Christians were thus scarcely a new religion; rather they represented a return – even a predicted return – to the most ancient and most true way of life of the pious men of Hebrew antiquity.

If Eusebius' proof could be sustained, the benefit for the Christian claim to possess a legitimate and, indeed, superior corporate identity would be immense. At a time when at least one emperor (namely Licinius) was still harassing the Church,[45] such a claim was a bold move that constructed a triumphalist vision embracing all nations and all times, even the most ancient, for a people whose future was by no means yet assured. Our modern narratives of a 'Constantinian turn' or a Christianization of the Roman Empire depend upon centuries of hindsight that Eusebius lacked. Yet his biblically formed historical vision was so powerful that we often miss the audacity of his project and its claims. His students may have heard a tone somewhat at odds with what was otherwise an uncertain time. This tone was, rather significantly, already present in his earlier *Introduction*, which likewise had alluded to contemporary persecution of Christians. Such triumphalism was due not so much to felicitous developments at the imperial level but to a sustained interpretation of all history through a thoroughly biblical lens – interpreted, of course, within a distinctively Christian, and Christocentric, framework and freed from 'fleshly' Jewish approaches.

Related to this first contrast with the *Introduction*, a second unique feature of the *Proof* is its restructuring of the order of the Hebrew Scriptures. Unlike the *Introduction*, which follows a strictly linear succession as it extracts passages for discussion, from the historical books through the Psalms and Prophets, the *Proof* organizes its selections of biblical texts around key themes. After the first two books' demonstration of the validity of the Christian appropriation of the Hebrew Scriptures for themselves, the third book centres on the person of the incarnate Christ (as neither a deceiver nor a sorcerer, but divine) and the fourth book sets up the basic themes of the remainder of the work (as we have it up to Book 10), namely the identity of the Son of God, whose existence preceded not only the Incarnation but the creation of the world, and the necessity and nature of the Incarnation itself.[46] The scriptural proof for the Christian doctrine of the pre-existent Son of God occurs in the entirety of Book 5; the proof of the basic fact and various features of the Incarnation (such as the time and place of Christ's nativity or His Passion) receive elaborate attention in Books 6–10.[47]

Even within the general thematic organization of the *Proof*, biblical passages are only sometimes considered using the linear approach followed by the *Introduction*. Book 5, for instance, begins with what became a central passage in fourth-century theological debates, Proverbs 8:12–31 (see

Chapter 5). Treatment of this passage precedes discussion of, in order: two Psalms, a passage from Isaiah, another Psalm, a second passage of Isaiah, various passages from the historical books (Genesis through Joshua), Job, a fourth Psalm, and finally several passages from the Prophets. The other books of the *Proof* are not so non-sequential, but nonetheless the linear pattern of biblical testimonies exhibited in the *Introduction* remains less important within the new rhythms of 'evangelic proof' presented in this later apologetic–pedagogical project. Interpretive tools already developed in the *Introduction* were now put to work for more thematic and systematic ends.

The *Proof* makes a number of important advances by formulating a broad Christian interpretive approach to the Hebrew Scriptures in all their complexity. Its systematization furthers techniques already adopted in the *Introduction*. One of these involves the interpretive principle of homonymy. While earlier Christian thinkers had noted the occurrence of *christos* ('anointed one') in various places in the Hebrew Scriptures, Eusebius deploys it systematically and couples it with examination of individuals bearing the name Jesus in the Old Testament. The two primary names used of the incarnate Word in the New Testament were Jesus and Christ. Tracing indications from the writings of Moses and the Psalms on the anointing of priests, the *Proof* concludes that those who are anointed (*christoi*) were those who partook of the Holy Spirit and especially that One who participated most fully in the 'fragrance of divinity' of the Father:

> Therefore the prophetic word by this analogy referring to the highest power of God, the King of kings and Lord of lords, calls Him the Christ and the Anointed, Who is the first and only one to be anointed with this oil in its fullness, and is the sharer of the Father's divine fragrance communicable to none other, and is God the Word, sole-begotten of Him, and is declared to be God of God by His communion with the Unbegotten that begat Him.[48]

Such an interpretation allows Eusebius to find in all the 'anointed ones' of the Old Testament types of Christ and of Christians who were likewise anointed with the oil of the Spirit. At the same time, it insinuates a prophetic valence that would have otherwise been missed by the less theologically astute and careful reader. Chapter 16 of Book 4 strings together an assemblage of passages (especially from the Psalms) in which the name *christos* appears. The prayers of the psalmist were now no longer simple supplications but prophecies of various aspects or episodes in the life of Jesus. Psalm 27:8, for instance, praises God for taking the place of 'the shield of salvation of his anointed one [*christos*]'. For Eusebius, this clearly signifies the time of Jesus' Passion, when the Son would have needed the protection of His Father the most. Importantly, the occurrence of *christos* in the eighth verse elicited an interpretation of other elements in the Psalm as now bearing a prophetic function. Thus, the first verse's exclamation, 'To thee, O Lord, have I cried; My God, be not silent before me, lest I be like unto them that go down into the pit,' refers to Christ's prayer at Gethsemane immediately preceding His Passion; the seventh verse's claim that 'the Lord is my helper and my defender [...] my flesh has revived', prophesies the bodily Resurrection of Christ after His suffering and death.[49]

The occurrence of the name Jesus in the Old Testament may at first seem startling to the modern reader who has not become accustomed to the Septuagint's rendering of the Hebrew name Joshua with *Iēsous*, Jesus. The most well known of the individuals bearing this name was the successor to Moses who gave his name to an entire book of the Bible. Eusebius pauses over the fact that this was not his original name, but one given him by Moses ('Moses gave the name Jesus to Nausē the son of Navē'[50]). Moses had, for Eusebius, proven his 'inspired wisdom' and deep appreciation for name changes in his writing of Genesis where the names of prominent patriarchs had been changed as they entered into a special relationship with God. Moses' purpose in changing his successor's name was typological, we are told, for Moses recognized that in the same way that he would die and be succeeded by Nausē/Jesus, so his Law would be replaced by the constitutional way of life (*politeuma*) of Jesus Christ. Moses appeared as 'the most wonderful of all the prophets' because of the prescient ways in which he named his first high priest, Aaron, a *christos*, and bestowed on his first successor, Nausē, the name Jesus.[51]

The second figure to be named Jesus in the Septuagint was the son of Josedek the high priest in the times of Zechariah the prophet. It was this Jesus who became the leader of the return of the Jews from the years of Babylonian exile. He was a 'manifest symbol' of Jesus Christ who became a high priest to afford redemption to those who were freed 'in this present life from Babylon, that is from the confusion and slavery, and are taught to hasten to the heavenly city, the true Jerusalem'.[52] Furthermore, Zechariah's vision of the prior Jesus' facing the accusations of the Devil and having dirty garments exchanged for new robes served as a prophetic type of the later Jesus' removal of humanity's sins. A pastiche of cross-references from Isaiah and various New Testament verses clinched Eusebius' typological reading: Christ had carried the sins of the world, clad in them as if in filthy clothes to be exchanged in His Resurrection and Ascension for 'the bright robe of His Father's light'. Christ 'made us who were slaves [of the Devil] His own people'.[53]

Another technique similar to the homonymy principle is the identification of passages that used the title 'Lord' twice. His adoption of this dual-Lord technique allows Eusebius to discern indications of the Son where the careless reader might have missed Him. The statement in Genesis that 'The Lord rained down from heaven brimstone and fire from the Lord' (Genesis 19:23) presents the reader with two Lords who were to be identified as the God over all and His Word (or Son), as Eusebius had already claimed in his *Introduction*.[54] The recognition of a 'second Lord' required nuance, Eusebius quickly adds:

> Yet if we openly confess two Lords, we do not apply similar notions of divinity to them both. We are taught in all reverence to admit an order, that One is the Most High Father and God and Lord, even God and Lord of the Second; but that the Word of God is the Second Lord, Lord of those below Him, and yet not in the same manner as the greater. For the Word of God is not Lord of the Father nor God of the Father, but His Image, and Word and Wisdom and Power, and Master, Lord and God of those that come after Him; whereas the Father is Father and Lord and God even of the Son.[55]

Eusebius' insistent monotheism here is often taken as an expression of a subordinationist theology, and indeed it is. But we should be cautious before evaluating such a pre-Nicene theological exegesis of a text by the standards of a later orthodoxy. Eusebius exhibits a concern to maintain the oneness of God in the face of an equal concern to emphasize the distinct identity of the Son through recognition of the duality of Lords in the Hebrew Scriptures. The dual-Lord approach alerts us to the priority Eusebius already placed on the distinct ontological status of the Son.[56] The characterization of Eusebius' later conflict with Marcellus (who denied a distinct hypostasis to the Word) as a chance to strike back at the more radical pro-Nicene party or as a personally driven vendetta against Marcellus must be restrained by this earlier overt concern to protect the Son's integral existence that had arisen out of his great exegetical–pedagogical projects in both the *Introduction* and the *Proof*.

Beyond the simple attention to the names used by ancient Hebrew writers such as *christos*, Jesus or Lord, basic interpretive tools of much wider application were required for Eusebius' 'proof' to incorporate greater swathes of scriptural material. We have already seen typological interpretation at work in his performance of the homonymy principle. The search for 'types' of Christ in the Old Testament writings could ultimately be quite open-ended: any just person who suffered, was revived or gave blessing or healing could be a type of Christ. Likewise, any priest was a potential type of Christ, whose atoning sacrifice for sins and mediating role between the Father and humanity had defined Him as the greatest and final priest. In this sense, typology was related to the prophetic signification: its initial instantiation carried a predictive valence of a future fuller embodiment.

Typology and prophecy, however, made up only part of Eusebius' exegetical project. A fundamental role was played by allegorical or symbolic interpretation as well. The *Proof*, like the *Introduction* before it and the biblical commentaries after it, applied a broad affiliated range of terminology to get at the search for deeper meanings. The ancient Hebrew writers had used allegory, symbols, metaphors and riddles to conceal mystical significations.[57] His interpretation of a passage from Numbers deemed to make prophetic reference to the star seen by the Magi marking the nativity of Christ exhibits Eusebius' interpretive approach well. The passage not only signified a prophetic fulfilment that would come centuries after the original oracle, according to Eusebius, but a deeper and even more divine meaning. Prompted by the claim in the Genesis creation account that all stars were placed in the sky 'for signs' (Genesis 1:14), Eusebius averred that the appearance of a new star, as indicated in the oracle at hand,

> portended a new luminary that should shine on all the Universe, the Christ of God, a great and a new Star, whose likeness to the star that appeared to the wise men symbolically showed. For since in all the holy and inspired Scriptures the leading object of the meaning is to give mystic and divine instruction, while preserving as well the obvious meaning in its own sphere of historical facts, so the prediction before us was properly and literally fulfilled in the matter of the star that was prophesied to appear at our Saviour's birth.[58]

But this was only a partial interpretation, for the passage also furnished a 'mystic and divine instruction' of the 'spiritual light coming to all humanity through the Saviour's Advent'.[59] The star of the oracle joined with the star visible to the Magi as a symbol of deeper theological import. The prophetic, historical and literal significations, on the one hand, conjoined harmoniously with the mystic and symbolic, on the other. The horizontal fibres of oracular writings were interwoven with the textual reports of their fulfilment, while simultaneously making vertically oriented symbolic relations between the visible or historical and the divine.

Consonant with recent studies that have questioned the neat demarcations of a singularly 'literal' (or Antiochene) against an allegorical (Alexandrian) approach to the interpretation of Scripture,[60] Eusebius saw literal or historical significations residing alongside an allegorical sense and refused to privilege one over the other. Such a conclusion has begun to be recognized in all his writings. Earlier arguments of a shift in Eusebius' exegetical sensibilities have not been able to withstand closer scrutiny.[61] Distinctive emphases in his exegetical works (from the *Introduction* to the *Proof* and commentaries) is largely due to the differing purposes of these works rather than to a change from an earlier escapist allegory during times of persecution to a later worldly, historical–literal interpretation in times of peace.[62]

The Commentaries

In spite of originally being at least ten books, the *Introduction* repeatedly claims to strive for brevity in its exposition of biblical passages. An introductory primer to the Scriptures required concision so as not to tire, distract or discourage the student faced with the complexities of a strange and difficult corpus. Periodically, Eusebius recommends that the interested student, the 'lover of learning', consult a commentary for fuller examination of a passage than that offered by the *Introduction*. At one point in the ninth book (on Isaiah), he states: 'It is not the right time nor is it our aim [*skopos*] to clarify each phrase [*lexin*] of the prophecy [...] We shall send the lover of learning to the commentaries on this passage.'[63] As already noted, the commentaries intended were those of Origen. Yet Origen's commentaries on Isaiah only covered the first 30 chapters of that prophet,[64] while if he did produce a running commentary on the entire book of Psalms Eusebius may not have had it.[65]

The scholarly community would like to know the degree to which Eusebius' commentaries arose from or were aimed at use in a Christian school for aspiring students of Christian philosophy, such as we find hinted at in the *Introduction*. Did Eusebius himself or others have these commentaries at hand during reading seminars similar to those of Plotinus mentioned earlier? If we could presume that Eusebius and other Christian teachers were conducting school in a manner parallel to Plotinus then we could conclude that the procedure would involve the reading of a passage from the Psalms or Isaiah, then consultation of the commentaries of Origen and Eusebius (and others?), followed by the teacher's interpretive determination. Unfortunately, we have little indication in the texts as we have them – and these are rather problematic. Eusebius' original *Commentary on Isaiah* seems to have lacked lemmata (that is, it did not quote the precise lines of scriptural text being expounded at the beginning of each segment of commentary).[66] If we compare it with the nearly contemporary *Commentary on Plato's Parmenides* (often attributed to Porphyry), the omission of a lemma introducing each section of commentary is less surprising.[67] It does, however, make it more difficult to determine any actual procedure or context for reading the commentary and the text being commented upon.

The *Commentary on the Psalms* provides even greater difficulties. Its single print edition (in the Patrologia Graeca series) was based on a combination of materials from different catenae of varying value. A critical edition is sorely needed (and is now, fortunately, under way).[68] At present, the student of Eusebius may find the commentary on Psalms 50 to 91:3 in Jean-Paul Migne's edition (drawn from a single direct witness) to be securely Eusebian, in addition to other portions of sound material.[69] Neither the Psalms nor the Isaiah commentary appears to have commented exhaustively on every single phrase of each biblical sentence. They do, however, proceed in a linear sequence and avoid any narrow thematic scope. Unlike the *Introduction*, which extracted only those passages that fit its Logocentric and prophetic aims (albeit in sequence), the two commentaries exhibit a much greater interest in treating these books in terms of their historical contexts in a way scarcely conceivable in the earlier introductory manual. In addition, along with the elucidation of prophetic significations of the central themes of his earlier works (namely the Incarnation of Christ, the defeat of the Jews by the Romans and the establishment of the Church from the nations), Eusebius incorporated much more discussion of an edifying and practical nature.

Importantly, historical concerns take a prominent position that had been omitted in Eusebius' earlier work (both the *Introduction* and the *Proof*). The elucidation of the historical context of a particular Psalm or a prophecy from Isaiah was naturally excluded from those works by their very genres (as conceived, at least, by Eusebius) and their fundamental purpose of reading the ancient texts in a prophetic framework. The commentaries recognize the deep historical import of these writings, and so, while not disrupting the prophetic and allegorical valences emphasized in his earlier expositions, they bring the historical and the prophetic into a fuller conversation with each other. The two were, in any case, close conceptual allies: the recognition of a text as possessing prophetic significance only meant that its historical impact fell at different, sometimes widely separated, historical intervals. In this sense, Eusebius is often found declaring that the lines of a passage, which were deemed to be prophetic of the life of Christ or the spread of the Church, were fulfilled 'to the letter', or according to the literal sense (*pros lexin*), and at the same time 'historically', or in accordance with history (*pros historian*).[70]

This principle was true of the *Introduction* and *Proof* as well. What is uniquely prominent in the commentaries, however, is a concern for the historical context of the composition of the Psalm or prophecy as an aid to proper understanding. In a more polemical vein, the earlier works had challenged Jewish opponents to find a historical fulfilment of prophetic utterances in the Psalms or Prophets that was closer to the immediate historical context of its composition. Such questions were rhetorically framed and presumed the impossibility of finding a fulfilment other than that embodied in the Incarnation or rise of the Church. The commentaries, on the contrary, exhibit less of the flair and bombast of diatribe and instead adopt the calm and studied tone of the patient scholar. In part this is no doubt due to the fact that the hostile context of the persecution and its aftermath was drifting farther away over the historical horizon and the need for polemical fuel was felt less intensely. The different aims, tone and form of a commentary were also, however, equally responsible for the increase in historical considerations. Even if not directly applicable to a 'proof of the Gospel', and therefore seemingly less pragmatic for the contestation over identity and interpretation, Eusebius' commentaries nurtured a care for the textual details and contextual information that might otherwise have been omitted in the persistent focus of the *Introduction* or *Proof.*

The commentaries fostered the full-scale and universal marshalling of knowledge for the sake of thinking through an ancient and authoritative text. The world could be charted, or 'mentally mapped', by pondering the peoples and places named in the Psalms or Prophets. For instance, in elucidating a rather obscure oracle against Idumea (Isaiah 21:11–12), the *Commentary on Isaiah* asserts that the prophecy had 'not been made idly', but arose within a context of conflict and assault by the Idumeans against Israel.[71] This fact was not made clear from the text of Isaiah itself, and so Eusebius, claiming that 'history bears witness to these things', cross-referenced a Psalm that complained of an attack in which a united coalition of Idumeans, Ishmaelites, Moab and the Agarenoi, Gebal, Ammon and Amalek were encamped against Israel (Psalms 82:6 LXX). The reader should notice, the commentator avers, the placement of the Idumeans at the beginning of the list of enemies. This was the great nation located in Petra of Arabia, 'which continued the succession [of its lineage] from Esau'. Because another name for Esau (who was noted for being the brother of Jacob and hence a son of Israel) was Edom, his descendants had taken the name of Idumeans. When the oracle mentioned those who called upon God from Sēeir, the commentary informed its reader that this was 'the mountain of Esau' located in Arabia, which was recognized 'even now' by its inhabitants by the same name.[72] The oracle gave hope to those Israelites being attacked by the Idumeans. The locating of the objects of the oracle both ethnically and geographically is not extensive (totalling roughly half a page of Ziegler's edition), but it is typical of the compiling of data (however suspect by modern critical standards) for the exegesis of biblical passages. This was not so much the 'organization of knowledge' as the amassing of information within the commentary that could pile upon verses or phrases of the ancient text. Each passage could become a congealed mass of ethnographic, linguistic and historical data. In the commentary's account of the oracle against the Idumeans its purpose was to fill out the historical context of the oracle's composition itself before turning to the identification of its equally historical fulfilment ('not even a whole year would pass' before the oracle would be fulfilled[73]).

The mechanism employed behind the historical reconstruction and hence the construction of knowledge about Isaiah's oracle was the cross-reference.[74] Eusebius' commentaries moved beyond the use of cross-references in the earlier *Introduction*, where we noticed that they were adopted in order to interweave the diversity of the Old and New Testaments into an organic self-interpretive and even interconnecting textual assemblage whose focal point was the revelation of the divine Logos. In the commentary, cross-references occur, whether through direct quotation or more subtle allusions, for more varied, but especially historical, purposes. In the case of the comments on the oracle against the Idumeans, Eusebius' historical contextualization rests on the single reference to Psalm 82 as its sole support. Its singularity makes it an integral component in his exposition; without it the exposition would dissolve entirely.

Elsewhere the historical cross-references can become more complicated through multiple references while at the same time seeking to make sharper historical distinctions. His comments on an oracle against Damascus (Isaiah 17:1–3) begin by cross-referencing an earlier occurrence of Damascus in Isaiah (Isaiah 10:9).[75] The earlier prophecy against Damascus had been fulfilled in the conquest of Assyria as 'history bears witness', proof of which came from a quotation from 2 Kings. Both the former prophecy and the historical confirmation were, however, only quoted so as to differentiate them from the present oracle and its prophetic signification. The oracle against Damascus of Isaiah 17 found its fulfilment 'to the letter' (*pros lexin*) in the times of Jeremiah, as a quotation from that prophet would confirm (Jeremiah 30:30–2). The fulfilment that was recorded by Jeremiah had only a temporal effect, contrary to the Septuagint's supplemental claim that it would be 'for ever'.[76] Eusebius quoted from the Apostle Paul for confirmation that Damascus' kingdom was restored and a king reinstated there (2 Corinthians 11:32).

This passage from the commentary exhibits the importance of multiple cross-references for the determination of the historical fulfilment of a prophecy. It is of interest that Eusebius invokes other translators than the Septuagint with reference to phrases of each biblical text quoted in this passage (not only the texts from Isaiah 10 and 17, but also those of 2 Kings and Jeremiah). A significant feature of Eusebius' commentaries (as well as his earlier exegetical writings) is the appeal to the multiple Greek translations of the Hebrew Scriptures, which had been made available in Origen's Hexapla (see Chapter 1). While the Septuagint seems to have been the most common translation of choice among early Christian communities and the other translators were rejected as being too Jewish (as Eusebius himself sometimes complained),[77] Eusebius' commentaries show a remarkable openness to other versions.[78] In the passage under discussion here, he even rejected the Septuagint in favour of the others, which of course aided in explaining and justifying a passage of Paul that contradicted the translation of the Septuagint. But not all appeals to the various translations of the Hebrew were so purposeful. Following his quotation of the Septuagint version of Jeremiah, he interjects the phrasing of the translator Symmachus apparently only to pause over the greatness of Damascus and so heighten the dramatic effect of its fall though it had been 'the mother city of happiness'.[79] Whether for rhetorical punch or for more important interpretive aims, Eusebius' frequent inclusion of the non-Septuagint translations provides us with one of the most important testimonies to the nature and importance of Origen's Hexapla, which, due to the difficulty and cost of copying such a large text, has largely been lost to us.

Eusebius' commentaries on the Psalms and on Isaiah were monumental achievements that surpassed the work of Origen on these biblical books and made an important impact on later patristic exegetical work on each. While throughout Eusebius' corpus the Psalms and Isaiah held a privileged place in his intellectual framework, he did not limit himself to commentaries on these two books. Significant remains from commentaries on Daniel, Luke and 1 Corinthians survive. Unfortunately, they have received only scant scholarly attention. They hold much important material that would aid our appreciation of key areas of Eusebius' thought, such as his eschatological notions, his prioritization of the ascetic way of life and of ascetics within ecclesiastical social hierarchies, his post-Porphyrian exegesis of Daniel, and so on. Eusebius had keen exegetical sensibilities that modern scholarship is just beginning to address adequately.

Reference Works and Study Aids

In addition to those treatises and commentaries that Eusebius composed within the context and for the benefit of a Scripture-reading curriculum, he turned his scholarly industry to other compositions that could function as reference works for the study of both the Old and New Testaments. These included his *Onomasticon*, letters to Stephanus and Marinus in question-and-answer format, and the *Gospel Canons*.

The *Onomasticon* (meaning 'on biblical place names') is the final instalment of a larger and otherwise lost four-book work dedicated to Paulinus, who was the bishop of Tyre until his death in 327 or 331.[80] It was probably written not long before Paulinus' death.[81] Fortunately, Eusebius himself describes the first three books: a table of Greek equivalents for ancient Hebrew place names, a narrative geography (a *katagraphē*, literally, a 'register') of Judea during the time of its organization among the 12 tribes of Israel, and a description of the city of Jerusalem with its famed Temple.[82] The *Onomasticon*, for its part, contains an alphabetical list of all the toponyms found in the Hebrew Scriptures with a brief entry providing additional information (especially their location if known to Eusebius). Each letter's section is further subdivided according to the book in the Bible in which the name occurs (beginning with Genesis, then Exodus, and so on).

The work would have been of immense help in determining whether a place name encountered in one's reading occurred elsewhere in Scripture and what had happened in that place up to the present (whether it was intended for use by pilgrims to holy sites is less clear).[83] Several cities were identified as Jewish in Eusebius' day; some were even identified as Christian (or Ebionite).[84] What precisely such identifications entailed is unclear, but their assignment to various cities or villages exhibits a fascinating insight into Eusebius' geographical vision of his world (even if the identifications were made by Eusebius' sources, rather than originating with him).[85] Contributing to the ethnic and religious valences of his geographical vision were the notices of what could 'still even now' be seen or performed at particular sites. Christians still sought baptism at the place where John baptized; the site of Lazarus' resurrection, the hill where the demons possessed a herd of pigs, the garden where Christ prayed before His Passion, or the rock from which water flowed under Moses' striking could all still be seen in the author's day. Pilgrims (of Jewish or Christian affiliation) could visit the tombs of Joshua, Rachel, Amos, Habakkuk or Joseph.[86] The *Onomasticon* thus served not only as a reference tool for students of the Bible and its geography. It was a catalogue that evinced the living sacredness of its sites even within a scholarly medium.

Another reference tool was more limited in scope, but equally powerful in its literary, scholarly and spiritual significance. The *Canons* allowed for the first systematic approach to what is now commonly called 'the synoptic problem'. The four canonical Gospels share much material that is similar and sometimes nearly identical (especially Matthew, Mark and Luke – the 'synoptic' Gospels). To enable the proper recognition and study of the similar passages, the *Canons* presents a compendium of ten tables. The first contains a list of the passages that are shared by all of the Gospels; the second a list of the passages shared only by Matthew, Mark and Luke; the third a list of those shared by Matthew, Luke and John; the fourth, only those shared by Mathew, Mark and John; the fifth, only those shared by Matthew and Luke; and so on.[87]

As the accompanying introductory letter to a certain Carpianus explains, his motivation behind compiling the tables was to avoid breaking up the narratives of each of the Gospels as an earlier 'four in one' (*Diatessaron*) parallel version made by Ammonius had done.[88] Eusebius' *Canons* with its copy of the four Gospels preserves each intact, while making it possible to locate comparable material in the others, through the use of section markers at different intervals in the text. This was, then, a first step towards the system of chapters and verses in all modern versions of the Bible. The *Canons* sharpened a reader's ability to see the diversity of expression and organization of the four canonical Gospels, while not forcing them into an artificially harmonized 'four in one' master version. Eusebius did not, however, shy away from the challenge of harmonizing the apparent contradictions between the various narratives about Christ's life.[89] He composed two works in the form of question-and-answer letters to address such problems.

The letters to Stephanus (*Gospel Questions to Stephanus*) and Marinus (*Gospel Questions to Marinus*) are not easily categorized as either pedagogical treatises or reference works. Both are presented in the form of questions followed by sometimes lengthy answers. In the case of the letter addressed to Stephanus the first 'question' appears to be somewhat hostile in tone: 'In vain they chatter that Christ is from the seed of David.'[90] It is impossible to know whether the addressee of either work was a patron of Eusebius or a student who had sought his teacher's answer on a critical question he had heard, though a hint of a close yet subordinate relationship is provided by Eusebius' address to Stephanus as his 'most industrious son' at the conclusion of the first letter and to 'my most honourable and industrious son Marinus' at the commencement of the second.[91] On the other hand, a bishop of Eusebius' standing might have addressed just about anyone as a son.

Even though our present witnesses to the letters do not preserve their original form (both survive in a single epitome and numerous scattered fragments), their genre was clearly that of question and answer.[92] The letter addressed to Stephanus comprised multiple books (probably two) focused on difficulties arising from the different birth narratives, especially the genealogies, in the Gospels of Matthew and Luke. The one-book letter dedicated to Marinus, which was apparently given to him along with the two to Stephanus, aimed to solve issues surrounding the conflicting narratives in the Gospels' accounts of Christ's death.

The application of the question-and-answer genre to interpretive issues arising from an authoritative text had already been composed in the form of 'Homeric Questions' by philosophers such as Heraclitus and Porphyry. Like these earlier examples of the genre, Eusebius' contributions sought to discover sound answers to interpretive difficulties or even details that might seem to present outright contradictions in the text. As with the 'Homeric Questions', Eusebius' letters to Stephanus and Marinus used the text itself to answer its own difficulties: just as Homer was to be interpreted by Homer, Scripture was to be interpreted by Scripture. The principle had already been adopted in Eusebius' earlier exegetical works, as we have seen. Here, Eusebius looked to etymology (for instance, the title 'Pharisee' came from 'Phares', a name given to a man included in Matthew's genealogy of Christ even though he was not, in fact, actually part of His lineage[93]), as well as to creative use of cross-referencing (for instance, the mention of Uriah's wife in the genealogy led to consideration of David's Psalms after his adulterous affair with her, which in turn indicated, through a further cross-reference to the prophet Micah, the place of Christ's birth, namely Bethlehem[94]), in order to find suitable answers to the questions posed.

Strikingly, these question-and-answer letters allow us to see a different side of Eusebius, one that had not found prominent expression in his other exegetical works. In contrast to his pervasively critical stance on the Jews, one answer indicates something of a conciliatory, even wistful, tone. In a discussion of the two sons of Tamar (who was mentioned in Matthew's genealogy), Eusebius claims that each represented a different way of life, the one under the Law, the other under the Gospel. Of the twin sons, the one representing the Gospel had stretched out his hand first, though the one representing the Law was actually born before the other. If only the second had awaited the proper order, there would have been harmony between the Law and Gospel.[95] While the harmony would only have come with the appropriate subordination of the two ways of life, Eusebius' remark nonetheless remains striking for its softer tone, in contrast to the sharper demarcations of Jewish from Hebrew/Christian identity we find in other works.

A second remarkable feature of the work is Eusebius' highly favourable account of the women in the Gospel accounts, in particular Tamar and Ruth, both of whom were mentioned in Matthew's genealogy of Christ. Tamar had dressed as a prostitute to sleep with her father-in-law, Judah. How could such a scandalous woman be included in Christ's lineage? Eusebius responds with a strong exculpation of Tamar: she had been wronged by her father-in-law and had played the prostitute only with pure motives to show strategically his wrongdoing. Far from being immoral, Tamar exhibited a 'philosophical and self-controlled life'; 'though a foreigner, she made it her prayer to be found worthy of the race of the friends of God.' Similarly Ruth, being a foreigner, represented the 'calling of the foreign nations'. By overcoming the Law's exclusion of foreigners she became 'the supreme example for all of us who are foreigners from the nations'.[96] In other works, Eusebius had declared the amazing exhibition of the philosophical life on the part of Christians from all categories, men, women, children, educated, uneducated, and so on. Here, he has elaborated on this inclusive tendency, basing it on the details of biblical genealogies.

Whether these reference works were used within an educational context at Caesarea cannot be known. It may be that they were aimed at individual readers outside of any institutional scholastic environment. Nevertheless, they appear to be scholarly by-products of a school context where texts were pored over in relations of interpretive apprenticeship between the master reader and his students. At the same time that he asserted his own interpretive authority, his exegetical investigations did allow for a certain degree of openness or 'exegetical prudence', rather than dogmatism.[97] Eusebius was a central figure both in a school of some sort at Caesarea as well as in the broader educational developments within Late Antique Christianity. Of the biblical scholars of Late Antiquity, Eusebius was the most innovative and industrious. His searching explorations of critical and creative ways of studying the Scriptures and learning to read them well were at once wideranging and incisive. His impact can still be felt to the present day.

IV

WRITING PAST
AND PEOPLEHOOD

OF THE MANY WORKS THAT survive from Eusebius' hand, the *Ecclesiastical History* has been translated and treated in scholarly discussion more often and in more languages than any other text.[1] Already in Late Antiquity it was recognized as the authoritative history of the first three centuries of Christianity. The great trio of fifth-century Church historians, Socrates, Sozomen and Theodoret, all began their own accounts where Eusebius' left off. His text is not merely the first 'ecclesiastical history' that happens to be extant, then; it marks an innovative and exploratory advance in the conception of the task of history-writing itself, one that would make an immense impact on history as a literary genre as well as on how to represent textually the people who identified themselves as Christians.

Eusebius himself remarked in the preface of the *History* that he was entering uncharted textual territory in his historical project:

> We are the first to enter on the undertaking, as travellers on some desolate
> and untrodden way [...] For nowhere can we find even the bare footsteps
> of men who have preceded us in the same path, unless it be those slight

indications by which in divers ways they have left to us partial accounts of the times through which they have passed.[2]

Some hints towards the new historical project Eusebius proposed for himself had been faintly indicated by earlier Christian authors, who stood as beacons to guide him, if only partially. From these earlier writers, Eusebius would draw 'whatever seems relevant' for the task of writing an ecclesiastical history, as though he were 'culling flowers, as it were, from literary meadows'.[3] Indeed, one of the unique features of the *History* is the great quantity of often lengthy quotations, paraphrases and direct discussions of the writings left by his Christian intellectual and episcopal predecessors. His is thus one of the first truly documentary histories (at least in terms of proportions – though the appellation of 'documentary history' also occludes much of what goes on in the pages of the *History*).

Eusebius' activity of plucking, however, should probably not be limited to the quotation or paraphrase of other texts. The history he produced also selectively incorporated a variety of earlier genres, including martyrology, apology, epistle, history, polemical treatise and commentary.[4] Quotations from such a wide array of diverse texts transformed Eusebius' work of history into a vibrant literary collage. Like so many of his endeavours, the *History* was a grand literary experiment.

Before the History

The *Ecclesiastical History*'s novelty was built not only on the careful selection of literary fragments from those who had gone before. Eusebius makes explicit his dependence on his own earlier work in the area of history. The *History* is marked out as an elaboration in greater detail of what his *Chronicon* (or, more precisely, the *Chronological Tables*) had collected in summary form.[5] The *Chronicon* was itself a striking innovation in the representation of the past. Of its two books, the first provides a lengthy account of chronographical knowledge that aims to be universal in scope and contains a compilation of the records of earlier chronographers. This account includes quotations from Eusebius' predecessors, including Porphyry, Julius Africanus, Josephus, Alexander Polyhistor and Manetho.[6] Comprising a mixture of narrative summaries and lists of kings and other major figures from the most important nations, this first portion of Eusebius' work provides a massive overview of the historical data on rulers, empires, athletic victors, thinkers, texts and wars. What might be sensed as awkward and incongruously presented blocks of narrative or repetitive lists evokes an aesthetic of erudition: this was a literary monument that charted and organized chronographical knowledge in a manner inclusive of varied forms of presentation and that represented a conglomerate of different types of historical figure (kings, emperors, archons, athletes, priests or holy men).

The material of the first book of the *Chronicon* can be broken into five basic segments. The first focuses on the various eastern empires: first the Chaldeans, then the Assyrians and Babylonians (Chapters 1–15); the second deals with the Hebrews and Jews, from Adam up to the time of the Romans (Chapters 16–18); the third addresses the Egyptians from the ancient pharaohs up to the end of the Ptolemies (Chapters 19–22); the fourth turns to the Greeks and then the Macedonians (Chapters 23–40); and finally the fifth section is concerned with the Romans (Chapters 41–8). The relative dating schemas differ between years of kingly rule, dynasties or Olympiads. Yet even with these differing schemas placed together in succession, this compilation preserves and categorizes the raw materials from what Eusebius deemed to be the best sources for charting a universal chronology.

Consonant with the first book, the second half of the chronographical project, the *Chronicon* proper, lays out in three or more columns a parallel synchronization of the data collected about each of the major nations. Following preliminary remarks on the difficulties inherent in the task of synchronization (such as the problems of the biblical numbers for the lifespans of ancient persons), Eusebius furnishes a series of bare lists that contain the number of years assigned to the kings of each nation (or the patriarchs, judges, kings and high priests, in the case of the Jews). These lists form the strands of the most important and innovative of this work's contributions to the study of chronography. The bulk of the second book then consists of a stunning synchronized collation of the dates of such historical figures in parallel columns. The foundation of the synchronism was the numbering of years from the birth of Abraham, provided in the left margin.

Given that chronological data was often used to fuel arguments in the development of cultural or nationalistic apologetics, it is surprising that Eusebius refused to alter the chronology to give Abraham precedence: year 1 of Abraham is made synchronous with the 43rd year of the reign of Ninus (in the column belonging to the Assyrians), the 22nd year of Europs (in the column of the Greek Sicyonians) and the first year of the 16th dynasty of the Egyptians.[7] Nations come and go from the columnar collation, however, while the years of Abraham remain constant from beginning to end.[8] Furthermore, it is fascinating to see the number of columns become progressively narrow as each of the Hellenistic dynasties fall, eventually leaving only the columns representing the Romans and the Jews. Then, in the second year of Vespasian, the year 2086 of Abraham, with a marginal note remarking on the destruction of the Jewish Temple by the Romans, the Jewish column disappears. The remainder of the columnar table consists of page upon page of the single national column of the Romans marked only by the Olympiads and the year of Abraham.

The effect of such a chronographical collation is (at least) threefold. First, the diversity of national histories was visibly united into a single, massive world-historical stream. The varied and independent trajectories of separate nations had become anchored to a single historical vision grounded in the Abrahamic dating system. Second, the reduction in the number of columns over time, ending with a single column representing Rome alone, expressed an assumption that what occurred within the Empire during the lifetime of Eusebius was of world-historical significance. The omission of Goths, Ethiopians, Indians and Parthians or Persians may appear to suggest an assumption of the lack of importance of the kingdoms in these different regions. Alternatively, their omission from the table may exhibit the presumption that these nations were actually subject to Rome – a claim that appears absurd to the modern historical understanding but which recurs not infrequently in Roman imperial literature. Third, the singularity of Rome in the final portion of the table makes a significant impression. On the one hand, the conquests of Alexander and the imperial control of his successor dynasties had created the context for extracting historical data from the conquered peoples and allowing for Hellenistic intellectuals to compile and begin collating the diverse pieces of information. On the other hand, Rome's Empire, following its appropriation of Hellenistic knowledge, had appeared in Eusebius' tables to put a stop to the discovery of new knowledge from further external peoples. The narrowing of national columns may appear to mark a narrowing of knowledge.

Both conceptually and textually, therefore, Eusebius' chronographical work made an impact upon Late Antique historiography that cannot be underestimated. One scholar's assessment even claimed that it 'must rank as one of the most influential books of all time'.[9] While many of his predecessors had made significant steps towards a universal chronography, none had achieved such a feat, both in the incorporation of sources and in the organization and layout of chronological data. Knowledge remains ever near to power: the resources required and the expenses accrued in the production of such a great exhibition of universal chronographical knowledge would have been immense. We would like to know Eusebius' sources for acquiring texts (only some of which could derive from Origen's library, but what of Longinus' library?), the materials for the book itself (who paid for parchment and ink?) and the manual labour involved (slaves or students?) in the years so closely following the Great Persecution. But no hints are given in the text of the *Chronicon* itself.[10]

The History of the Church

Much of the innovative work of the *Chronicon* found an echo in or became the basis of some of the most important features of the *History*. The task of synchronized collation, exhibited in the earlier work in the tabular columns adjoined to the dates of Abraham, was pursued in the later work. The closest resonance between the two works appears in the notations of episcopal succession in the *History*. There Eusebius traces the line of bishops at the major cities of Alexandria, Jerusalem, Antioch and Rome. But rather than enumerating all bishops in order from the first century to the third at a given city, the first seven books of the *History* follow a narrative organized chronologically by the reigns of Roman emperors, inserting reports on the deaths of bishops and the names of their successors at the appropriate moments. By avoiding the use of episcopal tables or formulaic lists of bishops, Eusebius' *History* approaches the form of an annalistic history. In such a history (the tradition of which stretches back to Thucydides) all the events deemed significant by the author would be narrated in year-by-year blocks. Those events might, therefore, lack narrative flow or integrity of their own, but the reader gained a more global (or at least, Mediterranean-wide) sense of all that happened in geographically or politically unconnected areas at a given time. In the past such annalistic histories were based on each year of a war (such as the Peloponnesian War) or on the tenures of consuls or emperors (as in the histories of Livy and Tacitus). Eusebius' structuring pattern for the most part followed the reigns of emperors.[11]

This meant that Eusebius' synchronized collation of information, documents and literary texts had to go beyond merely acquiring the names of bishops at any given time. It also involved making determinations about the dating of texts at his disposal based on internal or external clues. The imperial regnal structure produced a space for bringing together all the relevant or useful texts of a given period and reading them within the appropriate chronological frame. The reader acquired an impression of an age and its diversity of figures, texts and happenings. The *History* was a massive synchronism in narrative form. The regnal framework instilled the sense that one knew who the great Christians were in the reign of Marcus Aurelius, for instance, what texts they were producing (and reading), who their enemies were (whether heretics or persecutors) and where they travelled.

The fact that the narrative synchronisms followed imperial reigns seems to parallel the *Chronicon*'s final narrowing to the singular national column of the Romans. Indeed, the very first synchronic statement places the birth of Christ in the reign of Augustus and the governorship of Quirinius:

> It was, then, the forty-second year of the reign of Augustus, and the twenty-eighth year after the submission of Egypt and the death of

> Antony and Cleopatra (and with her the Egyptian dynasty of the
> Ptolemies came to an end), when our Saviour and Lord Jesus Christ, in
> accordance with the prophecies concerning Him, was born in Bethlehem
> in Judea at the time of the census which then first took place, while
> Quirinius was governor of Syria.[12]

This Augustus–Christ synchronism recurs elsewhere in the *History* and appears in other works, such as the *Preparation for the Gospel* and *Proof of the Gospel*. It is frequently taken as representing Eusebius' alleged attempt to unite the Empire and the Church, which had sprung up at the same time. While it was used for differing rhetorical aims in its various occurrences in Eusebius' corpus and, in any case, had already afforded a diverse and even contrary range of uses in earlier Christian texts (from the Gospel of Luke to the work of Melito of Sardis, Origen and Hippolytus), there is reason to pause before too quickly seeing this passage as an attempt at imperial-ecclesial unification.

Following the four introductory chapters of Book 1, the fifth chapter sets the precedent for many of the narrative synchronisms of the rest of the *History*. Eusebius ties together key figures and associated events in as chronologically precise a manner as possible (in the present instance, providing the year of Augustus' reign relative to the end of the Ptolemaic dynasty and Quirinius' governorship). Confirmation of the synchronism is then presented from authoritative sources; here, and elsewhere in Book 1, Josephus takes pride of place. Throughout the first book the Jewish historian, who lived to see the fall of Jerusalem, is a textual treasure trove from whom Eusebius extracts several choice quotations that 'confirm' or provide 'testimony' to the *History*'s narrative claims. Strikingly, Eusebius sought to synchronize Josephus' own works with each other as well as with passages from the New Testament.[13] Here, in the fifth chapter, two quotations from Josephus are explicitly referenced as coming from the 18th book of the *Antiquities of the Jews* and the second book of the *Jewish Wars*, respectively. Even though the first quotation appears to be used only because it parallels part of the second passage (that there was an uprising by a certain Judas), which is more relevant to Eusebius' purposes of confirming Quirinius' governorship and census-taking, the parallel quotations commence the practice of documentary cross-referencing that is one of the distinguishing features of the work.

Importantly, the choice of Josephus as the first source to be cited highlights the Jewish historian, and particularly his *Antiquities of the Jews*, as an important historiographical model that Eusebius chose to follow.[14] The *Antiquities* had traced the history of the Jewish people based upon a chronological framework attached to the reigns of various rulers, whether of Judea or elsewhere, as well as to Olympiads. The connection of his narrative to the reigns of foreign rulers had provided an organizing schema, and the remarks tying events to the reigns of kings, consuls and emperors or to Olympiads did not require a positive evaluation of those Greek, Roman or Macedonian nations who provided the markers of time (and, indeed, could even stand alongside an antithetical attitude to those nations). Eusebius' adoption of Josephus as a model prompted his own notation of emperors' reigns as synchronic pegs on which to hang his ecclesiastical narrative and the many reports of episcopal succession. It need not signify that Eusebius was pursuing a project of the promotion of that Empire in a straightforward or simple manner.

This observation is salutary for our assessment of Eusebius' Augustus–Christ synchronism in particular as well as the general occurrence throughout the *History* of chronological notes attaching events or figures of the Church to an imperial timeline. If recent reassessments have (rightly) been critical of flat and misleading modern caricatures of Eusebius as a 'court theologian' or panegyrist of the Empire and emperor, the reader of the *History* should be wary of finding a pro-imperial agenda in the Augustus–Christ synchronism when none is explicitly formulated.[15] The year of Augustus is noted – but no praise or elaboration of the deeds or character of the emperor is given. We need not have recourse to a purported pro-imperial ideology on Eusebius' part to account for the synchronism (and other imperial chronological notations throughout the work). A distinction must be drawn between the notion of the *History* as a Roman imperial text, modelled on an earlier imperial text (Josephus' *Antiquities*), and the claim that it is a Romanizing or pro-imperial text. Even the last books of the *History* (to which we shall turn below), which relate the rise of the first Christian emperor, may be less pro-imperial and more ambivalent than frequently claimed.

Quotation and History

The passages taken from Josephus in Book 1 are first in a long succession of quotations from earlier sources that pockmark the narrative surface of the *History*.[16] While the second book of the *Chronicon* constructed history as a visual affair – laid out on its pages one saw the several distinct threads that made up a world-historical tapestry – the *History* exhibits history in emphatically textual terms.[17] An apologetic tone pervades the work in its frequent invocations of documents as witnesses to the veracity of Eusebius' narrative.[18] The Augustus–Christ synchronism hinges on an allusion to the Gospel of Luke's naming of Augustus and Quirinius that was deemed to require textual confirmation from Josephus. Quotations, paraphrases or allusions to other texts combined to solidify the reliability of the account and to produce a textualization of history – that is, history-writing as a texture of earlier texts.[19] Josephus confirmed the sacred record; Gaius and Dionysius of Corinth 'certified' Eusebius' account, as did Ignatius; Hegesippus confirmed the narrative of the apostolic age, and even the anti-Christian Porphyry could be quoted as confirmation of Origen's great learning.[20] These and other quotations served a legitimizing role granting an authoritative status to the *History*.

Quotations could do more than affirm Eusebius' own narrative claims. In some instances, a quotation provided an authoritative evaluation of a person, school of thought or ecclesiastical problem. Therefore, Irenaeus' references proved that Justin was worth studying; Montanism was refuted through the quotation of various authors (some anonymous); it was shown that advice or opposition to the Church at Rome on the celebration of Easter came from different bishops; the heresy of Artemon was opposed; the bishopric of Asclepiades was affirmed; a letter of Alexander and Theoctistus was shown to defend the preaching of Origen.[21] In the preface, Eusebius claims that his history will be innovative, but in his theological stance or decisions about the orthodoxy or appropriateness of a historical figure's actions, he presents himself as conforming to the authoritative voices of the true Church. In terms of doctrine and practice, he wanted to say nothing new.[22]

Quotations or textual references could confer legitimacy not only on an individual or school of thought, but even on another quotation. Therefore, a passage from Justin Martyr was validated through appeal to Irenaeus; Clement was confirmed by Papias; Hegesippus agreed with Clement, while multiple quotations from Josephus confirmed Hegesippus; Irenaeus and Polycarp alluded to Ignatius' letters; one passage of Josephus confirmed earlier ones by the same author; Dionysius of Corinth confirmed the authoritative status of Clement's *Letter to the Romans*; Melito's work on Easter was quoted by Clement of Alexandria; Serapion cited Apollonius' writings.[23] Alternatively, a text's legitimacy could be criticized through quotation.[24] While it has frequently been emphasized that Eusebius is one of the first authors to show an interest in the precise parameters of a biblical canon, his concerns are as much about the texts that use the various biblical texts. Proofs of authoritative legitimacy rested in quotation and thus the *History* becomes a mass of cross-references. For Eusebius, the history of the Church was a history of those texts deemed foundational to its communal life, texts produced by its members, texts granting legitimacy to those other texts, or texts against texts deemed to be threatening to the life and thought of the Church. His was an unparalleled textualization of history.

Such a textualizing impulse meant that quotation was an end in itself. Beyond those that he used for a purpose, others were included, Eusebius claimed, merely because they were too good to pass up. Therefore: 'There is nothing better' than to quote from Josephus; 'There is nothing better than to listen to [Hegesippus] who tells us these facts'; 'I think it most necessary to give in this history the account [of the *Martyrdom of Polycarp*].'[25] Without needing to stake out legitimacy or confirm the narrative's accuracy, Eusebius could quote a passage merely for the readers' edification.[26] One of Eusebius' longest quotations, that of the letter about the martyrs of Lyons (totalling roughly 15 pages), likewise seems to have been offered purely for edification, though he makes no explicit claims.[27]

No doubt the *History* could have made a more discreet or concealed use of sources; texts could have been invoked in order to authorize the account given but their presentation could have been limited to paraphrase. Instead, we are confronted with a quotational pastiche that connects the text of the *History* to the venerable and authoritative texts of the Christian tradition in an aesthetically unmediated manner. The collage of quotations on the page elicits a feeling of walking with the master of the Caesarean library as he guides the reader to move from shelf to shelf (or cupboard) retrieving the works of great historians, bishops or Christian philosophers, opening (or unrolling) them, bidding him or her to read the relevant passage or passages before moving on to the next. Not all the quotations come from works of the library at Caesarea (the location or institutional setting of which we know nothing), however; some come from Edessa and several from Jerusalem.[28] One walks in the presence of the collected wisdom, struggles and triumphs of those who studied under the disciples, and who witnessed the deaths of martyrs, opposed heretics or wrote to alleviate conflict between and within churches.[29] An immediacy is fostered between reader and texts within the *History* when Eusebius recommends that we 'take up and read' or even reproduces an autograph of a letter. 'I, Aurelius Cyrenaeus, a martyr, pray for your welfare [...] I, Aelius Publius Julius, bishop of Debeltum, a colony in Thrace [...]'[30] The very reproduction by the hand of Eusebius would seem to destroy the legitimacy of an autograph by definition – yet it provides a sort of second-hand or deflected presence.

Similarly, the *History* acquires a shared sense of legitimacy as an accurate account when Eusebius quotes favourably from a passage of Irenaeus invoking Christ's judgement upon those who carelessly copy his books, remarking: 'May his [Irenaeus'] words be spoken to our profit and be narrated in order that we may keep those primitive and truly sacred men as the best example of the most zealous carefulness.'[31] A text praising accuracy in others thereby seeks to garner the trust of the reader in its own faithful precision. Not all modern readers have been willing to trust Eusebius on this score. Material that survives only in Eusebius has been accused of being inauthentic (such as the letter on the martyrs of Lyons), and even material that does survive in the independent manuscripts of other authors has been doubted and Eusebius assigned a role as potential forger.[32] In each instance, the critics face serious challenges: either the style of a quotation is sufficiently different from that of Eusebius (though he himself is no purist), or peculiar vocabulary shared by a quotation and Eusebius may only be the result of Eusebius' common chameleonic practice of adopting the diction of his sources well before he turns to quote them.

Even if Eusebius does not invent sources, his accuracy may still be impugned. He confuses the chronology of bishops at Rome and guesses at that of the bishops of Antioch,[33] and in any case, the sort of institutional establishment of single bishops of the great cities that Eusebius presumes is probably an anachronism imputed on earlier generations. Accusations and identification of Eusebius' errors, intentional or not, have frequently arisen.[34] His veracity as a historian has been severely questioned and his status as an apologist and spin-doctor has been declared. Too frequently the fault line has lain between Eusebius the historian and Eusebius the apologist, as if these are easily separable tendencies.[35] In fact, historians have never been able to write an objective account of a period, event or movement from a location devoid of moral, ideological, historiographical, theological or philosophical sets of assumptions. It is thus a felicitous shift in recent scholarship that seeks to move beyond the scholar/apologist dichotomy.[36]

Historical Vision and Christian Nation

Consideration of the *History*'s preface might leave the impression that there is no single historical vision, but only a cluster of loosely connected priorities. In rapid succession, five concerns are enumerated as the guiding themes of the work: the history of ecclesiastical leaders (the successors of the Apostles, the presiders over congregations and the ambassadors of the Word through oral or written means); the rise of heretics; the defeat of the Jews; the persecution of Christians by 'the nations'; and, closely related, the martyrdoms 'of our own times' and the recent end of persecution.[37] Here again, there may be an echo of Josephus' *Antiquities*. That work had concluded with the claim that its account of Jewish history from the creation to the end of Nero's reign had described: what had befallen the Jews in Egypt, Syria and Palestine; the persecution of the Jews by the imperial nations of the Assyrians, Babylonians, Persians, Macedonians and Romans; the successions of high priests; the successions of Jewish kings; and all that was written in the sacred books of the Jews.[38] The parallels between Josephus and Eusebius are almost too close to be coincidence. The concerns central to Josephus' *Antiquities* are thus exhibited and transformed in Eusebius' *History*.

Importantly, what had united the basic themes of the *Antiquities*, namely the identity of the Jews as an *ethnos* (a nation or people) possessing shared history, territory, religious texts and practices, and other cultural customs, likewise provided the unifying crucible for the closely parallel themes of Eusebius' *History*. Later in the preface, Eusebius explicitly identified the Christians as an *ethnos*:

> For when the advent of our Saviour, Jesus Christ, recently shone forth
> on all men, it was confessedly a new race [*ethnos*], which thus appeared
> in such numbers, in accordance with the ineffable prophecies of the
> date, and is honoured by all by the name of Christ, but it is not little nor
> weak, nor founded in some obscure corner of the earth, but the most
> populous of all nations, and most pious towards God, alike innocent
> and invincible in that it ever finds help from God.[39]

Eusebius had set this bold declaration against the sweeping backdrop not only of world history but of the very origins of the universe. Christ, who had given His name to the Christians, had been no ordinary founder of a city or progenitor of a race. Here he adapts an argument already developed in his *General Elementary Introduction* and *Proof*: while individuals from the ancient history of the Hebrews (as recorded in the Old Testament) had been named Jesus (the Greek equivalent of the Hebrew name Joshua), and while some individuals had received the title of Christ (or 'anointed one'), none had given their name to an entire nation.[40] Christ was God and the 'living Logos who was, in the beginning, God by the side of the Father, the first and only offspring of God, before all creation'.[41] The founder of the Christian nation was thus the creator of the entire world as well. As such,

He had not been inactive during the centuries before His Incarnation and establishment of the Church. Even if the name of Christians was 'clearly new', the way of life and teachings of piety (*eusebeia*, which is almost always misleadingly translated as 'religion') were of the greatest antiquity. Those men who long ago had become 'friends of God' by living according to reason (or 'the Word', *logos*), the most famous of whom was Abraham the forefather of the Hebrews, 'were Christians in fact, if not in name'.[42]

It is only in this 'archaeology' of Eusebius' *History* that the pre-incarnational history of the 'Christians' (that is, the Hebrews who lived before the Jews and thus did not follow the Mosaic Law but true wisdom) is found.[43] Yet it sufficed to meet a common criticism found in ethnic and cultural polemic of the imperial era, namely the chronological belatedness of peoples other than one's own. The dominant assumption behind such polemic was that the most ancient humans were wiser, because untrammelled by the vices and moral confusion of later generations; they were closer to the gods (or God), and lived according to nature. Later luxury, sophistry and discord would mar the primal purity of the first humans (a historiographical vision elaborated in the *Preparation*, as we saw in a previous chapter). Hence, any nation who could claim ancestors among the earliest humans could stake a valuable claim to continue to have access to the ancient wisdom and piety in a direct way that was not available to other peoples. Together with his apologetic treatises, Eusebius' *History* made just such a claim.

Leaving ancient history behind, important and necessary though it had been, the remaining ten books of his *History* trace the interwoven developments of the five central themes laid out in Eusebius' opening lines. What united these themes was that they were all integral elements of the shared history of the Christian people. First, the continuity of leadership of the Church, that is, those who presided over the 'assemblies' (*ekklēsiai*) of members of the Christian nation at the largest civic centres of the Mediterranean (Jerusalem, Antioch, Alexandria and Rome), marked the strength of the Christians over the course of their history. As leading intellectuals and expounders of the Scriptures, their texts likewise became a central component of the *History*. In addition to the quotations from many great Christian writers of the first three centuries, Eusebius periodically included lists of their works accompanied by brief descriptions of their purposes, contexts or contents.[44]

This feature of the *History* not only provided Eusebius with a chance to record (and ostentatiously parade) a catalogue of some of the major works he possessed in the library at Caesarea. It also provided him with the means of exhibiting an important convergence in two of the most central models of Christian identity: Christianity was simultaneously conceived as a nation and as a school of true philosophy. Sometimes acknowledged, though not properly studied, are the persistent similarities between the Christian historian's account of the succession of ecclesiastical leaders and the histories of philosophical schools by Diogenes Laertius and Porphyry.[45] Just as Diogenes' history of the lives of philosophers traced the successions of teachers and students, while evincing a concern with the range, nature and content of their writings, Eusebius exhibited a concern with episcopal continuity, smooth transitions of leaders, their written contributions to true philosophy (that is, Christianity) and sometimes even their roles as teachers and the forms of their curriculum.

In spite of challenging episcopal authority (inadvertently, as Eusebius would have it), the greatest teacher of the *History* is certainly Origen, the polymath of liberal arts and the Scriptures in Alexandria and then Caesarea. In spite of the frequent declarations that Book 6 of the *History* is a 'Life of Origen',[46] that book maintains the tone and structure of those that precede it. It is an account of persecution, heretics, bishops of the major cities and the important writings produced by Christian thinkers from the reign of Severus to that of Decius. What has given rise to the characterization of this book as a biography of Origen is partly Eusebius' own reference to the amount and importance of material that would fill a whole book on the life of Origen, but also his artful manner of connecting Origen to all of these themes.

Eusebius gives the synchronism for Origen's birth: 'Severus was in the tenth year of his reign, and Laetus was governor of Alexandria and the rest of Egypt, and Demetrius had just then received the episcopate of the communities there in succession to Julian.'[47] The persecution of Christians from Severus up to Decius is a strand of Origen's own life and activities that receives due emphasis throughout Book 6: Origen's father died a martyr; he sought martyrdom as a boy but was diverted by his worried mother; he wrote on martyrdom; many of his students became martyrs; and, finally, he is nearly described as having died a martyr.[48] Indeed, contrary to modern suggestions that he was wrong or confused about the facts of Origen's death (who did not die until a few years after Decius' reign), Eusebius' description of his tortures under Decius, combined with his omission of any account of Origen's final years and eventual death, attempts to elide the years intervening between his imprisonment and later, unrelated death.[49] A sentence of 19 lines advises that any reader who wishes to learn of 'the nature and extent of that which happened to Origen at the time of the persecution, and what was the end and what sort of sayings he left behind him after this' may find all the details in Origen's letters.[50] The 'end' (*teleutēs*) must surely refer to the end of persecution, though the word hangs ambiguously by itself allowing the reader to think of Origen's death (for which the word would be most appropriate). While the *History* does not deny that Origen lived on after the Decian persecution, the evocative description of his mistreatment, imprisonment and tortures under that emperor creates the impression that Origen was properly to be classed a martyr.

Origen is thus portrayed as a valiant and enduring contender in the wars waged against the Christian nation (to use the language of Book 1). Any national history would need to include the vicissitudes of its fortunes against foreign opposition. Therefore Eusebius' narrative of Christianity as a nation incorporated accounts of martyrs undergoing persecution – the equivalent of battle narratives in traditional national histories.

> Other writers of historical works have confined themselves to the written tradition of victories in wars, of triumphs over enemies, of the exploits of generals and the valour of soldiers, men stained with blood and with countless murders for the sake of children and country and other possessions; but it is wars most peaceful, waged for the very peace of the soul, and men who therein have been valiant for truth rather than for country, and for piety rather than for their dear ones, that our record of those who order their lives according to God will inscribe on

> everlasting monuments: it is the struggles of the athletes of piety and
> their valour which braved so much, trophies won from demons, and
> victories against unseen adversaries, and the crowns at the end of all,
> that it will proclaim for everlasting remembrance.[51]

The fact that traditional national histories were presented as the fundamental point of comparison provides the key to the historiographical conception of the *History* as a whole. Origen's encouragement of the martyrs, the peaceful soldiers in the wars waged against them by the impious, is fully embedded within this larger concern.

Wars fought against Christianity by 'the nations' (*ta ethnē*, frequently translated as 'gentiles' or 'heathen') were not the only threat to the Christian nation and its champions. Though living in the same house as a heretic during several of his intellectually formative years, Origen was able to resist the seductive sway of heresy from an early age. As with the Christian nation, so with a school of Christian philosophy, any change from the pure truth and piety residing at its origins was a deleterious threat that needed to be uprooted. The *History*'s portrayal of Origen's opposition to heresy was therefore not only an attempt at a favourable characterization of a thinker who would face years of posthumous controversy and eventual official rejection as a heretic himself; it was also an expression of Eusebius' persistent concern to identify and 'out-narrate' rival schools of thought (*haireseis*, from which we derive the word 'heresies').[52] These heresies polluted the pure stream of the Christian nation. Because Eusebius seems to have adopted the view that Christians were 'a nation of philosophers' (an appellation given to the Jews already by Hellenistic philosophers), and because, for him, true philosophy was shown best by those who scorned their ephemeral bodies and found death at the hands of persecutors to be the swift and noble release of an immortal soul from its body, heretics were frequently excluded from Eusebius' accounts of martyrdom.[53] Though representatives of several suspect groups were persecuted and executed by Rome's imperial judicial machinery, Eusebius' narrative leaves an insistent picture of martyrs as true philosophers and defenders of right belief (*orthodoxia*). Origen's learned and powerful opposition to heretical teachers combines with his great courage in the face of terrifying ordeals of persecution to form a narrative apex near the centre of the *History*.

While Origen was something of an independent figure whom the bishop of Alexandria would ineffectually attempt to keep in check, his life was not, for Eusebius, at odds with episcopal authority. Instead, Eusebius describes Origen's teaching activity as directly connected to many of the most important bishops of his day. A future bishop of Alexandria was one of his star pupils; he engaged in positive and mutually encouraging intercourse with bishops at Rome, Caesarea and Jerusalem. Though a travelling intellectual and ascetic celebrity like Origen might be seen as a rogue figure, not easily controlled by the upholders of a developing ecclesiastical hierarchy, Eusebius' narrative marks out a man who complemented more than undermined the stability and authority of other Church leaders.

The account of Origen in Book 6 of the *History* is thus scarcely a distinctive 'life' of an independent charismatic thinker, different from or somehow at odds with the broader tone and purposes of the *History*. Instead, it is representative of Eusebius' exploration and delineation of the key themes he had set out in the programmatic opening lines of the entire work. The account of Church leaders, heretics and martyrs intersect in the portrait of the person of Origen. His travels to speak with and for bishops, to argue against heretics, to exhort confessors and martyrs or to conduct the daily regimen of a school of ascetically driven intellectuals extend the life of the man inextricably into the life of the Church.[54]

A single theme from the *History*'s preface is noticeably missing from Book 6, and indeed from most of Books 4–10. Eusebius had declared that the fate of the Jews would be a key element of his narrative; and indeed, it played a significant role in the third book. The obvious historical and theological reason for their destruction would seem to be their rejection of Christ as the Messiah prophesied in the Jews' own sacred books.[55] There is, however, more at stake in Eusebius' historical vision. The continuation of the national integrity of the Jews (as defined by their possession of land and performance of religious rituals at a common sacred site, the Temple at Jerusalem) was one of the stark realities that could question the viability of Christianity's claims to be the true inheritors of the ancient Hebrew way of life. If Christ was the reviver of an original true piety, if He was the legislator for a new nation's rational law and heavenly citizenship (*politeia*), establishing friendship with God through the work of the Son of God, then history had to exhibit in clear and overwhelming fashion God's rejection of the Jews in favour of the nation named after Christ.

The *History*'s silence about the Jews after Book 3 clearly articulates this historiographical conception. A new nation has replaced the 'former people' as God's chosen ones. Two elements deserve note. First, the early discussion of the Jews at the time of Jesus and the Apostles reaches descriptive height when it arrives at the final destruction of Jerusalem in Book 3. The use of quotation is more extensive than at any previous point in the *History* as Eusebius diligently reproduces lengthy material from Josephus comprising several pages.[56] There is a singularly powerful irony here, since the single source quoted at this point is Josephus, a Jew who had been displaced from his Judean homeland to the metropolis of the Empire. Josephus' narrative of the tragic last days of the Jewish people was a poignant and powerful means of rendering the Jewish way of life obsolete for Christians. Whereas Josephus' *Antiquities* had ended with Rome's occupation of Judea and defeat of the Jews, Eusebius could at that point pursue the history of the new nation unhindered by its rival for God's favour. Just as the *Chronicon* had charted the final years of the Jews until their tabular extinction under the reign of Vespasian, one of the primary goals of the *History*, which was made explicit in its preface, was to memorialize the dissolution of the Jews as a result of their rejection of Christ. That goal found definitive achievement in the quotations from Josephus in Book 3.

Secondly, following the Roman defeat of the Jews a couple of significant mechanisms function to displace the Jews entirely from (Eusebius') history. Eusebius remarks on the change of name from Jerusalem to Aelia Capitolina under Hadrian (though he continues to use the former name).[57] Furthermore, the succession of bishops at Jerusalem becomes decidedly non-Jewish: 'the Church there was welded together from the nations.'[58] The history of the Church after the fall of Jerusalem was a story of non-Jews, those from the nations, who had become identified with the nation named after Christ.

The Ends of the History

The beginning of the *History* had commenced at the cosmic level. Christ, the founder of the Christian people, had been the incarnate Word of God through whom God had created the universe. In spite of a repeated claim in modern discussions that the *History's* concluding books were aimed at narrating an ultimate unity of Church and Empire in the person of Constantine, the work makes a significant return to, or rather a narrative summation of, the power of Christ.[59] We must pause over the dynamics of his narrative in the last books if we are to avoid a misleading, if popular, understanding of the aims of the work and simultaneously of the ends of Eusebius' performance of the historical task.

The problem of the end of the *History* is particularly complicated due to a number of competing scholarly arguments regarding the ends of different supposed editions of Eusebius' work. Until recently most modern discussion of the *History* had argued that Eusebius was responsible for multiple (three or more) editions of the work.[60] Before the analysis of Andrew Louth in 1990 and Richard Burgess in 1997,[61] two studies now widely accepted, a number of scholars had posited that a first edition contained most or all of Books 1–7, or 1–8 (and so had been composed either just before the Great Persecution of 303 or after the issue of Galerius' palinode in 311, respectively); a second edition (or third, depending on what one concluded about the range of the first edition) would have seen the addition of material up to the period of joint rule by Licinius and Constantine (*c.*315); a penultimate edition would not have been written until after the death of Licinius (*c.*324); then a final edition would have eliminated the name of Constantine's son Crispus following his execution (*c.*326). One of the principal aims of several of the proponents of a multiple-edition approach has been to reconstruct Eusebius' varied reactions to contemporary events – especially the Great Persecution and the rise of Constantine and deaths of other emperors. How could a historian who is often seen as averse to eschatological tendencies compose a history of the Church when the Church was being shaken so visibly all about him?[62] The *Introduction*, which was written during the persecution, had addressed the sentiment among many Christians that apostolic succession had dissolved in their own days.[63] What sort of historiographical vision could possibly inform the writing of a Church history at such a bleak moment? Or, with respect to the emperors, it is presumed that Eusebius would not have written any overtly critical material until after their deaths, only then inserting unflattering comments or removing their names altogether in an act of *damnatio memoriae*. Likewise, it is assumed that Eusebius would have made positive remarks about Licinius only as long as that emperor was still alive.

An attempt to determine the ways in which Eusebius might have sought to make historiographical sense of a rapidly changing world is possibly the most important tendency in discussions of the editions of the *History*. Other concretely textual factors have contributed to the sense of legitimacy attaching to such a tendency. The first is the existence of a short work (possibly a companion tract to his earlier, now entirely lost *Collection of Martyrdoms*[64]) providing an account of martyrdoms that occurred in the province of Palestine. The so-called 'shorter recension' of the *Martyrs of Palestine* is found in a group of manuscripts at the end of Book 10 (these are abbreviated as the A, T, E, and R manuscripts), while two of these manuscripts note that the *Martyrs* had been placed between Books 8 and 9 'in a certain manuscript'. A longer recension of the *Martyrs* survives separately in a Syriac translation and several Greek fragments.[65] It is possible – though not necessary – that the very existence of the work (whether in longer or shorter recensions) would seem to hint at an edition of the *History* that ended without treating of the persecution, since this little work would seem to fill (temporarily) the need to record and memorialize the martyrs under that persecution; the present Book 8 would then seem to hint at Eusebius' considering that the *Martyrs* was insufficient to fill that need and that it would better fit within the frame of his historical project. In fact, the shorter recension of the *Martyrs* (which otherwise lacks a proper introduction and conclusion) seems as if it would have fit nicely after 8.2.3 (especially as the beginning lines of the *Martyrs* and those of 8.2.4 are identical); while 8.17 (Galerius' palinode) would have made a good fit following the end of the *Martyrs* (especially given the fact that the final segment of the shorter recension specifically mentions an imperial recantation[66]). Positing an edition that ended with the *Martyrs* material has thus appeared attractive.

The second textual factor that hypotheses about editions have drawn upon involves the manuscript witnesses to emperors, especially Licinius. One group of manuscripts (the four abbreviated as A, T, E and R) preserves the name of Licinius along with Constantine when describing imperial policy or the issuing of edicts; another group (the three abbreviated B, D and M, along with the Syriac translation, abbreviated S, and the Latin translation by Rufinus, abbreviated L[67]) either frequently omits Licinius' name and imperial titulature[68] or makes hostile jabs at him (for instance, positive references receive the additional note that 'this was before he went mad').[69] To complicate matters a good deal, the second group is not entirely uniform: one of them (M) seems to have had access to an exemplar of the first group and made determinations accordingly (including a dossier of imperial documents in Book 10, Chapters 5–7, which is otherwise omitted from the second group of manuscripts).[70]

The precise relationship of the various manuscripts to each other and to hypothetical editions is likely irresolvable. Nonetheless, the many variations on the theme of multiple editions (even when providing carefully nuanced displays of scholarly ingenuity) may cause more bewilderment than the evidence warrants. An approach that values the most economical explanation of the textual evidence can avoid the proliferation of hypothetical and often unverifiable schemas while offering an adequate account of the problems.[71] The following observations may be made in favour of such an economical approach.

First, as noted above, the preface of the *History* mentions the *Chronicon* as a necessary building block for its own composition; the latter work has now been conclusively shown by Richard Burgess to have been composed no earlier than 306, and more probably (according to him) *c.*311.[72] The existence of a pre-persecution edition of the *History* can only be maintained by supposing that the reference to the *Chronicon* in the preface was an addition in a later version. Such hypothesizing is unverifiable and hence must be avoided.

Second, the preface of the *History* declares that it will contain a narrative of the persecution 'of our own time' and the final cessation of that persecution. The suggestion that Eusebius added this remark only in a later edition is (again) unverifiable since it occurs in all the manuscript witnesses. It can be warranted only by appeal to hypothetical constructs and not to evidence in the text itself.[73]

Third, the removal or alteration of the various references to Licinius can just as adequately be accounted for by appeal to a copyist's hand as to Eusebius' own.[74] Eusebius could have maintained the mention of Licinius' name or even positive statements about that emperor even as late as 324/5 and beyond (indeed, he would continue to name Licinius in his latest work, the *Life of Constantine*[75]). Assumptions about Eusebius' reactionary attitude to changes at the imperial level (combined with imputations of what is frequently taken as a pro-imperial attitude in his later writings) require assigning the deletions and alterations to Eusebius. While a *damnatio memoriae* against Licinius would be most natural during Constantine's lifetime, any time during the fourth century is equally possible. As Eduard Schwartz admitted, there seem to have been several copies in circulation in Eusebius' own lifetime.[76] Indeed, in the 360s there are indications of a desire to leave Licinius unnamed in otherwise clear allusions to him.[77] Importantly, the manuscript evidence itself does not necessitate assigning the textual *damnatio memoriae* to Eusebius himself. None of the Greek manuscripts can be dated before the tenth century,[78] while the manuscript traditions of the Latin translation are also too late to be helpful. The two manuscripts of the Syriac translation are much earlier (the first dating to *c.*462), but exhibit an abbreviative technique that renders them of a rather problematic usefulness.[79] To make matters worse for any multiple-edition hypothesis, which would base itself on the Licinian references, the alleged *damnatio* is only partial: as Hugh Jackson Lawlor observed as long ago as 1912, aside from the negative material enumerated by Schwartz, much positive material remains in both manuscript groups of Book 10.[80] Positive and negative references to Licinius (including his defeat by Constantine) occur in all the manuscript witnesses. To suppose with Schwartz that the exemplar of the ATER manuscripts combined elements from multiple editions becomes merely an unverifiable and circular appeal to account for a complete absence of unambiguous textual proof for the hypothetical editions. Evidence of different manuscript families should not be confused with different authorial editions of the text. Furthermore, I can find no serious evidence to discount entirely the possibility presented by Lawlor that the process could have gone the other way – that the name of Licinius was added to an earlier exemplar where a vague reference to a ruler (or tyrant) was unclear to later readers.[81]

Fourth, the fact that Eusebius claims in Book 8 of the *History* that he will later compose a work memorializing the martyrs should be taken as a reference to the work we have, namely the *Martyrs*.[82] It seems fairly safe to assume the shorter version was composed before the longer,[83] though both of them could be by the hand of Eusebius. In any case, the presence of the Greek version (the shorter recension) of the tract at the end of Book 8 need not imply that it originally stood within an earlier edition of Book 8, since the end of that book is an appropriate location for a copyist or Eusebius himself to place a preliminary narrative of Palestinian martyrs that he had composed at the time of the composition of the *History* or soon thereafter. Recognizing, however, that the draft was too narrow in scope to incorporate into his project and wanting to return to it in a later work (such as the long recension), he left it as an appendage to Book 8. If it once formed the bulk of an early version of Book 8, as has been frequently supposed, it would have been noticeably inadequate at the time of its composition given the much wider scope of the preceding books of the *History*. In other words, the composition of the short recension could be closely approximate in time to the composition of the later books of the *History* without necessarily ever being intended for inclusion in that work as one of its books or as part of its coherent organization.

Fifth, Book 10 is explicitly addressed to Paulinus of Tyre and claims to include Eusebius' own speech delivered at the dedication of the basilica at Tyre at Paulinus' request. The dedication speech has been dated to either *c.*314 or *c.*316.[84] In the spring of 325, Eusebius was summoned to a synod at Antioch to be investigated for his support of Arius. Paulinus was at that synod and it is possible that Eusebius delivered the *History* to him at that time. While an edition of the *History* that went up to Book 10, Chapter 7 could have been sent to Paulinus at any point following the dedication of the basilica of Tyre,[85] an edition containing the whole of Book 10 (that is, up to the death of Licinius), intended for Paulinus in 324/5, is a possibility. The opening statement that he now dedicates the tenth book to Paulinus after having written nine books does not entail an earlier publication of the nine books separately. Indeed, had they been circulating already, it would be more natural for Eusebius to refer to them and possibly responses to them (on the part of Paulinus or others). The belated dedication may, rather, indicate the final stage of a composition whose production had been of long duration. The incremental addition of material to his *History* once he had arrived at his own times finds confirmation in the fact that some manuscripts include additional material (Constantine's letter to the eastern provincials, which would be included later in the second book of the *Life of Constantine*) after the end of Book 10.[86]

Sixth, the fact that no addressee is named until Book 10 is puzzling, but not entirely without precedent, if we take the epitome of the *Gospel Questions to Stephanus* as a faithful representation of its original, as there Stephanus is not addressed until the very last lines. In addition, while we are missing the first three books of the four-book project on biblical toponymy, the fourth book (the *Onomasticon*) addresses itself to Paulinus of Tyre.[87]

Seventh, the final sentence of Book 10 repeats nearly verbatim the final sentence of Book 9,[88] describing how God's help had alone come to the aid of the victorious party and the tyrant had been destroyed, thus showing what happened to those who hated God. This repetition exhibits a consistent historiographical vision of God's work in the rise and fall of emperors, even if we were to suppose that the passage from Book 10 comes from a later edition than that of Book 9.[89] Such 'self-plagiarism' occurs in other works of Eusebius where it is clearly not indicative of different editions (such as the *Preparation*).[90]

Finally, the only books whose numbers are explicitly declared are 7, 8 and 10. A recent discussion has suggestively argued that Eusebius wanted to evoke subtly the symbolism behind just these numbers. Therefore, just as Christ's Resurrection occurred on the eighth day, that is, the day after the Sabbath or the seventh day of the week, so the significance of Christ's work in the revival of the Church through the martyrs narrated in Book 8 of the *History* was indicated by Eusebius' explicit numbering of the seventh and eighth books; then, just as ten was the number of completeness, so the tenth book was declared as the completion of the *History*.[91] If so, it would seem that these three books were united (along with Book 9, which they embrace) in a single edition.

We may conclude from these observations that a single edition comprising all ten books is not beyond the realms of possibility. The fact that no serious scholar has supported a single-edition position may therefore seem surprising.[92] Recent discussion has begun to move towards a two-edition position: the first comprising Books 1–9, with the addition of Book 10 in the second (which may also have included alterations to earlier books).[93] A significant obstacle remaining for a single-edition thesis is the seemingly disjointed structure of Book 10. It begins with a dedication to Paulinus, followed by Eusebius' oration at Tyre, continues with a dossier of imperial documents, and ends with a narrative of the downfall of Licinius and final triumph of Constantine. While the documentation (the oration and the imperial letters) seems excessive, it is not entirely out of keeping with Eusebius' earlier documentary choices. Book 5, for instance, had commenced with the quite lengthy letter on the martyrs of Lyons, while Book 6 had ended with a lengthy dossier of episcopal letters from Dionysius of Alexandria. The fact that the dossier of letters in Book 10 still seems to break what otherwise might seem like a certain thematic and narrative flow, from the context and delivery of the oration at Tyre and then the account of Constantine's defeat of Licinius, may have been what prompted the scribe of the exemplar of one group of manuscripts to omit the dossier altogether (in other words, its omission from B and D need not be a result of different editions but only of different editorial choices by a copyist seeking to alleviate Eusebius' ponderous quotational choices, or possibly even seeking to cut out a document headed by Licinius, namely the so-called 'Edict of Milan' in Chapter 5).

Reasons to suppose that Book 10 would have functioned as a unit are that there is no manuscript evidence for any alternative ending to the one we have (namely Chapter 9), there are thematic links between the end and beginning of Book 10, and there are links as well between the ends of Books 9 and 10. The arrangement of this book may not be to our taste, but such dissatisfaction – something that has been felt with respect to other works by our author as well – is not sufficient grounds for supposing distinct editions (and, in any case, it would only shift modern judgements from Eusebius' supposedly poor compositional practices to his supposedly poor editorial practices). While a good deal of more nuanced investigation is required, at the possibility of which this discussion is only meant to gesture, a reassessment of many of our assumptions is in order as scholarly conversations on the *History* continue.

The concluding sentences of both Books 9 and 10 would suggest endings for the *History* that would conjoin the identities and fates of the Church and Empire. Yet like the hypotheses of multiple endings of multiple editions, here too the purposes towards which the *History* was aimed might be in need of more cautious reflection. There is something of a scholarly consensus that Eusebius was a Christian intellectual who invested his historical labours on the task of envisioning a Christian Roman Empire. And to some extent he did.

Yet the end of the *History* brings us to a point similar to its beginning. He had commenced his historical work with an account of God's work in ancient history up to God's work in the Incarnation of Christ and establishment of the Church. Throughout the *History*, especially during narratives recounting the persecution and deaths of martyrs, a providential concern for the affairs of the nation who followed Christ appears woven into the lives and texts of Eusebius' work. Book 10 brings this theme to its climax: the bishop of Tyre in Eusebius' oration, quoted in Chapter 4, acts in a mimetic fashion as a representative of God on earth; the dossier of imperial documents that follows the oration are signal testimonies to God's providential work; the failure of the last persecuting emperor, Licinius himself, at the hands of a ruler who had submitted himself to God was the final act of Providence and a powerful end point to a historical narrative that had sought to preserve and confirm the superiority of the Christian people. Rather than being an attempt to legitimize an emperor within a Christian framework (though this could no doubt be an effect of his narrative), the final book of the *History* provided proof of God's favour upon the Christian nation. A persistent theme of various articulations of imperial ideology in antiquity and especially in the Roman Empire was the notion that triumph and prosperity in the affairs of a nation confirmed the divine favour and theological rightness of the nation's way of living in the world and relating to the divine.[94] The ending of the *History* is not so much a religious legitimation of the Roman political sphere, but a narrative exhibiting the political confirmation of the true piety and wisdom embodied in the lives of Christians.

V

ARTICULATING
THE WORD

IN SPITE OF THE MODERN dearth of recognition for Eusebius' abilities
as a theologian and philosopher in his own right,[1] he stands as one of the
foremost Christians of his age who brought together the scattered threads
of the major intellectual traditions of the Graeco-Roman world. His corpus
reflects, often explicitly, a sustained and critical conversation with many of
the great thinkers who preceded him. The voices of Hellenistic Judaism,
early Christianity and Platonic theological speculation are all brought
into a productive tension (or fusion) in Eusebius' thought. The works we
have discussed so far (from the *General Elementary Introduction* to the
Preparation for the Gospel and the *Ecclesiastical History*) are the products of
a lifetime of engaging with the philosophical traditions of the Greeks, Jews
and Christians. In the last years of his life, a little over a decade after the
Council of Nicaea, he turned his erudition against Marcellus, the bishop
of Ancyra, who represented a theological position that Eusebius viewed as
a form of the Sabellian heresy, which Marcellus had manifested in a work
against Asterius (who in turn had sought to defend Eusebius of Nicomedia,
the foremost leader of the 'alliance' that had sided with Arius).[2] The latter's

theology held that God's absolute unity entailed the denial of the Son's separate existence from the Father; the Son was merely a different mode of expression of the one God's nature and activity. Eusebius, too, sought to protect the oneness of God – but he did so in a way that simultaneously aimed to protect the distinct hypostatic integrity of the members of the Trinity. His critique of Marcellus was not the result of an attempt to lash out at a radical supporter of Nicaea by one who still felt the sting from having been theologically bullied at the Council. It was, rather, a natural continuation of Eusebius' long held theological concerns. Eusebius was neither an 'Arian' nor a 'modified Arian'.[3] Furthermore, in spite of the modern contempt for Eusebius' theological abilities, he seems to be the only one in the 330s to have developed a coherent and thoughtful middle ground between the poles of Marcellus and Arius in a way that was consistent with Nicaea (we should not require an appeal to or a defence of *homoousios* from him as proof of his orthodoxy, since all sides ignored that term until the 350s).[4]

Informed by contemporary Platonists and his own predecessors in biblical theology (from Philo to Origen)[5] and disciplined with a greater philosophical sophistication than his opponent, Eusebius composed two treatises against Marcellus and his position. Adopting the sort of quotational methodology he had explored in earlier works such as the *Preparation*, the first treatise, entitled simply *Against Marcellus*, refuted the bishop of Ancyra through his own words. It was hastily composed and deemed by its author to have been inadequate. It did, however, fulfil the task of legitimizing Eusebius' key role in pushing for the denunciation and exile of Marcellus at an ad hoc synod in Constantinople in 336 (just following Eusebius' involvement in a synod at Tyre dealing with Athanasius, who had been aligned with Marcellus, and then the dedication of the Church of the Holy Sepulchre in 335).[6] During the same visit to Constantinople, Eusebius delivered an encomium in honour of Constantine's 30-year anniversary (the *Tricennial Oration*, to be discussed in the next chapter). The second treatise, the *Ecclesiastical Theology*, dating to sometime between 336 and 339, took a more systematic approach to the theological issues that had been such a source of contention between the two. Although both are polemical in nature, the *Against Marcellus* and *Ecclesiastical Theology* together represent a theological vision coherent with the formulations presented in the earlier works. The present chapter will, therefore, focus on these treatises in an attempt to elaborate the concerns that drove Eusebius' theological reflection throughout most of his life. In what follows, we shall find within that coherent vision an entangled web of connections between Eusebius' formulations on key theological themes and earlier (and contemporary) thinkers.

Theological Hierarchy in Eusebius

Several thinkers outside, but tangential to, the Christian tradition had developed theological systems through adherence to and sustained reflection upon the dialogues of Plato that maintained a separation between a First and a Second God. The First was utterly transcendent, indivisible, simple, at rest and beyond the reach of adequate identification or definition by human language. The Second became divided in the thinking of Ideas and in its engagement with matter (which for most Platonists was coeternal with God).[7] The Second God was readily identifiable as the Demiurge of Plato's *Timaeus*, while the First could be aligned with the One or the Good of Plato's *Parmenides* and *Republic*. Articulation of a third entity began to arise in reflections on an enigmatic passage of Plato's Second Letter, which stated: 'Around the King of the universe are all things, and all are for His sake, and that is the cause of all things beautiful; and around the Second are the secondary things, and around the Third the tertiary.'[8] Plotinus seems to be the first to have worked out a thorough and systematic tripartite theological ontology as the result of over a century of persistent reflection among Platonist circles. The One stood resolutely 'beyond being' and beyond language. In a procession from the One, which maintained its ineffable unity and transcendence, Intellect contemplated the One and its own ideas, from which emanated the World Soul at a third remove. It was through these three hypostases that an ontological hierarchy exhibited ever greater levels of multiplicity as being proceeded further from the One. For both Plotinus and his student Porphyry, any of the three hypostases could be deemed the 'Father' of the lower orders and likewise the 'Son' of the preceding.[9] For both, the distinction between the One and Intellect needed to be maintained in recognition of the 'beyond-ness' of the One.

Eusebius knew several of the writings of Plotinus and Porphyry, as well as a good number of earlier Platonist philosophers. In the *Preparation* he quoted from Plato, Plutarch, Numenius, Atticus, Severus, Longinus, Plotinus, Amelius and Porphyry. He may have known only two treatises of Plotinus[10] and we cannot determine whether Eusebius possessed the more narrowly metaphysical works of Porphyry, such as the *Sentences*, the *Philosophical History* or his commentaries on Plato and Aristotle. At the very least, we may acknowledge that a Platonic view of reality was an integral part of the intellectual air he breathed, so to speak; he was cognisant of the broad contours of the metaphysical rumination of imperial-era Platonism, and he was aware of the triadic hypostatization in the system of Plotinus and his school.[11] The precise degree to which all of this made a determinate impact on Eusebius' theology is a difficult and possibly insoluble problem. No doubt there was an important influence, for there are strong echoes of Platonic language in many of his works.[12] As we shall see, however, his thinking was so deeply formed by an incessant and prolonged engagement with the biblical texts that there remains little possibility of distinguishing any intact Platonic elements from his biblically formed thinking. With some small exceptions, the philosophical and biblical components of his thought were thoroughly fused.

The problem is not peculiar to Eusebius' thought. The long-standing modern question of the relationship of Christianity and Hellenism is a scholarly dead end. There has been little success determining a pure or essential Christian religion, culture, identity or, to use an ancient term, *Christianismos* – and likewise an essential Hellenic religion, culture, identity or *Hellēnismos* – so that there are always multiple variations of the relationship between the two, or even of what the definition of either of them was on its own. It is nearly impossible to chart a singular or linear relationship between two such variable and fluid 'things' that are perpetually under negotiation and rhetorical manipulation in ongoing performances of a literary, ritual, communal or isolated nature. As we have seen in an earlier chapter, it is important to examine closely individual moments of the articulation of a relationship between Christianity and Hellenism in the pages of Eusebius (and other Late Antique authors), but to explain Eusebius' theological work within a modern master narrative of such a relationship is not always helpful. Eusebius himself would have denied any impact of Platonic or Greek ideas on orthodox Christian doctrine and opposed thinkers who he claimed had inadvertently brought Greek ideas into their Christian theology.[13]

The consequence of these observations is a recognition that not only is it impossible to delineate the Platonic from the Christian (or biblical) in his thought, but that he would not have wanted us to make such an attempt in the first place.[14] Recalling Platonic philosophical developments in the period up to the time of Eusebius may not, then, allow us to determine precise points of impact, but it does remind us of a broader context of reflection and the possibility of multiple resonances and layers of theological formulation in Eusebius' corpus (and indeed, in most third- and fourth-century Christian theology). These multiple resonances had arisen because of Eusebius' project of allowing for Platonic theological language and conceptions insofar as they were deemed amenable to the ancient truths of biblical language and conceptions.

A proper account of his theology, therefore, must begin with the principal biblical texts that exerted a sort of magnetic pull throughout his thought. There were three passages of the New Testament that proved fundamental to Eusebius' theological formulations. Without being simplistic, we may recognize throughout his writings an attempt to align all theological knowledge, from both philosophical and biblical sources, within the conceptual focus provided by these verses. They are:

> In the beginning was the Word, and the Word was with God, and the Word was God. All things were made by Him, and without Him was not anything made. [John 1:1]

> Who is the image of the invisible God, the firstborn of every creature, because in Him were created all things, things in heaven and things in earth, whether thrones or dominions, or principalities or powers. All things were created by Him and for Him, and He is before all things, and by Him all things consist. [Colossians 1:15]

> To those whom God has called, both Jews and Greeks, Christ [is] the
> power of God and the wisdom of God. [1 Corinthians 1:24][15]

Much of Eusebius' exposition of the nature of the relationship of the Father and the Son or the character and activity of the Logos throughout history is best explained as a wide-ranging exploration of the implications and logic of these three passages. They provide us with the terminological and conceptual linchpins of his theology of the person of the Son. The Son is to be identified with the Word, who is the image of God, the creator of all things, and the Wisdom of God. Eusebius would use each of these as a key for interpreting the Old Testament: wherever reference was made to a word of God, or to wisdom, or to God's creative work in the world, an opportunity was afforded to Eusebius of finding material for fleshing out his theology of the Son (from the earlier *Introduction* to the later *Ecclesiastical Theology*). Each term deserves to be considered independently.

The Word

The first verse of the Gospel of John was itself a clear allusion to the first verse of Genesis ('In the beginning God created the heavens and the earth'). God's creative activity was there portrayed as dependent upon God's speech: 'And God *said* "Let there be light"'; 'and God *said* "Let there be an expanse"', and so on. The verb 'said', *legein*, in the Greek translation of Genesis, is cognate to the noun 'word', *logos*. That speech through which the world was created was, therefore, the Word, which, according to John furthermore, was 'with God and was God'. But John continued: 'The Word became flesh and dwelt among us.' So Christ was the Word, and therefore all the New Testament claims about the divinity of Christ applied to that Word as well. The challenge for Eusebius was not the elucidation of the Word's identity as God in the New Testament texts, however, but the identification of Word and God in the Old Testament. How could the Word *of God* in the pages of the Old Testament be reread to signify that the Word *was God*?

While Eusebius had explored the problem at length in his *Introduction* and again in the *Proof of the Gospel*, it became particularly acute in the latter years of his life when he became embroiled in controversy with Marcellus of Ancyra. For Marcellus, the Word was *in* (Greek *en*) God and therefore did not have an existence (*hypostasis*) of its own; it was merely the speech that God used in creation. Marcellus claimed that God was like a human artist speaking to himself, thinking out loud, as he crafted creation. When God said in Genesis, 'Let us make humanity in our image,' it was to be compared to a human example, declared Marcellus.

> When an expert sculptor wants to make a statue he first looks at his own forms [*typoi*] and characters [...] then makes preliminary impresses on what is going to be the statue with his mind [...] and understanding that his reason [*logos*] works with him by which he calculates and usually does everything; so he encourages himself saying, 'Come let us make, let us fashion a statue' [...] the whole creation came into being by a word.[16]

The word that God spoke at creation was, therefore, just like a word spoken by a human being. Elsewhere, Marcellus would apparently assert that God's word was no different from an indicative (*sēmantikon*) or imperative (*prostaktikon*) statement made by humans.[17]

Using John 1:1 as his touchstone, Eusebius opposed this formulation of Marcellus on two fronts. On the one hand, the Gospel did not claim that the Word was *in* (*en*) God at creation; to be precise, the Word was *with* or *at the side of* (*pros*) God.[18] Eusebius understood this way of describing the Word as denoting a distinct existence and identity from God the Father.[19] Furthermore, if the Word was *in* the Father as Marcellus claimed, then the possibility would be opened up for conceiving of the Word as a part of God; but the God over all was indivisible. He could not be lessened by having parts of Him broken away. While proceeding from the Father, the Word must be described as having its own identity and existence (*hypostasis*) in order to avoid the partitioning of God.

On the other hand, Marcellus' appeal to a human analogy for God's speech was misplaced. Drawing on Stoic theory, though most likely it was mediated through Plotinus or Porphyry, Eusebius noted that human words fell into two categories.[20] First, internal speech (*endiathethos logos*) involved the use of mental words in discursive reasoning. Then, when the mental words were verbalized and were 'carried forth' from the person's mouth they became uttered speech (*prophorikos logos*).[21] For Eusebius, the Word of the first verses of both Genesis and John was not *in* God but *with* God, and hence could not be identified as an *endiathetos logos*, or a word in God's internal self-talk. But, likewise, the Word could not be analogous to the uttered words of humans since this would exclude the possibility of a separate existence of the Word, and hence any further possibility of the Word being God or becoming flesh in the Incarnation. Emphasis was placed on the precise wording of John: the Evangelist did not say that the Word was *of* God (just as an uttered word would be the word *of* a person), but rather that the Word *was* God.

The exploration of the implications of various moments of the Word's activity from the New Testament received less discussion in Eusebius' theological writings than its activity before the Incarnation. Through the Word all things were created and sustained. Adapting a formulation developed by Stoics and Platonists alike, and already applied to the explication of biblical texts by Philo of Alexandria, Eusebius described the Word's creational work as performed through creative and productive principles (*dēmiourgikoi kai poiētikoi logoi*).[22] Pagan philosophers had explained the rational workings of God in the cosmos, the natural world and human reasoning by appeal to seminal principles, which pervaded the created order and caused it to work according to a divine Reason.[23] Eusebius found such a conception useful in accounting for the Bible's assertions that the Word created all things and sustained them. Unfortunately, Eusebius does not elaborate in his various works his own conception of these *logoi* in a manner sufficient for us to determine whether he would have aligned himself more with the Stoics, who assumed the embeddedness of these principles in the material world, or the Platonists, who asserted the immateriality of these principles, acting upon but not presiding within bodies.[24] It is likely that, if pressed, Eusebius might have sought a dual-*logoi* approach that posited a class of immaterial principles working in the intelligible level of reality and a lower set of material principles at work within bodies. The incarnational theological tendency within Christianity could have prompted such a thorough interweaving of *logoi* at both intelligible and sensible levels. Because Eusebius nowhere lays out a systematic theology and metaphysics, however, we can only suspect the possibility of such thinking.

The Word acted also in identifiable though mysterious ways in human history. Beyond the creative rational principles that pervaded the world, key theophanic moments had occurred in which the Word spoke to particular people. In fact, the Word claimed the entire race of the ancient Hebrews as His special province of activity; the other nations were instead placed under the governance of angels (though one by one the control of these nations was usurped by the Devil).[25] Under the guidance of the Word, the Hebrews could be truly said to exercise rightly the best part of their soul, which was simultaneously 'the rationality' and also the part 'belonging to the Word' (*to logikon*). But such a claim could not carry much power in marking out the Hebrews as a distinctly superior race from the others. After all, any human who used reasoning could be said to belong to the Word even if inadvertently. Marcellus had granted that the Word was revealed only in a mystic and hidden manner to the Jews in the Old Testament. If the Word was no different from human reasoning, then how could that be deemed a mystery? Greeks, Jews and barbarians all granted that God was wise and 'rational'; no one believed God to be 'without a word' or 'irrational' (*alogos*). If it were so simple, there could be no special claim that Christians were those to whom 'the mystery had been revealed', as the Apostle Paul remarked. For Eusebius, the mystery concealed in the Hebrew Scriptures 'is not that which is known to all by natural conceptions'; rather it was Christ, the Son of God, who was the mystery – 'mystically the Prophets glorified Him with different titles, concealing what is unutterable.'[26]

Even before the Prophets, the Word revealed Himself directly in a theophany at special times and to special people among the Hebrews, as recorded in Moses' history of the Hebrew race (especially Genesis). To each of the patriarchs, Abraham, Isaac and Jacob, the Word (or Son) had spoken, speaking prophetically of the future blessing that would come to all nations when the Word became incarnate.[27] Because the 'Angel of the Lord' in many of these occurrences had allowed humans to worship Him and address Him as 'Lord', the best interpretation of this shadowy figure was, according to Eusebius, identification of Him as the Word. Even after the age of the patriarchs, when Moses led the descendants of the Hebrews (who were now given the name of Jews, Eusebius argued, to distinguish them from the holiness and piety of their forefathers), the Word continued to work. 'Before, the Word, like a pedagogue, gave the ABCs [the elements or letters, *stoicheia*] to the former people, who were infants, keeping them from the error of polytheism; but he concealed the mystery of grace from them.'[28]

Thus, while the description of the Word in John 1:1 emphasized the cosmic, creational frame of reference, Eusebius expanded the work of that Word beyond Genesis 1. In His theophanic revelatory activity, the Word appeared in nearly every book of the Old Testament. Even though Eusebius' terminology appears to be drawn from the philosophers, it was always located within biblical contexts. The clearest adoption of philosophical conceptions, the *endiathetos/prophorikos* distinction, is only invoked to be rejected. In spite of Marcellus' claims that it was his opponents who Platonized (in particular Origen), Eusebius pinned Platonic (and Stoic) ways of thinking onto him. Contemporary Platonism is thus seen as an influence on Eusebius not in his own substantive articulations about the Logos but in his construal (or misconstrual) of the positions he attacked in polemic.

The Begotten Son of the Unbegotten Father

A large part of what was at stake in his anti-Marcellan defence of the separate existence and identity of the Word was a deep-seated conviction that the Word was to be identified with the Son and that the Son was the unique offspring of the Father. The identification seemed to arise naturally from a coherent reading of the Gospel of John: the Word, which was with God and was God, and which became flesh and dwelt among us, was the person portrayed as consistently naming God as His Father and referring to himself in the third person as the Son. A well-known passage in the third chapter of John had designated Christ as the 'only begotten Son' of the Father (John 3:16). This sonship of the Word was threatened by Marcellus' attempt to draw an analogy with human words. Furthermore, the begotten nature of the Son was critical for preserving the notion of the Son's eternity and divinity. One could not allow for expressions of the Son being made or created like other creatures. To do so would certainly have granted an existence (*hypostasis*) to the Son (or Word), but it could not appropriately express the Son's divinity.[29]

Marcellus had, in Eusebius' estimation, erred in the opposite direction. In spite of his overt criticisms of Sabellius, Marcellus had inadvertently followed the latter's heretical theology by holding a position that sought to protect God's oneness and the Son's divinity by denying a separate existence to the Son.[30] Instead, Eusebius claimed, for both Sabellius and Marcellus the Son was only a mode of God's activity in His interactions with humanity. Marcellus would have rejected the existence of the Son as a second 'person' of the one Godhead (though admittedly, such language was not adopted as orthodox until later in the fourth century); instead, the Son was only a name taken by the Father. Eusebius responded to such a position with an alarm that arose from the inevitable conclusion of such a conception. If the Son was only a name for a particular mode of the Father's interaction with humans, then not only must one see the biblical representations of the Son praying to or struggling with the Father (in the Gospels) as ridiculous nonsense, but one must suppose that the Father suffered in the Passion of Christ (a thing that no orthodox Christian could countenance). In a manner somewhat resonant of Neoplatonism's attempt to protect the transcendence, impartibility and impassibility of the Father (the One), Eusebius declared the hypostatic integrity of the Son as a clear and necessary ontological step that preserved the Father's transcendent status. The Father could not, by His very nature, suffer as the Son had suffered; therefore, the Son possessed necessarily his own existence (*hypostasis*).

The concern of Marcellus and Sabellius was legitimate enough in Eusebius' eyes, however, since their assertions had rested on an emphasis upon the oneness of God. Whereas Plotinus and other Platonists were content to designate the three hypostases – One, Intellect, World Soul – as first principles (*archai*), Christians had become wary of such language. To preserve God's transcendent uniqueness from all else, grounded as it was in biblical passages declaring that the 'Lord God is one' (the Shema), Christians were reluctant to speak of a multiplicity of first principles. In spite of his over-whelming emphasis upon the separate hypostasis of the Son, Eusebius agreed:

> Are you afraid, oh man, that if you confess two hypostases you would introduce two first principles and fall away from the monarchic divin-ity? Learn, then, that because God is one, without beginning and unbegotten and the Son is begotten from Him, there will be one first principle, one monarchy, and one kingdom. Do you struggle [because of the supposition] that the one confessing two hypostases of Father and Son will need to accept two Gods? Know this as well, that it does not necessitate granting two Gods.[31]

In a defence of Origen against the aspersions of Marcellus on this topic, Eusebius averred, 'What fellowship is there [between Origen's orthodoxy and] Plato in these things?' In his treatise *On First Principles*, Origen did not conceive of 'first principles in a way similar to Plato, knowing there is only one first principle, unbegotten, without beginning, beyond all, and that He is the Father of the only begotten Son'.[32] Though some philosophers would also assert a single first principle (as Porphyry had argued against Atticus), Eusebius declared that belief in many first principles was a distinc-tive feature belonging to the Greeks (among whom he classed Porphyry).[33] The position of

> the Church of God recognizes an indivisible monad, confessing a single first principle, the one unbegotten God who is without beginning [*anarchon*]; and [it recognizes] His only begotten Son [...] who is not without beginning [*anarchon*] nor unbegotten, lest there be supposed two first principles and two Gods.[34]

Porphyry had defended the belief in one first principle while granting that the One, Intellect and World Soul were three hypostases.[35] He even adopted the language of Father/Son to describe the relationships between each ontologi-cal level with that above or below it, respectively. Plotinus had asserted that the One was 'pure activity' from which the Intellect proceeded at the will of the One.[36] In the context of describing the Father's begetting of the Son, Eusebius would use similar language. Against Marcellus, but in harmony with Plotinus' metaphysics, he declared that the Father, as monad, neither increased nor decreased in His activity, but, 'being a monad, He begot the Son, not enduring division, alienation, turning, flowing [or emanation], or suffering.'[37] Elsewhere, Eusebius would describe this begetting as performed by the will of the Father. Such was the resonance of the Christian's formulations with those of his Platonist contemporaries.[38]

The differences between Eusebius and the Platonists, however, are equally striking. For the Christian bishop, the Son was the image of the invisible God and the unique mediator between the transcendent Father and the materially bound, embodied souls of humanity. The Son had done what would have been unthinkable of the second hypostasis of the Neoplatonic system – He had become flesh, suffered and died. Furthermore, the second hypostasis would never have been designated the 'visible image of the invisible' Father, in the way that the Christian notion of the Son could be.

The Visible Image of the Invisible God

Even if the Intellect of Neoplatonism might be described in an oblique manner as the One's image, perceptible visibility arose only at a third or fourth remove from the One, when World Soul luminously shone upon otherwise formless matter and gave it order. Eusebius seems little concerned with alleviating the metaphysical problems that would have arisen for a Neoplatonist at the Christian collapse of such ontological distance between invisible transcendence and visible, embodied immanence. It seems, however, that Eusebius wanted to limit the ontological collapse to an important degree. Marcellus, on the other hand, had claimed that the 'image' spoken of in Scriptures was none other than the body of Christ. After all, Marcellus reasoned, God had spoken at creation of human bodies: 'Let us make humanity in our image.'[39] Images were visual 'indicators of things that are absent'; God's word was, like any human word, whether interior or uttered, invisible. The word of God, Marcellus further argued, could only become visible once it entered the body of Christ; it was the word of God that spoke through the image of the body, saying 'I and the Father are one' (John 10:30). He concluded: 'One can know neither the word nor the Father of the word apart from the image.'[40]

Eusebius' response to this line of reasoning was firm: the Word was the unique image of the invisible God before, during and after the Incarnation.[41] This theological assertion based itself on three considerations. First, the body-image notion had to be rejected since it diminished Christ's exceptional status as Saviour. 'If we grant that the flesh is the image of God then the flesh of all humans are images of God,' and the Saviour's is nothing exceptional.[42] Elsewhere, Eusebius would interpret the passage from Genesis that recorded God's words at the creation of humanity ('Let us make humanity in our image') as designating the *rational* element in the human soul, not the corporeal existence of humans.[43]

Second, and somewhat in tension with the first consideration, was the theological prioritization of the Son's status as a mediator between the transcendent God and embodied humanity. The body inhabited during the Incarnation was too much on the one side of the divine/human split. In order to bridge the divide the Saviour (in both the incarnate and pre-incarnate periods) had to be distinctive from the rest of embodied humanity, while at the same time being somewhat ontologically below the Father. This 'ontological reduction'[44] was expressed through the language of the image just as much as through the language of begottenness. Here, Eusebius stands well within the Platonic philosophical tradition.

Plato's mimetic metaphysics is well known. The most real entities (like the sun or the 'Form of the Good' in the allegory of the cave) existing in the non-sensible, intelligible realms were imitated by (or participated in by) less real entities that were copies of the higher realities (like the reflections of the sun, the fashioned images of things or the shadows of those images in the allegory of the cave). At the lowest levels of the metaphysical chain the shadows of the higher levels could indeed be steeped in confusion and only bear the truth of their exemplars in the faintest manner. The sensible world was an ontological level of obscurity and even distortion of the truth, like a mirage or the warped image of an object under water. On the other hand, the situation of embodied souls, who had fallen into the 'mud' of materiality, was not entirely hopeless.[45] For while images were deemed copies at various removes from reality, they were also said to participate in those higher forms. This was the conception that lay behind Socrates' discussion of beauty in the *Phaedrus* and elsewhere: because beautiful bodies in this world participated in higher forms of beauty, the very sight of them could prompt one's memory of a pre-embodied existence, when souls flitted about among the astral gods and beheld the beauty of the intelligible spheres.

While Eusebius consistently denied the possibility of souls pre-existing their embodied states, the vision of higher intelligible realities being perceived through images in the physical world had a powerful hold on him. The second hypostasis was an image of the first, which conveyed an ontological reduction while being a necessary mediating step in the chain of being.

> Whoever has seen the Son has seen the Father, the unbegotten divinity, as in an image and mirror, being impressed in the Son [then follows a quotation from Wisdom of Solomon 7:26]; the Son receives the glory of divinity from the Father, but the Father from no one; being first principle, spring and root of good things, He is called one and only God [anarthrous].[46]

This statement emphasizes the transcendence of the Father's divinity, while maintaining a close relationship between the Son as image and the Father as model. Elsewhere, Eusebius heightens the proximity between image and source:

> Hear [from the Gospel of John that] the Word was God [anarthrous] Himself, as an image of God [articular], an image not as in lifeless matter but as in a living Son, likened most precisely after the archetype, the Father's divinity.[47]

A Platonist reading this statement might have recalled a similar assertion made by Plotinus, but with reference to the world's imitative relationship to its model: 'The universe comes from Intellect and Intellect is prior in nature, and the cause of the universe as a kind of archetype and model, the universe being an image of it and existing by means of it.'[48] Eusebius has, however, sharpened the notion of image in order to apply it to the closest of relationships between two hypostases; in existence, life and divinity the living Son was the only image of the only God.

The sheer closeness of image to archetype, on the one hand, allowed for the demiurgic work of creation; on the other, though, Eusebius avoided the pervasiveness of Plato's and Plotinus' mimetic metaphysics. He preferred to use the concept of seminal principles (*dēmiourgikoi logoi*) rather than images to denote the Son's relation to the lower ontological levels. Though the world 'came to be through Him', as John had attested, Eusebius was reluctant to name the world an image of the Son (or Word). Rational humans alone would receive the honourable appellation of 'images of the image' of the God over all, a title predicated upon humanity's sharing in the Word as rational, *logikon*. This feature of Eusebius' thought importantly found expression in his apologetic work where he developed claims to Christianity's superior philosophical and theological system and engaged in dialogue with the Greek philosophical traditions (see Chapter 3).

Eusebius' conception of the divine image in his later theological works is most concerned to mark out the nature of the Son. Since his interlocutor, Marcellus, had denied that the Son was the eternal image of the Father, Eusebius' emphasis is understandable. Yet, the relationship between Son and Father had important implications for the relationship of the Son to the created order as well. Without the image, the transcendent Father would remain in solitary aloofness and ontological simplicity without any procession of being – there would be no possibility of a world. Were one to maintain the existence of the world, one would necessarily have recourse to matter as a second eternal first principle – a concept that remained a strong possibility and even a deeply held doctrine among Platonists of Late Antiquity (though they all maintained mediating ontological levels through which matter was informed). Yet, even if one did allow for a sort of severe metaphysical dualism, a soteriological problem was felt acutely by at least some Christians, including Eusebius. Eusebius recognized the necessity of a visible image of the invisible God in the process of human salvation. Without the unique image of the one God, humanity would be abandoned to the pursuit and worship of deceptive images that distorted theological truth. In other words, the soteriological problem was also an epistemological problem: humans needed the image of God in order to see and know God.

The frequent prohibitions against polytheism and idolatry in the Old Testament were delivered by the Word himself. 'Who is the Lord and God of the commandment to "have no other gods?"' asked Eusebius, quoting Exodus 20:3; 'It was the Son, having the image of the Father in Himself, giving commands to those who were sick with idolatry.'[49] Or again:

> The Son is the image of the Father, and the Saviour teaches that the Father is the only true God; and it is unavoidable that He confesses that He is the true God [anarthrous], having obtained this as in an image, in order that the addition of the word 'only' would harmonize with the only Father as of an image with its archetype.[50]

Not only was the visible indication of invisible truth necessary for humanity, but the centrepiece of Christian doctrine – a point that unnerved the metaphysical sensibilities of Platonists – was the claim that the unembodied Word or image took on a body for the redemption of embodied humanity. By the Platonist vision, this was a metaphysical intrusion of the higher into the lower that was unthinkable. Yet the Apostle Paul had firmly stated that the divine Son 'emptied Himself' and laid aside equality with God in the Incarnation (Philippians 2:6–8). Had Eusebius possessed a more theologically articulate opponent in Marcellus, we would probably have a more elaborate examination of this point in Eusebius' writings. Unfortunately, he limited himself to opposing Marcellus' emphasis on the 'form of a slave' by balancing it with the 'form of God' in Paul's same statement.

The third broad consideration in support of the conception of the Word's (not the body's) identification as the image of the invisible God, which has already been hinted at in the foregoing remarks, comprised the attempt to legitimize the Christian worship of the Son. Given Marcellus' positing of a strict union between Father and Son so that these became only names of a single hypostasis, Eusebius' counterclaims of the Son's separate hypostatic identity and the image's proper existence close beside the archetype would seem to move a person out of the bounds of strict monotheism and hence open up the problem of idolatry in one's worship of the Son. But God remained one in Eusebius' system:

> No one who thinks well could say there are two Fathers or two Sons; just as when one image of a ruling emperor is brought forth through all the earth, no sensible person would say these are two rulers but that there is one honoured through his image. The Church likewise worships the one God through His Son.[51]

The conceptualization of the Son's relation to the Father as one of image to model allowed, by the visual and cultural logic of imperial images current in the Roman Empire, for a sharing of honour, worship and (as noted earlier) divinity. Because such a formulation nonetheless came dangerously close to polytheism, Eusebius was careful to limit as firmly as possible the number of images of the Father that were ontologically possible. One God could only be mirrored by one image. Plurality would of necessity await later levels of being.

Earlier in his *Ecclesiastical Theology*, Eusebius elaborates the unique worship of which the Son is worthy as an image of the Father. Since the Son is the Saviour, Lord and Demiurge of all, 'so much should He be called God [anarthrous], master, Saviour and king. For this reason, the Church is taught to worship and honour Him as God [anarthrous].' Though the Son is given the title of God in this passage without the article (as the Father is), the Son remains unique from all other entities in the universe. He is not to be honoured, Eusebius emphasizes, like prophets, angels or spiritual powers, but like the Father. As Thomas had recognized the incarnate, resurrected Son as God, 'we too worship the Son alone with divine [*theïkē*] honour.'[52] The analogy with imperial images is again adopted:

> We honour the Father when we honour the Son; for just as we honour the prototype of the image when we honour an image of an emperor, so

the Father is honoured through the Son since He is also seen through the Son.[53]

Before we close our discussion of Eusebius' image theology, it is fruitful to consider the broader place of images in his writings. There are two important contexts for engagement with images in his thought: the representation of humans in various media, from the visual to verbal, which occurs especially in his methodological comments about memorializing saints; and the representation of the Son in visual iconography. Because discussion of the former will become the focus of the next chapter it may be postponed for the moment, except to note that the visual images of Constantine himself would be highly significant both for connecting Eusebius' literary representation of the emperor to such visual copies and for extending towards a broader range of application the hierarchical metaphysics of images that we have seen in his theological writings.

The second area is the topic of his *Letter to Constantia*, the sister of the emperor and widow of the dead Licinius.[54] Constantia had enquired about the legitimacy of producing icons of the Saviour with the hope that such a practice might aid devotion. The bishop responded with caution and firmness: a visual image could only capture the features of his body; the divine nature and qualities of the Son could not be so easily reproduced. Just as he had rejected Marcellus' assertion that Christ's body was the image of God, Eusebius dismisses the visual image as only a copy of the body, which was 'the form of a slave' – an allusion to the words of Paul that had been a key part of his polemic against Marcellus. In the letter, Eusebius sagely avoids the polemical tone, but nonetheless resolutely moves past the viability of such image production. This sort of iconographic practice would not be a true 'image of an image' as the rational soul of a human could claim to be the image of God through the mediation of the Word (*logikon-logos*); it was, rather, a copy of a body and not of the Word that had taken on the body. Even if a visual image attempted to represent the Word in its divinity, such an attempt would fall under the prohibition against graven images contained in the Ten Commandments. In a manner resonant of his anti-Marcellan writings, the *Letter to Constantia* thus presumed the unique status of the Son as the image of the Father. While the image could share in the worship rendered to God, it could not become the object of further images (aside from its own living images, the human souls, which it created). Just as Marcellus' analogy of the Word with human words was misplaced, so his correspondence of the divine image with human bodies marked a significant deviation from ecclesiastical truth, the Church's proclamation of God the Son.

Sophia the Son

If we can trust Eusebius' rendering of Marcellus' argument (which is not always a safe assumption), his opponent seems to have made a consistent exegetical move of interpreting key biblical passages about the Son as referring to the Incarnation in particular. As we have seen, Marcellus declared the image of God to signify the body of Christ, and by extension the bodies of humans generally. He went further, however, and claimed that the title 'Wisdom [*Sophia*] of God' also applied to Christ's body. Marcellus 'casts the meaning on the ground claiming these verses [describing God's 'creating' Wisdom] refer to Christ's body'.[55] In both instances, that of the image of God and that of the Wisdom of God, Marcellus had used Genesis as the interpretive key. Biblical passages referring to the image of God, even when naming Christ as the image, had to be taken as designating bodies since Genesis had presented God as saying: 'Let us make humanity in our image' (Genesis 1:26–7), just before the fashioning of human bodies. Likewise, when Wisdom spoke in her own voice in the book of Proverbs, proclaiming that she had been 'created [...] before He made the earth' (Proverbs 8:22, 24 LXX), Marcellus identified the 'earth' as the human body which will return to earth, an interpretation based squarely upon another verse from Genesis: 'earth you are and to earth you shall return' (Genesis 3:19).[56]

The conclusion to be drawn, for Marcellus, was that 'He created me' could only be spoken of God's making 'not that which was, but that which was not', namely, the body that the Word took on.[57] The precise meaning of the verb 'created' meant the production of something out of nothing; hence the phrase, 'He created me the first of His ways,' could not refer to the Son himself, who was, for Marcellus, only a name used interchangeably with 'Father' for God and, therefore, did not hypostatically exist separately from the Father. The thing created from nothing was, if not the Son, then the Son's body.[58] As in the case of the image of God, this somatic interpretive focus allowed Marcellus to steer clear of attributing a separate existence to the Word, image or Wisdom that would raise the frightful prospect (he thought) of the existence of two Gods. If the Word was like a human word, being uttered or remaining in the mind, and if both the image and Wisdom were designations of Christ's incarnate body, an interpretive option rendered legitimate by the lens of Genesis, then the oneness of God could be preserved from any taint of plurality.

Eusebius, in a manner that would become the orthodox position,[59] refused to grant this somatic reading of Wisdom. The eighth chapter of Proverbs was the crux. While portions of it have already been quoted or paraphrased in the preceding paragraphs, it is beneficial to have the relevant verses before us as we trace out Eusebius' understanding of this key passage for his theology. Wisdom is speaking:[60]

> The Lord created me the first of His ways unto His works, He established me in the beginning, before eternity, before He made the earth and before He made the abysses, before the springs of waters went forth, before the mountains were settled, before all the valleys, He begot me [...] When He prepared heaven, I was present with Him. [Proverbs 8:22–7 LXX]

Because 1 Corinthians 1:24, which named Christ 'the Wisdom and power of God' through whom everything was created and sustained, provided a focal lens for reading the Hebrew Scriptures, Eusebius sought to develop a reading of the Wisdom of Proverbs in light of his Logos theology. Important theological expressions that were formative of his interpretive apparatus came from Hellenistic Judaism and possibly also from Middle Platonism. Eusebius had made connections between these already in the 11th book of his *Preparation*, where he quoted the verses from Proverbs alongside material from Wisdom of Solomon, in proximity to a quotation from the Middle

Platonist Numenius. A quotation from the Wisdom of Solomon alerted the reader that its author would reveal the mysteries of Wisdom, 'constructor' of all things, 'from the beginning of creation'.[61] In words that, for Eusebius, would have clinched the identification of this Wisdom with that of the New Testament, the Wisdom of Solomon went on to pronounce:

> She pervades and penetrates all things by reason of her pureness. For she is the breath of the power of God and a clear effluence of the glory of the Almighty [...] She is an effulgence from everlasting light, and an unspotted mirror of the operation of God, and an image of His goodness.[62]

Most of the key features of the New Testament Wisdom (and Logos) theology are present here (and indeed, the New Testament authors probably had the Wisdom of Solomon in mind): Wisdom existed at the beginning (John 1:1; Colossians 1:15); She pervades all things (Colossians 1:15); She exudes the power of God (1 Corinthians 1:24); She radiates with divine glory (Hebrews 1:3); She is a mirror and image of God (Colossians 1:15).

Yet a significant feature of the Wisdom of Solomon (especially in material not quoted above) was the clearly non-corporeal nature of Wisdom. Furthermore, this precursor to Eusebius attributed the goodness and order of the created world to a pervading presence of the divine Wisdom. Wisdom was an 'intellectual spirit [...] only begotten [...] which pervades through all intellectual spirits'.[63] This non-corporeal conception was precisely at odds with Marcellus' somatic interpretation of the Wisdom of Proverbs. Significantly, it also required a pre-temporal existence of Wisdom before the creation of the universe (or, at least, 'at the beginning' of creation). This was sufficient for Eusebius' concerns: Wisdom could not be identified as a body (even Christ's), but nonetheless had an existence of its own, which pre-existed bodies and was responsible for, or involved in, the creation of everything. But did this amount to a hypostatic identity for Wisdom? Even if Marcellus' somatic interpretation was deflected, the main thrust of his position had been the denial of the Son's hypostasis – Eusebius was obliged to meet this challenge. While the Wisdom of Solomon may have played a significant role in the formation of his thinking on the Son as Wisdom and Word, that text plays less of a role in his anti-Marcellan writings, being displaced by the passage in Proverbs 8 (a passage which would prove to be one of the most significant proof-texts of fourth-century theological debates over the nature of the Son). His reading of that passage attempts to leave the issue beyond doubt: it does not say Wisdom was 'of God', just as in John 1:1,

> it does not say the Word was 'of God', lest anyone think He is said to be among those things which are relative to [*pros ti*] God and that He happened to be in [*en*] God [that is, an *endiathetos logos*], since He is substantial and living [...] just as in the case of Wisdom.[64]

She is, furthermore, not named *a wisdom* of God, but *the Wisdom*, 'lest we think Her to be some accident [*sumbama*, that is, a chance quality] of God, like knowledge in a knowledgeable man, but a substantial and living Wisdom, being the same as the Son of God'.[65] If anyone should suppose the Wisdom mentioned in Proverbs 8 to be

> a wise condition in God, according to which we consider God to be wise, let them hear the verse 'Wisdom is your sister'. Who would be so mad as to suppose that the God over all and the wise condition in Him should be called sister of our accomplishments?[66]

He concludes that the Wisdom spoken of in Proverbs must be the same as that mentioned in 1 Corinthians 1:24. Wisdom, with its own hypostatic integrity, is the Son.

Eusebius' exposition of the Proverbs passage furnishes a platform for articulating the role of Wisdom in creation in a manner distinct from the Father. The biblical passage itself was focused on key aspects of God's creation: He 'created' Wisdom 'the first of His ways [...] Before He made the earth and before He made the abysses', springs, mountains and valleys, Wisdom was begotten by God; 'when He prepared heaven', Wisdom 'was present with' Him. As we saw earlier, the term 'created' was of considerable concern to Eusebius. It certainly seemed to lend itself either to Marcellus' somatic interpretation or to Arius' claim that the Son was a 'creature' like other creatures.[67] Eusebius, however, had discovered that the Hebrew term translated by the Septuagint as 'created' could more appropriately be rendered 'obtained'. Wisdom could thus maintain hypostatic distinctiveness from the Father without being classed a creature. The adoption of the language of begetting in the Proverbs passage was likewise helpful in bolstering Eusebius' interpretation (Proverbs 8:25). Since the abysses, springs, mountains and valleys were not to be taken as the Apostles (as Marcellus had declared) but were instead to be read either as the literal features of the physical creation or as symbolic of heavenly powers,[68] Wisdom could clearly be shown to have an existence before these things, and hence to have existed 'before creation'.

When Eusebius turned to Proverbs 8:27 ('When He prepared heaven, I was present with Him'), he found a riddle of the only begotten Son as 'living and subsistent, being before all generated things [...] for She was with Him and was beside Him before the heavens and what is beyond the heavens came to be.'[69] But what was Wisdom's precise role in creation? The answer for Eusebius lay in the notion of God's 'preparation' of creation. God prepared the moment of creation

> by legislating and making outlines [*diatupoumenos*] before [the heavens] came to be [...] Therefore, the Father would make outlines and would make preparations, conceiving how to establish such a heaven [...] While [the Son] looking intently [*enatenizōn*] at the Father's calculations and alone looking at the depths in Him, proceeded in deeds, ministering forth the Father's will.[70]

Before the heavens or anything else was created, then,

> the Son was beside and with [*parēn... sunēn*] the Father, when He was still planning the establishment of everything [...] then like a good painter [*grapheus*], receiving the archetypal ideas from the Father's calculations, He transferred them to the being of things, forming living things [*zōoplastōn*] and establishing them such as He saw laid down beforehand in the mind of the Father.[71]

The same Son who spoke as Wisdom in the Proverbs would later, in the Gospels, confirm these claims about being an active and instrumental link in the work of creation: 'I can make nothing from myself unless I see the Father making it; whatever He makes, the Son makes' (John 5:19).[72] If anyone were to ask how the Son made things that had already come into being by the Father, Eusebius could answer in good Platonic fashion that the world consisted of two levels, the intelligible and the sensible.

> The things coming into being by the Son are likenesses of archetypal things established beforehand in the Father's calculations; looking intently at these things in the Father's mind, the Son makes representations of what He sees; He shows that His looking at the depths of the Father is an act of the Father's love, saying 'the Father loves the Son and shows Him all that He makes.[73]

This description of an ontologically mediating role performed by the Son expressed a strong tradition rooted in Plato's account of creation in the *Timaeus*.[74] There, Plato's Demiurge had 'looked intently' at the paradigmatic forms in creating the intelligible universe, which in turn formed a model for the sensible universe.[75] In contrast to Marcellus' ephemeral uttered word that would dissolve like a wisp of wind (as well as a body that would be abandoned at the consummation of the universe), Eusebius tapped into the most powerful sublimation of the created order of ancient thought in Plato's cosmogony.

Wisdom's creational work, as described here, becomes more complicated, if richer, when held simultaneously with Eusebius' theology of the Son as image. The Son was the visible image of the invisible Father. At the same time, humans, in their most human element – that is, their rationality – were images of the Son. The human soul was an 'image of an image'.[76] Whether through participation in the Word's words (or rational principles, *logoi*), or more clearly through reflection of the Word's model, itself an image of the Father's model, for Eusebius humans at their best are 'those who are wise with Him who is Wisdom, those fashioned to be rational [*logioi*] with Him who is Reason [the Word, *logos*]'.[77] Thus, in Eusebius we find a thorough interweaving of the Platonic account of the Demiurge looking at a divine paradigm and moulding created things according to what He sees there, and the biblical declarations of humanity made in the image of God and the Son being the very image of God. If asked, Eusebius no doubt would have claimed that his formulations were entirely and solely rooted in Scripture alone (any resonance with Plato would only be felt because Plato had copied or even 'translated' the Scriptures, as discussed in Chapter 3). We know, however, that his reading of the Son's fecund mimetic work of creation is not the only, or the natural, interpretation of the biblical texts. As with any reading, Eusebius' was a product of ongoing processes of making sense of particular texts, of associative engagements with both classical and biblical literature, and of tracing and retracing interpretive routes, with all the false starts, rests, jumps, detours and circuitous paths for which such a metaphor allows.

The Holy Spirit

It is appropriate to discuss the Holy Spirit last in our examination of Eusebius' doctrine of the Trinity, since he himself only treats of the Spirit in any detail last in his *Ecclesiastical Theology* and only briefly in the rest of his corpus.[78] Extensive consideration of the nature of the Spirit and its relationship to the other members of the Trinity would arise later in the fourth century in the struggle against the Pneumatomachians ('those who fight against the Spirit'); even later, it would become a source of contention between Byzantine Christians and Roman Catholics in the 'Filioque' controversy. Though brief, Eusebius' discussion became an important early participant in a much larger discourse on the Spirit (that is, pneumatology), one that would play a decisive role in intellectual and ecclesiastical history.

The source of Eusebius' account of the Holy Spirit in the *Ecclesiastical Theology* lay in Marcellus' reading of key verses from Christ's 'Farewell Discourse' in the Gospel of John combined with His post-Resurrection words (in the same Gospel). Christ taught His disciples that, though He would soon depart, He would send the 'Comforter' ('Paraclete'), namely the 'Spirit of truth who proceeds from the Father' (John 15:26); somewhat confusingly, this same Spirit is also described as receiving truth from Christ and announcing it to the disciples in times of need (John 16:13–14). Later, after His Resurrection, Christ 'breathed on them and said, "Receive the Holy Spirit"' (John 20:22). In these verses, 'By an ineffable word the monad is shown,' Marcellus asserted, 'broadening into a triad, but not submitting to division.'[79] The three could not be three distinct hypostases, since both the Son and the Spirit proceeded from the Father, and yet the Spirit was breathed out of the Son on His disciples. How, Marcellus asked, can the Son say to his disciples 'Receive the Holy Spirit' after earlier declaring that 'the Spirit proceeds from the Father,' unless the Son and Father were one hypostasis?[80]

Eusebius claimed there was an 'easy solution for those contemplating [the verses] piously', if they recognized that the Son was 'together with the Father, being inside as though He were in the inner chambers and unapproachable places of the Father's palace; then for the salvation of humans He was sent out from the side of the Father'. The Spirit, too, was beside the throne of God and was sent forth from 'the palace of the Father's divinity', at one time in the form of a dove (at the Saviour's baptism), at other times to each of the Prophets and Apostles. A careful reading of the passages from John exhibited, for Eusebius, the necessity of positing a difference between the Son and the Spirit. They could not be the same hypostasis since Christ had named the Spirit 'another Comforter'. 'Who is so stupid as to say after so many verses [from John] that the one speaking and the one spoken about are one and the same?' Likewise, when He breathed on the disciples, the giver and the thing given (the Spirit) were not the same; the breath (*pneuma*) of Christ was only a 'cathartic breathing', preparing the disciples' souls for their later reception of the Spirit.[81]

Though his dominant concern was the strengthening of his claim of the separate hypostatic identities of the three members of the Trinity, Eusebius offered further remarks on the activity of the Holy Spirit. The Spirit served a dual role as both comforter and teacher of truth. The disciples would face both persecution and partial knowledge; hence, the Spirit was necessary not only to comfort the disciples in persecution, but also to 'teach them all the truth of the new covenant, with respect to which they had not advanced to be taught by the Saviour when he conversed with them, because they were still enslaved to the Judaic way of life.'[82]

This was a significant claim on Eusebius' part, which evinced an acknowledgement of the limited and partial nature of Christ's teachings for a full 'ecclesiastical theology'. Whereas modern scholars frequently suppose a rift between Christ's original teachings and later accretions of oral and written traditions, and furthermore a divide between the Jesus of the Gospels and the Jesus of Paul, Eusebius saw such growth in doctrine as a direct result of the progressive force of the Spirit on the minds of Christ's followers. Christ's teachings and post-Resurrection breathing marked partial stages in a teleology of engagement with the Spirit that would culminate in the day of Pentecost – when the disciples received the Spirit and spoke in other languages (Acts 2:1–13). His breathing on them only gave them 'a portion of the gift' of the Holy Spirit: 'He gave to them in part while he was present with them, but after this He filled them with greater and more perfect power.'[83]

While this exposition would seem to limit the role of Christ (at least as a teacher) Eusebius maintained a position for the Holy Spirit that was subordinate to both the Father and the Son. While the Spirit is 'preeminent in honour, glory and priority, and greater and higher than every intellectual and rational being (for which reason He is also included in the holy and thrice-blessed Trinity)', He nonetheless 'has been subordinate'.[84] The reasoning for Eusebius' subordinationist pneumatology was threefold. First, Christ had taught (in the Gospel of John) that He spoke only what He heard from the Father, while the Spirit announced to the disciples only what He received from the Son; the Spirit thus 'leads out' from the Son what the Son passed on from the Father.[85] Second, each member of the Trinity was named a spirit in the Scriptures, so there was little unique in the Holy Spirit's being described as such. It was for this very reason that the Son had given Him a special title, the Paraclete, to mark Him off from the other two members of the Godhead as well as from other holy spirits, like angels.[86] Third, His special province of activity was more limited: the Spirit worked only in the minds and lives of believers, performing the processes of sanctification (that is, the Holy Spirit made believers holy). 'The Holy Spirit,' averred Eusebius, is fond of dwelling only in holy ones, proceeding through the Son to whomever the Father should determine. This would be His work: to sanctify everyone to whom there is a share of one or even many of the gifts [...] and it is even reasonable that the ruling and divine powers [that is, angels] receive their holiness from Him.[87]

The chain of command looked like this: 'The Father has full power (or, is independent) and gives grace, the Son is a minister of this grace [...] and the Holy Spirit is Himself the leader over the divisions of the gifts, which are in Him.'[88]

These considerations led Eusebius to the formulation of a strict separation between the Spirit and the other members of the Trinity in a way that seems sharper than that between the Father and Son. 'But the Son alone having been honoured with the Father's divinity, would be creative and demiurgic of all generated things, visible and invisible, and indeed, even the very existence [*hyparxis*] of the Paraclete–Spirit.'[89] Such an assertion highlighted both an ontological distinction between the three members of the Trinity and an ontological dependence of the lesser upon the higher in a hierarchical manner. The theology 'handed down by the holy and catholic Church' articulated belief in 'one God and Father' and the Son as the 'only begotten God being in the lap of the Father' – but the Spirit

is neither God nor Son, since He did not take His birth from the Father like the Son; but He is one of those things generated through Him, since 'everything came to be through [the Son] and apart from Him not one thing came to be'.[90]

Such a hierarchy, which denied full divinity to the Spirit as part of the created order, would not sit well with later orthodox theologians.

In seeking to preserve the distinct existence of the Word, Eusebius' two theological treatises display a concern with textual words: whether those of his opponent Marcellus or those of the Scriptures. His argumentation remained persistently within the methodology of earlier works of exegesis (such as the *Introduction*) as well as of polemic (such as the *Preparation*).

His basic doctrinal system seems largely to have remained consistent (with the notable exception of his avoidance of the phrase 'second God' in the theological works), though with a greater elaboration of his Logos theology and with deeper interpretive work being performed on central passages that were relevant for the debate over the nature of the Son of God. Furthermore, his concern to pursue further the precise nature and role of the Holy Spirit stimulated later pneumatological formulations. He thereby stands as a critical contributor to theological discourses in one of the most exciting periods in the history of doctrine.

VI

SPEAKING, TRUTH
AND POWER

BY THE TIME CONSTANTINE DIED in 337, Eusebius had taken many
occasions to reflect upon the person and role of the Roman emperor and
his predecessors. While the *Chronicon* and *Ecclesiastical History* sought to
be comprehensive, those emperors who had loomed largest in a variety of
literary contexts, from the *Preparation for the Gospel* to the biblical commentaries, were Augustus (under whose reign Christ was born), Vespasian
and Hadrian (under whose separate reigns the Jews had been defeated
with different, though equally devastating, effects), and the Tetrarchs or
would-be Tetrarchs (especially Maxentius, Galerius, Maximinus Daia and
Licinius). Each of these emperors was invoked within the articulation of
themes central to Eusebius' thought. Christ's birth was synchronized with
the reign of Augustus in order to solidify his historical and theological
claim that the worship of many gods was eradicated by Christ at the same
time that the first Roman emperor had defeated the many rulers who vied
for power over parts or the whole of the Empire.[1] The final destruction and
dispersion of the Jews under Vespasian and Hadrian represented the end
of the Jewish nation and showed the illegitimacy of their continued claims

to be the chosen people or to possess the life of piety.[2] The Tetrarchs were examples of the savage bestial life promoted by daemons, who attacked the stalwart confessors and martyrs, but were ultimately crushed by the 'saving sign', the 'trophy' of the cross, which was carried into battle by Constantine.[3] Each of these emperors, therefore, stood within a careful historical vision that vividly expressed the triumph of Christ and his followers over hostile enemies and their permanent replacement of the old Jewish way of life for a new (and yet most ancient) life of piety and wisdom.

In addition to these main themes, several interesting allusions to emperors occur throughout Eusebius' corpus as well, which help to fill out our picture of his political sensibilities. Galerius (or Maximinus Daia) receives oblique mention in the *General Elementary Introduction*. Readers who had become disconcerted by the ongoing attacks against Christians are encouraged not to let

> their faith be shaken by the persecutions in [our own] times, and especially the present one breathing against us more violently than any of those before, even exhibiting such things against the churches and all the people as no one has recorded in Scripture or in the tradition of the ancients.[4]

Eusebius' oration on the basilica at Tyre reflects a happier relationship with emperors: 'the supreme emperors' spit on dead idols.'[5] However, written at a time roughly contemporary with the oration, the *Proof of the Gospel* seems to make a negative veiled reference to Licinius and his supporters when it declares: 'nations, rulers, peoples and emperors have not ceased their combined attack on Him and His teaching.'[6] Though the plural use of 'emperors' in the oration is often taken to designate the joint rule of Constantine and Licinius, it is just as likely to refer to Constantine and his son Crispus (or merely to be a rhetorical amplification of Constantine alone – after all, the only imperial activity that is specified sufficiently in the oration is that of Constantine at Rome).[7] There were periods of tenuous peace between the two emperors during the second decade of the fourth century, during which Eusebius might have thought to refer to both in favourable terms.

The evidence of the *Proof* shows that he was well aware of the uncertainties of the times. In the oration, then, Eusebius sagely avoids giving a precise identity to the imperial figures he had in mind, and thus eliminates any taint of subversive tendencies in a public declamation at a period in which Licinius may have begun to see Christians as potential supporters of his rival in the West.

Strikingly, even after the establishment of Constantine's sole rule over the Empire, Eusebius limited references to the reign of the first Christian emperor to those writings that necessarily included matters of imperial politics, namely the *History* and the speeches and biography in honour of Constantine (to be discussed in this chapter). The *Commentary on Isaiah*, for instance, declared that a prophetic reference to 'nurses' had been fulfilled in the emperors and rulers (always in the plural, and explicitly designating both the emperor and governors, prefects, and so on, and possibly the emperor's sons), who had provided for the construction of church buildings. 'Who, seeing with their own eyes the "rulers and authorities" genuflecting in the Church of God [...] would deny that the prophecy is fulfilled literally [*pros lexin*] and historically.'[8] Earlier in the commentary, a prophecy of the overthrow of idols was seen to have been fulfilled: 'Now in our own times polytheism has been said to be unable to help itself. Idol-worshippers have to hide their statues in caves so that the emperor's men may not take them for their costly material.'[9] Both passages in the commentary make clearly positive appeals to the emperors or their subordinates insofar as they confirm or embody Eusebius' assertions of the fulfilment of prophecy. Otherwise, however, the commentary avoids any imperial references. Even a discussion of the cross as the sign of Christ that offers protection to Christians makes no allusion to the importance of this sign in the military successes of Constantine. The praises of Constantine we encountered in the *History* are absent from both of Eusebius' major biblical commentaries. Likewise, his theological writings, in spite of dealing with issues that brought Eusebius before Constantine himself, make only sparse though positive references to the emperor.[10] There is thus a remarkable minimization of imperial matters in works that come from later in the reign of Constantine, a time when any earlier suspicions about the depth of his concern for ecclesiastical well-being or authenticity of his faith would have been assuaged.[11]

What has most abetted his characterization as a 'court theologian' of Constantine is the presence in Eusebius' corpus of what is often misleadingly labelled the 'official biography' as well as two speeches in honour of the emperor. The four books of the *Life of Constantine* strike many general readers today as a welter of fawning praise and blind sycophancy. More sophisticated and scholarly readings of it have declared it to be the result of combining the biographical genre with what was originally intended to be a laudatory panegyric.[12] Whatever his original plans had been as a prolific author who actively sought to rethink history and his own times, Eusebius no doubt had a multitude of varied impulses when writing during the years in which Constantine reached his 30-year anniversary as emperor (335), prepared to march on Persia, fell into ill health and soon thereafter 'was united to God' (337).[13] Faced with an irrecoverable cluster of authorial intentions we find it fruitful to approach the *Life* as an organic whole.[14]

Speaking Truth in the Presence of Power

Before we dismiss too quickly the idea that eulogistic tendencies or even an embryonic eulogy lie behind the *Life*, we should examine briefly the two speeches Eusebius purportedly delivered at the imperial court, one of which was itself a panegyric on the emperor. We know that Eusebius spoke before the emperor on more than one occasion since he tells us so himself.[15] Because the second speech, the *Oration on Christ's Sepulchre*, which is not so much a panegyric as an apologia for Constantine's building of a church at the site of Christ's burial, is abruptly appended to the first speech, an encomium honouring the emperor's 30-year anniversary entitled the *Tricennial Oration* (often called *Laus Constantini*, 'in praise of Constantine'), it had been thought they were both parts of a single long speech. But as the editor of the critical edition Ivar A. Heikel pointed out, changes in style and tone, in addition to clear evidence in the manuscripts, indicate that Chapters

11–18 belong to a different speech from what had gone before.[16] The argument was convincingly elaborated and strengthened in an important study by Hal Drake, and there is now little to support the supposition of a single lengthy oration.[17] The style, tone, argument and even named audiences of these orations differ in significant ways.

Adopting the language of the mysteries, the prologue of the *Tricennial Oration* addressed itself to listeners and readers who were already aware of and adherents to deeper theological truths. Unlike a typical encomium on a mortal human being, this oration would leave the human aspects of Constantine's reign to lesser minds and pursue the more significant divine power at work in the emperor:

> So let those who have penetrated the sanctuary of the holy palace, that innermost, most inaccessible of places, having barred the gate to profane hearing, narrate the sovereign's ineffable mysteries to those alone who are initiated in these things. Let those who have purified their ears in the streams of piety, who have attached their intellectual faculty to the exalted wing of the soul itself, pay homage to the Ruler of All, performing divine rites with decorum.[18]

In the speech that follows Eusebius offers an extended reflection on the true nature of sovereignty. As a result of the oration's dense rhetoric, the precise identity of the sovereign under discussion at any given point can be somewhat confusing, as is explicitly noted at the outset:

> This is a celebration of the Supreme Sovereign [...] I mean by Supreme Sovereign the One who is truly supreme; this One, I say – nor will the sovereign who is present resent it [...] – is the One who is above the universe.[19]

The reason for the confusing adoption of homonymy (alleviated here by the translator's capitalization of the divine Sovereign) resides in the fundamental argument of the oration: the existence of one God over all necessarily entails the propriety of one king on earth over one empire.

Eusebius' Logos theology enriches this 'political theology'.[20] For this bishop–orator, the God over all transcended all words and any attempt to comprehend Him would inevitably and quickly end in failure. Yet, just as imperial subjects came to know of their emperor through his images, so humans could know the Ruler of all through His singular image: the Word. It was the Word that mediated between the Father and the creation, providentially ordering and guiding the created world by means of his rational administration.[21] Constantine was both a friend of the Word and its copy, imitating its wise order and defeat of impiety.[22] Such a political theology was not new. Fragments from Neopythagorean philosophical texts of the later Hellenistic period had already applied this form of mimetic theology to human rulers – the proper political state on earth needed to model itself monarchically on the one God in heaven.[23] Eusebius' adoption of the mystery terminology in the prologue may have been intended to invoke the rarefied philosophical mood of the Neopythagoreans, though Christians had employed such language for centuries.

If the mimetic political theology marks no innovation, its adoption in an imperial panegyric as an excuse to transfer the orator's focus away from the emperor and onto a particular God who had traditionally not found a place in such orations is a noteworthy feature whose significance cannot be dismissed. Comparison with pagan panegyrics of the time is revealing in this regard. The *Tricennial Oration* entirely omits to narrate Constantine's parentage or youth, which was a staple feature of other panegyrics.[24] The virtues of wisdom, goodness, justice, prudence and courage, all of which are typical of panegyrics, are explained and emphasized only insofar as they are evidence that the true sovereign on earth 'has modelled himself after the archetypal form of the Supreme Sovereign'.[25] The opposites of these virtues are those vices displayed by illegitimate pretenders at sovereignty, who cannot properly be deemed rulers since they themselves are ruled by daemons.[26] Even more significant is the difference between the traditional concern for elaborating on an emperor's military victories and its reconfiguration in Eusebius' speech.

Even the distinctively Christian and biblically informed narratives of the Battle of the Milvian Bridge told in the *History* and *Life* (discussed below) were resonant of pagan panegyrics. Pagan orators, too, would attribute the victory to divine aid worthy of a great emperor. Over a decade before the *Tricennial Oration*, the pagan Nazarius had remarked on Constantine's victory over Maxentius as God's beneficent act on behalf of the good emperor.[27] Incorporation of divine miracles was likewise not limited to Christian versions of a battle. Nazarius, too, declared the miraculous appearance of a heavenly army who fought on Constantine's behalf.[28] Indeed, Eusebius' historical and biographical works are thus closer to the pagan panegyrical tradition, as exemplified by Nazarius, than the *Tricennial Oration*. The battles that receive the most attention in this Christian panegyric are those victories over the temples of daemons, rather than those representing the triumph over human enemies such as Maxentius at the Milvian Bridge.[29]

Modelled on an earlier discussion from the seventh book of his *Preparation*, Eusebius provided in the oration a brief narrative of daemonically driven decline in human history to provide a sort of 'archaeology' for the spiritual conflict that had taken place in his own day.[30] The deification of human passions or fears (Aphrodite and Death), or the elements of nature and procreation (Demeter, Dionysus, and so on), eventually led to the rise of even human sacrifice. Human sacrifice was then turned upon the pious devotees of the Sovereign of All in the time of persecution. The 'soldiers of God' stoutly withstood the most hideous of tortures and so fought 'with steadfast spiritual resolution the battles against the armies of polytheism'. Receiving many martyrs into their eternal abode, the divine Sovereign preserved some Christians, 'a spark, a seed of piety', to be 'interpreters of what had taken place'.[31] Constantine, a single man against many, like the one God against many daemons, appears belatedly in the narrative, receiving a victory that God had performed for him. 'For while the common Saviour of the Universe punished the invisible beings invisibly, [Constantine] as the prefect of the Supreme Sovereign proceeded against those thus vanquished, stripping their long and utterly dead corpses and distributing the spoils freely.'[32] The remaining account of Constantine's battles depict the despoliation of pagan temples by only a small number of the emperor's men, who melted down statues of precious metal for more fitting uses.[33] Only a small number was needed since God had already achieved the victory in battle.

Constantine and his men are merely the recipients of the benefits won by the true warrior and victor, God Himself. The brief and obscure mention of the Milvian Bridge is a passing gesture to what, in a typical encomium, would have taken a more central role in the speech.

While the emperor certainly shared in the glories of such spiritual warfare as a mirror of the divine ruler, the emphasis of Eusebius' speech remains on God. This, therefore, was a rather powerful shift from the traditional panegyrical mode of representing the military might and courage of the subject. The modern concern to find in Eusebius the source of Byzantine political theology and the 'father of Caesaropapism' has rightly appreciated the importance of this shift.[34] Yet while Eusebius' development of a thoroughgoing vision of the emperor as a copy of God may have sublimated the emperor through the Christian adaptation of Neopythagorean political theology, the oration's minimization of the emperor's role in the events of Eusebius' time must have been sharply felt in an Empire whose inhabitants remained awestruck at the seemingly invincible might and nearly unlimited power of emperors who had themselves received divine honours while alive or dead, and in the presence of whom even the most highly trained orators quailed with trepidation.

Eusebius' declaration that the emperor was a copy of the Logos, a sole ruler under a sole God who was the real hero of the encomium, was a striking ideological move. Insofar as the text of the oration is a faithful witness to the words delivered in the emperor's presence, other features, though slight, were similarly bold. To begin with, the oft-repeated modern assertion that Eusebius promoted a 'realized eschatology' that no longer looked to a future second coming of Christ as a result of the exhilaration at having a beneficent and godly emperor in the here and now is misleading. Instead, the bishop maintained a vision of a future eschatological establishment of Christ's kingdom throughout his corpus, even in the *Tricennial Oration*. Those who devoted their lives to the Logos 'foreknow here the promised hope of the heavenly kingdom.'[35] Even the God-loving emperor sought 'the highest kingdom':

> he is aware that the mortal and perishable state is like a river, ever-flowing
> and vanishing. And so he longs for the incorruptible and spiritual

kingdom of God, and prays to come into it [...] He cherishes in his heart
an indescribable longing for the lights there, by comparison with which
he judges the honours of his present life to be no more than darkness.
For he recognizes that rule over men is a small and fleeting authority
over a mortal and temporary life.[36]

Though the emperor looked to the archetype of the kingdom of heaven,[37]
his efforts in the kingdoms of earth remained partial.

In addition, the admiration of the martyrs, who looked 'with contempt'
at the rulers who waged war against them, and the identification of them as
God's soldiers or army,[38] exhibited a stance firmly independent of the Empire.
A good emperor who looked to God as his model would find Christians
as favourable supporters; those who failed to mirror their divine archetype
would receive the triumphant determination of martyrs who laughed at
death. Those Christians who were saved from death became 'interpreters'
of God's work – Constantine's role as 'an interpreter of the Logos' was thus
not an exclusive one.[39] One might catch the hint of a democratization in
this dispersal of interpretive work, especially since all Christians could be
claimed to be participants in the Logos, exhibiting His salutary work in their
own submission to reason (*logos*) in their individual lives.[40] The imperial
virtues of wisdom, prudence and justice could equally flourish in the life of
any individual who followed reason, for it was humanity that had received
the Logos in its rational abilities, its 'kingly' rule over all things on earth as
a 'sovereign species'.[41]

The features noted here suggest that at least some restraint should be
exercised in characterizing the relationship of Constantine and Eusebius
and any hasty assumptions about fawning flattery and uncritical acceptance
of the first Christian emperor by the bishop should be tempered. As with
any panegyric of the later Roman Empire whose very composition seems
so foreign to students in modern democratic contexts, we should proceed
cautiously in our interpretive determinations. A panegyric speech may
have sought to accomplish goals – political, ecclesiastical or theological –
other than that of the orator's ingratiation with the powers that be, and
could be more than a facile outflow of gratitude for imperial benefactions.

An oration delivered in praise of an emperor might also have had deeper purposes of swaying imperial policy or pressuring courtiers and dignitaries of the imperial administration (whether hearing it personally or reading the written version). As with many other contemporary panegyrics, we have no firm evidence to discern whether the emperor had requested the topic of an oration, or whether the orator had chosen the theme. While the emperor would have had to approve in advance any proposed oration to be delivered in his presence, the later written version could take on a life of its own with different audiences and thus different purposes from those of its oral delivery.

The *Tricennial Oration* may have been the result of an emperor's deploying a well-known Christian bishop to provide a strong theological rationale for his gradual dismantling of the Tetrarchy or his destruction of some token pagan temples. Alternatively, it may have been Eusebius' attempt to emphasize those elements of Constantine's policies that he considered to be beneficial for the Church (and its episcopal hierarchy), in order to assure the continuation of favourable policies or to pre-empt any reversals. Another possibility is that Eusebius hoped to garner favour from the emperor for his group of bishops who had left the synod at Tyre and the celebrations at Jerusalem (335) to travel to Constantinople to represent their interests. After all, a significant segment of the oration was dedicated to number symbolism (and thus reminiscent of its opening esoteric tone),[42] including the concepts of monad and triad – concepts that lay at the heart of Eusebius' controversy with Marcellus who unduly emphasized the monadic nature of God to the detriment of His triadic nature. What at first may appear as putting a Pythagorean number symbolism to the service of imperial politics, may in fact have import for theological politics within Christianity as well. The ideal listener or reader of the oration may not have been Constantine as much as his sons, in particular Constantius II, since Eusebius refers to the 'royal children' (unless this should be taken to mean any Christian in the audience) and even to Constantine's assigning 'this son here to us who inhabit the East'.[43] What precisely Eusebius' relations with Constantius II were at this or any time are difficult if not impossible to assess. We must, therefore, keep our interpretive possibilities open. But what remains clear is the firm ideological focus on God and the striking boldness of consistently putting the emperor in second place.

The second oration, often entitled in modern accounts *Oration on Christ's Sepulchre*, which seems to have had some transitional material added at its beginning to smooth over the break following the first oration (and may thereby have lost some limited material), bears unmistakable marks of having been intended for a different audience even though the emperor is several times addressed directly in the second person. A section containing indications of being its prologue occurs in Chapter 11 (if this is not still some of the intervening transitional material), in which the criticisms of Constantine's building of the Church of the Holy Sepulchre by an anonymous pagan are aired.[44] On the one hand, it was inappropriate for the emperor to concern himself with 'memorials to human corpses'; on the other hand, if Christ's tomb was worthy of honours it seemed inconsistent to reject the honours due to the ancestral heroes and gods.[45] Eusebius was a master of articulating an apologetic response to just such problems raised by an adherent of the ancestral religious traditions. Using the recent construction of the Church of the Holy Sepulchre and the responses it may have aroused as an excuse, Eusebius' oration provided a streamlined eight-chapter encapsulation of arguments previously presented in longer form in the *Preparation* and *Proof*, and their already shortened summary in the *Theophany*.

The *Oration on Christ's Sepulchre* commences with an exposition of Logos theology just as he had performed in the earlier oration – but with a noticeable difference. Even though the focal point of the *Tricennial Oration* had been God and His Logos, it continued to note the mimetic effects of the Logos upon the person of the God-loving emperor. The second oration, on the other hand, while describing, as the *Tricennial Oration* had done, the acute need for a mediator between the absolute transcendence of the Father and the lower material creation, and the ordering administration of the Logos' providential care over creation,[46] nowhere mentions the emperor as a copy of the divine model. There is a complete absence of political ideology in the latter oration's exposition of the Logos. The mimetic political theology would occur only later in a limited instance of the well-known Augustus–Christ synchronism.[47] Its ultimate purpose there, however, was to exhibit Christ's victory over daemonic polytheism not as a claim about the first Christian emperor.

Throughout the oration, Eusebius takes up elements that distinguish this speech from its sister but place it squarely within the main tendencies of his historical and theological thought. The narrative of decline provided in Chapter 13 begins with the fall into deifying astral phenomena and elements of nature, then human qualities (such as naming the mind 'Athena') and passions, and eventually individual humans, thus returning to the more robust narratives of the *Preparation* and *Theophany*, which had been largely diminished in the *Tricennial Oration*'s trimmed-down version, which omitted astral worship and euhemerism altogether.[48] Likewise, the *Oration on Christ's Sepulchre* repeats the enumeration of specific examples of human sacrifice among various nations,[49] though the *Tricennial Oration* had only appealed to the general practice of human sacrifice as a step towards the killing of Christian martyrs. Indeed, the purpose of the narrative of decline in the *Tricennial Oration* was to provide the background for God's defeat of daemons and Tetrarchic tyrants as could be seen in Constantine's despoliation of temples. The narrative of decline in the second oration, on the other hand, exhibited the need for the coming of Christ.

Discussion of the necessity of the Incarnation, with Christ's death and Resurrection,[50] became central components of this oration that, again, were largely lacking in the *Tricennial Oration*, though they had found extensive development in his earlier *Proof* and *Theophany*. In an interesting variation from what we find in the later *Life*, Eusebius declares that the 'trophy of victory' was the resurrected body itself of Christ (not the cross, as in the *Life*), which thus became a 'trophy over death' and a 'prototype of immortality' or 'the prototype of our common salvation'.[51] Constantine's recent construction of a church at the site of Christ's Resurrection was thereby a visible reminder of a cosmic event.

Together, the *Tricennial Oration* and the *Oration on Christ's Sepulchre* exhibit two contrasting ways in which Eusebius could speak to different audiences and for different purposes in the presence of the emperor. The first oration addressed an audience of the initiated (Christians) and referred to the emperor and his son as present (though in the third person). The second addressed the emperor in the second person while aiming at critics of Christianity and Constantine's Christian activity. The first oration emphasized the true reality behind Constantine's reign and, by persistently prioritizing the heavenly kingdom and its Sovereign, limited the powers and importance of the earthly sovereign. The might of the armies of Christ (the martyrs) were greater in triumph and virtue. This oration circumscribed – even as it legitimized – Constantine's sole rule. The second oration, in turn, legitimized Constantine's Christian activity while using it as an occasion to defend the faith and provide narrative significance to a particular church building. The person and activity of the first Christian emperor was thus a figure around whom rather divergent orations could be constructed. Eusebius showed himself a master of Christian control over rhetorical discourse in order to transform an emperor's 30-year anniversary and an imperial church building into signs pointing to more universal and cosmic truths.

Written Memorials of a Life

The preface of the *Life* seems at first to place it within a panegyric context. Eusebius recalls his own delivery of the recent oration at the celebration of the 30-year anniversary of Constantine's reign and heralds the elevation of the three sons of Constantine to the rank of Augustus.[52] Presenting a Christian twist to the usual *captatio benevolentiae*, he expresses his inability to memorialize one who not only received such wealth, property, praise and honours among mortal humans but had now ascended in soul to the very presence of God and was receiving the honour of everlasting life. 'Thought in its mortality stands agape, uttering not a word, but convicted by itself of its impotence; it condemns itself to silence, and concedes to the superior and universal Thought the right to utter worthy praises.'[53] Whereas humans frequently sought to memorialize great individuals through the visual arts, in portraits, statues and inscriptions, God Himself had turned such memorialization on its head by furnishing a mortal monument of a future immortal state that surpassed the imagination. That mortal monument was Constantine himself – or rather, the blessings bestowed upon

Constantine by God at the end of his earthly life.[54] Because of the emperor's piety and devotion, God

> crowned him with the prizes of immortality [...] So may God Himself, since He both exalted the blessed one when he was still among us with divine honours, and dying adorned him with exquisite perfection from Himself, become also his recorder, inscribing his successful conflicts on tables of heavenly monuments for long eternities.[55]

The rhetorically convoluted prose of the preface thus claimed that human attempts at giving proper honour to an emperor who honoured God were inadequate for the task. Such an emperor had been honoured by God and hence human representations paled in comparison to the 'heavenly monuments' erected for eternity by God, who was the ultimate author of the events of Constantine's reign. Implicit within such declarations was the assumption that the work to follow would, indeed, be a record of what the divine recorder had inscribed on eternal memorials. In spite of Eusebius' repeated claim that he was inadequate to the task, the *Life* had to speak the truth it recognized. His account, 'feeble though it is', would furnish much benefit to the reader: 'the recording of actions dear to God shall provide reading not unprofitable, but of practical benefit to well-disposed minds.'[56]

Struck though many modern readers are by the overwrought hyperbole and what seems a stifling onslaught of laudatory rhetoric, we see in the preface the clear hallmarks of the ancient biographical genre as well as strong indications of unique features that will arise throughout the *Life*'s four books.[57] In fact, though imperial-era biographies might convey a less than flattering tone towards their subjects (as we find, for instance, in Suetonius' *Lives of the Caesars*), the earliest phase of the genre seems to lie within the context of the funeral eulogy.[58] In the fourth century BCE, both Xenophon and Isocrates had crafted eulogizing 'lives' (*bioi*) of kings whom these authors admired. To honour the dead, they composed written accounts that recorded the basic features of the lives of these illustrious men before recounting their great traits of character. Significantly, each biographer made explicit contrasts between the sort of memorials they were constructing and those

manufactured by artists. Sculptors and painters could only portray the outward appearance of a body, while the written word could pursue more lofty
aims of exhibiting a person's character. The rhetorician Isocrates could thus
conclude that 'well-crafted words were much more worthy' as a memorial
befitting the greatness of soul of his subject.[59]

Plutarch, two centuries before Eusebius penned the *Life*, took up the task
of composing written *bioi* so as to provide the philosopher with concrete
details of a human life upon which moral evaluations might be made and from
which lessons might be learned. The preface to his biography of Alexander
the Great is well known. Avoiding the battle narratives of the history genre,
his writing of lives would focus on the delineation of character.

> Therefore, just as painters derive likenesses from the face and the forms
> of his appearance in which character is manifest, caring least for the
> other parts of the body, so we must be granted to undertake rather the
> signs of the soul and to portray each one's life through these, leaving to
> others the great deeds and struggles.[60]

The composition of a biography was, therefore, explicitly like 'painting a life'
(*bios* + *graphia*). Such literary portraiture aimed at providing moral character
sketches for the ethical instruction of readers. Like a distinctive wrinkle or
wart in a person's physical image, for the biographical portraitist the unique
anecdote, the passing quip or the more mundane rhythms of everyday life
became the object of the written life. Not in the military struggles but in the
behaviour or words restricted to friends lay the details to be memorialized
and judged by the philosophical biographer.

Eusebius' *Life* continued the eulogistic strains of the early proto-biographies
of Isocrates and Xenophon while extending the moral programme of Plutarch.
Like these earlier lives, the *Life* imitated and supplanted the human painting
by composing a 'verbal portrait in memory of the God-beloved' emperor.[61]
A striking feature of the *Life* is, in fact, its concern with producing a beneficial image of its subject while at the same time incorporating physical
descriptions of Constantine within its narrative. Following a staple feature
of both panegyric and biography, the emperor's comportment and visual

presence are descriptively conveyed (especially in Eusebius' account of Constantine's entry at the Council of Nicaea).[62] But the *Life* goes further, describing those visual products of imperial propaganda such as paintings, statues and coins. While artistic representations of the subject had not been excluded from earlier lives (such as, particularly, those of Plutarch) and while literary descriptions of visual art marked an important subset of epideictic rhetoric (the *ekphrasis*), Eusebius seems to heighten the importance of these imperial images.[63]

Each description of visual art seems to have been included for the single purpose of exemplifying the emperor's piety. Eusebius emphasizes the power of the sign of the cross, for instance, by describing a painting of Constantine's defeat of a dragon with the cross lifted high above his own head. The painting was an allegory, for Eusebius, of Christ's defeat of 'the invisible enemy of the human race [...] by the power of the Saviour's trophy which was set up over [Constantine's] head'.[64] Similarly, the portraits of Constantine on coins signified visually a deeper spiritual engagement of the emperor with the divine. 'The great strength of the divinely inspired faith fixed in his soul' was represented on gold coinage depicting the emperor gazing upwards, 'in the manner of one reaching out to God in prayer'.[65] Eusebius thus perpetuated and even legitimized the frequently remarked visual agenda of Constantine's representational propaganda.[66]

Eusebius claimed to set to the side Constantine's battles and triumphs, decrees and laws, in order to explore only those elements that 'relate to the life which is dear to God'. As in the case of Plutarch's biographies, such a claim did not entail the complete eradication of battle narrative from the work; instead, it marked the purpose for which a military exploit might be narrated and the benefit the reader might gain from considering a particular angle or context of such a narrative. Indeed, all of Eusebius' descriptions of battle have a single aim: to exhibit the divine involvement on the battlefield and thereby indicate the true nature of such conflicts as spiritual, not merely physical, engagements. For instance, before the Battle of the Milvian Bridge, in which Constantine took on the first of his imperial opponents, Eusebius describes an emperor circumspectly looking for the right divine patron. He recognized the folly of the ancestral deities, sought counsel from God-fearing advisors regarding a divine revelation and received divine benefits on the battlefield for such diligence in religious affairs. Or, when facing Licinius, Constantine is described as placing his trust in the 'saving trophy' of the cross. An anecdote about the protective effects of carrying the cross into battle, related by the emperor himself, became enshrined within the *Life*'s literary portrait of the emperor.[67]

Both instances of battle narrative convey the same aim of exhibiting the emperor's godliness and pure faith in the divine, while establishing proof of Eusebius' initial claim in the preface that God was the author of such victories, furnishing gracious honours on those who had honoured Him first. Directly connected to this claim was the narrative proof that the pagan gods and their human followers were weak and pathetic opponents when faced with the power of the cross and those who carried it into battle. In this way, the accounts of military conflict are part of the same project as the descriptions of visual art. Both sets of literary descriptions aim at solidifying the representation of Constantine's character as a 'friend of God' and demonstrating the blessings abundantly poured out on those who develop such a character. There is thus a deep moral lesson to the *Life*, to which we shall return below. The reader did not here learn a new way of conceiving of an imperial religious ideology. An emperor continued to be seen as achieving victory through propitiating the proper deities and obtaining a divine companion. What had changed in this Christian biography of an emperor was the identity of that divine companion and the interpretation of the already cross-shaped military standard as bearing a new signification (a 'saving sign') of the new deity.[68]

There remained an additional, very powerful, fund of significations that did provide new ways of representing the emperor's literary portrait. Both the visual depictions and the battle narratives had become deeply formed by the alternative literary heritage of the Hebrew Scriptures. Though the *Life*'s theology of victory and its explicit claim that it was painting a picture were continuations of Roman imperial and Greek biographical discourses, the stories, oracles and universal vision of the Scriptures infused the *Life* with a powerful, ancient narrative framework that provided the biography with a world-historical import and scope.[69] Constantine's conversion to

Christianity had marked his incorporation into the people of God, whose roots lay in the distant past and whose spread after the Resurrection and Ascension of Christ had filled all the nations of the earth. The types of holy leaders portrayed in the Scriptures were models providing explanatory frames of reference for Constantine's own behaviour and motives. The battles of the Bible had begun to be waged again with results that could only be predicted from an awareness of ancient patterns, in which saving signs provided protection, enemies were drowned in the sea, revelations were shown from heaven, synods were gathered from all nations, and demonic adversaries were defeated by the aid of God.

While Eusebius drew on a broad range of biblical texts (for instance, bishops from all nations gathered at Nicaea just as those from all nations had gathered at Pentecost in Acts of the Apostles; the painting of Constantine defeating a serpent represented visually the defeat of Satan spoken of in Isaiah[70]), the most sustained series of biblical allusions were centred on the person of Moses as a model for the Christian emperor. Though at least partly influenced by Philo of Alexandria's earlier philosophical biography of Moses (especially since this earlier work sought to depict the life of 'the friend of God'[71]), Eusebius' *Life* performed a freer range of associations and bore the twin tasks of crafting a Christian (and imperial) vision of Moses and a biblical vision of Constantine. Eusebius explicitly draws several parallels between the two holy leaders.

First, Moses grew up in the court of a tyrant (Pharaoh), as did Constantine (in the court of Diocletian and Galerius); both escaped the tyrants through flight. Second, the opponents of each were drowned: Pharaoh in the Red Sea, Maxentius in the Tiber. Third, the heart of Moses' opponent, Pharaoh, became hardened, as did that of Constantine's opponent, Licinius. Lastly, both Constantine and Moses pitched a tent outside the encampment as they travelled, in which prayers could be offered to God and divine revelations could be received.[72]

Eusebius' persistent recollection of biblical episodes was instrumental in crafting a vision of Constantine who 'preserved his likeness to the great prophet Moses'.[73] Beyond these explicit parallels between the imperial and biblical figures, however, are other associations that are only hinted at (or at least open to the reader's imagination). These include the fact that Moses and Constantine both received visions from God in response to which they enquired into the identity of that God, both led their people out of slavery into a state of freedom, and both crafted a saving sign by which their people could find protection: Moses made a bronze serpent (which Christ Himself had already likened to His cross) and Constantine had the trophy of the cross carried into battle for the protection of his troops.[74] Alternatively, the holding up of Constantine's trophy parallels Moses' holding up of his staff during war. The description of the trophy could signal the biblical description of the Ark of the Covenant.[75]

Furthermore, both served as arbiters between disputing parties among the people of God, or set up judges for deciding such disputes, and both were at the same time lawgivers. Both had a close association with the Scriptures: Moses was considered to be the author of the first five biblical books and Constantine ordered copies of the Scriptures for use in Constantinople. Both could be depicted as angels, and both opposed idolatry, even the distinctively Egyptian form of idolatry, and promoted worship of one God. Both were responsible for establishing important festivals: Moses established the Passover for the Jews; Constantine established the date of Easter (which continues to be called 'the Pasch', that is, Passover) so as not to follow the calendar of the Jews.[76] Likewise, it was at the time of the Easter celebrations that Constantine dedicated a shrine to the 12 Apostles, whose description might briefly recall that of the tabernacle.[77] And just as Moses instituted the consecration of the Sabbath day, so Constantine consecrated Sunday as the Lord's Day.[78] Finally, both died before being able to make a definitive military invasion, which would have involved crossing (or being baptized in) the Jordan River.[79]

Such allusions are not clearly marked. The few explicit parallels, however, prompt such intertextual possibilities. Once the precedent has been set for discovering biblical exemplars for the emperor's acts, the practice of looking for more can become almost endless. The guiding principle in such a procedure is that the Scriptures are an authoritative and profound source informing the narrative vision of all later events and figures. Such wholesale rethinking and renarrating of history in terms of biblical stories, oracles, teachings and words marks one of the greatest contributions of Eusebius to a Late Antique literary culture and imagination.

Indeed, Eusebius incorporates himself into the narrative of Constantine's activity as a God-beloved emperor and the proliferation of the Scriptures and biblical stories into the Empire. As proof of Constantine's attention to theological matters Eusebius quotes a letter to himself from the emperor requesting copies of the Scriptures for the Church in Constantinople. The letter entrusts to Eusebius the making of 50 copies of the Scriptures, 'the provision and use of which you well know to be necessary for reading in church'. Eusebius' response was swift: 'we sent him threes and fours in richly wrought bindings.'[80] Whatever the meaning of this obscure phrase, which has caused a good deal of scholarly disagreement, the biographer has clearly insinuated himself into the portrait of his biography. Furthermore, the context of his quotation of the letter is rich in self-authorization. It is preceded by an account of an episode in which Eusebius delivered an oration at the court. Constantine, he declares, resolutely honoured the speaker and his topic by standing throughout its entire delivery.[81] The reason alleged for describing the scene is to show the emperor's manifest reverence for divine matters; more pointed, however, is the fact that the emperor had paid the highest respect to a bishop – and this was none other than Eusebius himself. This episode is quickly followed by a letter addressed to Eusebius from Constantine, which is followed in turn by the emperor's other letter requesting copies of the Scriptures. This first letter confirms the receipt of a treatise composed by Eusebius on the proper date of Easter. The emperor had read the treatise and approved of it. Interestingly, a hint of Eusebius' own self-promotion may lie behind it, for Constantine adds, 'as you desired, I have ordered it to be published for the large number who are sincerely attached to the worship of God.' An additional piece of self-promotion comes in the very quotation of this letter, which utters flattering words about how greatly the emperor enjoys works from Eusebius' pen and hopes to receive further pieces in the future from one 'so well trained'.[82]

The entire segment containing the description of Constantine's attitude to divine matters and the Scriptures themselves makes a powerful self-representation of the author by means of the personal responses he received from the emperor. Like a painter who slips an image of himself into the portrait of another, so the literary portrait of Constantine became a space for Eusebius' own self-display. Some of the stimulus behind the modern proclivity for viewing Eusebius as a court theologian is thus his own doing. The several instances in which Eusebius claims to have obtained his information from eyewitnesses are as old as the genre of contemporary history (beginning, at least, with Thucydides, who frequently appealed to oral reports of witnesses). Their purpose is to confirm the veracity of the biographer's account. Eusebius goes further, however, in his repeated claims that he himself has heard a story from the emperor's own mouth or seen with his own eyes a painting in the emperor's palace. Such declarations at once confirm the reliability of his narrative and buttress his own authorial status. Eusebius saw the emperor when he was still a youth. He heard the account of Constantine's vision before the Battle of the Milvian Bridge from the emperor himself, as well as the narrative of the protective effects of the cross on the field of battle. He saw with his own eyes the saving trophy.[83]

The quotation of Constantine's letters allows the reader to share in the purportedly close relationship Eusebius had with the emperor. Eusebius quotes from a letter that bears Constantine's own autograph. In spite of the fact that his autograph by definition could not be reproduced in Eusebius' composition of the *Life*, his declaration of its presence before Eusebius' eyes as he wrote was like hearing the emperor himself. 'We may feel that we are listening to the voice of the emperor himself as he makes this proclamation for all mankind to hear.'[84] Though the four letters addressed to Eusebius in the *Life* may be the only letters he received from Constantine, we are made to sense an intimacy between the author and his subject when these are read within a narrative dotted with reports of other personal conversations between the two – and, of course, we are not given details as to the contexts of these conversations, which may not have been as personal as Eusebius seems to indicate (was he alone with the emperor when Constantine swore oaths as to the truth of his tale of the vision of the cross? Or was he in a room crowded by dozens of auditors?).[85]

The use of conversations and letters contributed to a project of self-authorization. The *Life* both commemorated the recently deceased emperor and monumentalized Eusebius' authoritative role as an interpreter of his reign. It also confirmed the bishop's status in the Empire-wide affairs of the Church. In the first letter, Constantine entrusted the oversight of church-building in Palestine to Eusebius. The second letter commended Eusebius' rejection of the offer of the bishopric of Antioch by the Church there. The biographer no doubt relished the letter's open declaration that 'by the testimony of practically the whole world you have been judged worthy to be bishop of any and every Church'. The third and fourth letters, mentioned above, praised Eusebius for his industry and wisdom in arriving at the correct interpretation regarding the date of Easter and requested him to supervise the production of 50 copies of the Scriptures.[86] Together these four letters provided a potent affirmation of Eusebius' importance in ecclesiastical affairs and theological matters, as well as sealing his legitimacy as the privileged biographer of Constantine.

By brief comparison with a nearly contemporary biography of a holy man we may also appreciate another significant effect of Eusebius' self-authorizing programme in the *Life*. In the first years of the fourth century, the Platonic philosopher and critic of Christianity, Porphyry of Tyre, composed a biography of his teacher Plotinus to serve as a sort of preface to his edition of the latter's essays (the *Enneads*). Like Eusebius, though to a lesser degree, Porphyry quoted from letters in order to affirm his own authoritative status as an interpreter and editor of his master's writings. There were, however, rival claimants to the position of favoured student. Amelius had been a pupil of Plotinus before Porphyry's arrival in the 260s and had copied and distributed some of the master's lectures. A letter from one of the top literary critics of the day, Longinus, confirmed that Amelius' versions of Plotinus' writings only led to misunderstandings. Of equal importance to the affirmation of Porphyry's editorial work was an anecdote revealing Amelius' misunderstanding of the proper relationship between religion and philosophy. Amelius represented a distinctive position that, for Porphyry, marked him as a 'lover of sacrifices'.[87] Plotinus' rejection of an invitation by Amelius to attend a religious ritual provided affirmation of Porphyry's own more guarded position towards traditional religion.

The biography of a recently deceased holy man thus allowed for more dynamic ways to develop the biographer's own authorial identity than would the biography of one long dead (as in the case of Plutarch). Furthermore, it could be used not only for garnering privilege and authority for the biographer as author, but also for the establishment of proper philosophical or theological positions. Along with self-promotion in the *Life* was Eusebius' careful control of the narrative of theological disputes during Constantine's reign: the disagreement of Alexander and Arius was about inconsequential theological matters; Nicaea was mostly about Easter; and the synod of Tyre was to regain peace from the wayward controversies of a small minority. The *Life* is silent on the synod of Antioch that convened just before the Council of Nicaea and, in effect, put Eusebius and two others on a sort of theological probation. His contacts with Arius are likewise absent, as is his somewhat uncomfortable explanation of the credal formulation accepted instead of his own at Nicaea as preserved in a letter he addressed to his parishioners at Caesarea.[88] The Donatist and Melitian schisms receive only the slightest glosses. His deep involvement in the ecclesiastical politics before and after the synod at Tyre is entirely omitted from the *Life*, though the letter of Constantine to the bishops gathered there implicitly affirmed his role.

A different biography might have depicted the emperor as the defender of Alexander and Nicaea or, alternatively, the guardian against Donatist or Melitian extremism. Instead, a theology of consensus pervades the entirety of the *Life*.[89] Eusebius allowed for hostilities and criticisms of the emperor by bishops at synods or councils; yet their angry voices become largely muffled under the representation of a firm and placid imperial disposition. In the *Life* the declaration is reiterated that it was episcopal discord that most grieved the emperor.[90] In response to the claims disputed at Nicaea, Constantine 'received the proposals with patient flexibility; he took up what was said by each side in turn, and gently brought together those whose attitudes conflicted.'[91] We learn nothing of what those actual issues were or what sorts of proposals the emperor heard. Within the frame of the *Life*, harmony is the chief aim and highest goal of both emperor and biographer. A rhetoric of the harmony of orthodoxy persists in many of Eusebius' works though he himself was not averse to conflict if the cause was right. He could be a harsh disputant against the Greeks, a stern critic of the Jews and their methods of interpretation, and a vociferous opponent of those he deemed to be heretics, like Marcellus. The particular emphasis on consensus and concord in the *Life* is not simply an inconsistency in Eusebius' outlook or an attempt at concealing his own questionable engagement in theological controversies. We must look to the broader aims of the work as a whole and its possible audience.

The Ideal Emperor: The Life *as* Speculum Principis

A popular and plausible understanding of the *Life* considers it an early example of a 'prince's mirror' or *speculum principis* (or *Fürstenspiegel*). Such an interpretive approach to Eusebius' biography is impossible to prove without any explicit indication of its intended recipient. But it does provide a fruitful angle through which we may discern a clearly identifiable moral programme that sought to crystallize an image of the ideal emperor. Such a moral programme is, at least, openly expressed near the end of the biography. After noting the various forms of education his sons received while young, Eusebius goes on:

> But when they reached manhood their father by himself was the instruction they needed. Sometimes he encouraged them while they were with him with personal admonitions to copy him and taught them to make themselves imitators of his godly piety. Sometimes when communicating with them in their absence about imperial matters he would express his exhortations in writing, the greatest and most important of these being that they should prize the knowledge of God the King of all and devotion to Him above all wealth and even above Empire.[92]

When they were given more control over public affairs, Constantine 'urged them that one of their prime concerns should be the Church of God, instructing them to be frankly Christian'.[93] Eusebius informs us that the sons duly responded and freely sought to live Christian lives. Whether Constantius II, who presided in the East after his father's death, was the intended reader of the *Life* and hence was here being reminded to maintain a youthful enthusiasm for the pursuit of piety, may be immaterial to the impact such a narrative could have upon the imagination of any reader. The Constantine depicted in the *Life* became an exemplar of piety and the pursuit of imperial and ecclesiastical harmony that his sons would do well to follow. To do otherwise would be to adopt the stance of his opponents and receive the just punishment for such 'tyranny'.

Indeed, an integral part of a persuasive *speculum principis* would be a portrait not only of the good emperor but of his opposites, bad emperors, who were given the appellation of tyrants to mark their illegitimacy. In contrast to the earlier *History*, which offered a literary pattern of two good emperors (Constantine and Licinius) countering two wicked tyrants (Maxentius and Maximinus Daia), the *Life*, with many years separating its composition from the reign of Licinius, portrays a single good emperor (Constantine, who had already been morally foreshadowed in the person of his father) against two bad emperors (Maxentius and Licinius).[94] None of the other emperors, we are told, was capable of defeating Maxentius under whose cruel bondage the city of Rome suffered.[95] Maxentius, the son of an earlier emperor (and hence, in the eyes of the established Tetrarchy, a usurper like Constantine), was represented as an advocate of sorcery, sacrifices and divination, whereas Constantine sought out the one true God who had been the source of his special revelation.[96] The tyrant's religious proclivities were exhibited in tandem with his equally unsavoury behaviour. The *Life* narrated his conquests of well-born Roman matrons, massacre of the urban populace and murder of senators.[97] Constantine, on the other hand, came as the triumphant liberator freeing Rome from such oppression.

Licinius, in addition to turning to pagan deities for support like Maxentius had done, renewed persecution against Christians and explicitly conceived of his conflict with Constantine as a test of the power of his gods over the one adopted by his opponent. His depravity of character was displayed in his infidelity towards his imperial colleague and abuse of his subjects. In spite of the examples of divine punishment against the earlier persecuting emperors Galerius and Maximinus Daia, Licinius persisted in hostility towards God, attacking the Church and its newest imperial convert.[98] Although shown repeated kindness with an aim towards concord by the triumphant

Constantine, Licinius finally received the fitting penalty of death following a conspiratorial attempt to overthrow the emperor. Licinius was a 'God-hater' in contrast to Constantine, the 'friend of God'. Adopting classical metaphors, the *Life* described the tyrants as 'God-battling giants' with Tantalus-like appetites.[99] In stark opposition to the belligerent and greedy behaviour of tyrants, and also consonant with the theology of harmony that Eusebius was intent on depicting in his portrait of Constantine, the emperor is shown as slow to anger and merciful towards the conquered.

With vigorous rhetoric, the *Life* highlights the contrast between Constantine and the tyrants in a lengthy series of antitheses that open the third book.[100] While they forced the worship of non-existent deities, Constantine used persuasion to turn his subjects towards worship of the true God. Whereas the tyrants blasphemously slandered Christ and the cross through which He had brought salvation, the emperor adopted it as his own saving sign. They attacked the Christians, he restored them. They sought to humiliate the Christians, Constantine sought to honour them. And so on. Eusebius' *speculum principis* exhibited a portrait of the good emperor as a distinctively Christian emperor.

Nonetheless, the theology of victory undergirding the assertions of legitimacy for Constantine's reign, that is, the conception that whoever obtained the victory on the battlefield must be under the patronage of the right deity, was a staple of Roman imperial ideology. Furthermore, as remarked earlier in this chapter, Eusebius' well-known 'political theology', which claimed that one emperor on earth was merely a tangible likeness of one God in heaven,[101] was itself not a distinctively Christian feature, but had already been expressed by Hellenistic philosophers. Many of the virtues that Eusebius laboured to depict in his emperor were likewise standard features of Roman imperial ideology. Constantine came to the help of the oppressed. His clemency was heralded and his refusal to give in to anger was praised. Even his ascetic regime and discipline in spiritual exercises had been evinced by non-Christian emperors such as the philosopher-king Marcus Aurelius.[102] What differentiates Eusebius' *Life* from the ongoing imperial discourses in which it participated is largely the massive inscripturation process by which the contemporary world was made sense of through the narratives and vocabulary of Scripture. It was a biography rooted in the biblical vision(s) of God, daemons, nations, kings and adversaries.

Following the 'summer of blood' – which has been characterized as the bloodiest transition of power in the Roman Empire – three of Constantine's sons had cleared the Empire of any potential rivals to Constantine's throne.[103] Constantine, after a reign marked by a clearly Christian series of actions combined with a more open stance in the interests of a broad consensus, had only belatedly received baptism and made the unambiguous claim on his deathbed that he would 'from now on' be numbered with the people of God.[104] The situation was precarious and the future uncertain. Eusebius, as a veteran crafter of a Christian historical vision, made a bold move to narrate the reign of Constantine from a distinctively Christian perspective so as to delineate relations between emperors and bishops in a way he deemed appropriate and beneficial.

> Alone therefore among emperors and unlike any other, [Constantine] had honoured by acts of every kind the all-sovereign God and His Christ, and it is right that he alone enjoyed [post-mortem honours among mortals], as the God over all allowed his mortal part to reign among mankind, thus demonstrating the ageless and deathless reign of his soul to those with minds not stony-hard.[105]

This powerful image of an emperor as a friend and beneficiary of the Christian God had a long-lasting effect upon later articulations and attitudes to imperial–ecclesiastical relations. It is only with the hindsight of centuries that we forget the potential dangers and anxieties of the time of its composition.

As in so many of his works, Eusebius was both bold and careful; his vision of the world and its historical figures and peoples, both in the distant past and the uncertain present, performed a creative and thoroughgoing transformation of traditional genres and forms of literary, rhetorical, historiographical or philosophical expression. The *Life of Constantine* with his other literary experiments resolutely mark out Eusebius' centrality to late antique thought and letters.

GLOSSARY

anarthrous   Relating to a noun that is 'without an article'. Especially important in the case of the noun 'God' or 'a god', its occurrence in Eusebius with respect to the Son has sometimes been thought to contribute to a concept of the Son as a separate god, existing below the Father. See 'articular'.

Arianism   A label for the theologies of the supporters of Arius, or of non-Nicene thinkers generally. It usually refers to Arius' rejection of the belief that the Father and Son were of the 'same substance' (*homoousios*). It is now recognized as a polemical term (as well as the more hostile 'Ariomaniacs'), one that was not, in fact, adopted by non-Nicene thinkers to describe themselves and instead obscures the diversity of their thought.

articular   Relating to a noun that is joined with an article; especially important in the case of the noun 'God' and often understood in Christian texts as designating 'the [one] God'. See 'anarthrous'.

catenae   Literally 'chains', the term (also in the singular form, 'catena') is used to refer to medieval works that strung together quotations from patristic authors on biblical passages in sequential order.

christos	Literally 'anointed one', which became a common title for Jesus (equivalent to Messiah) in the New Testament but had occurred many times in singular or plural form (*christoi*) in the Old Testament.
chronography	A genre directly addressing events, personages or reigns in chronological order, which was expressed in narrative or list form, or a combination.
damnatio memoriae	Literally, a 'condemnation of one's memory', the term refers to the practice of defacing inscriptions and images of a particularly disliked emperor, though it has been extended to designate the removal of particular emperors' names from some manuscripts of Eusebius' *Ecclesiastical History*.
Demiurge, the	The 'craftsman' or creator whose act of creating the cosmos was described paradigmatically in Plato's *Timaeus* and became highly influential in Late Antiquity among both Platonist and Christian philosophers.
Donatism	A schism in North Africa originally involving Donatus and his supporters who upheld a rigorist notion of episcopal legitimacy and opposed those ecclesiastical leaders who had turned traitor and handed over the Scriptures or church plate during the Great Persecution. Not only their official positions but their sacramental work were deemed invalid by the Donatists.
Edict of Milan, the	A modern shorthand label for a document issued by Licinius and Constantine following their meeting in Milan in 313. It granted toleration to Christians who had suffered under the Great Persecution and called for restoration of confiscated Church property; more generally, it granted toleration to adherents of any religion.
eisagōgē	Literally 'introduction', this was a loose genre of works dedicated to introducing a student to a particular subject of study; *eisagōgai* in the areas of mathematics, medicine, philosophy and the Christian Scriptures survive from antiquity.
ekphrasis	Literally a 'description' or 'exposition', but referring in particular to a literary description and interpretation of a work of art or visual image.

ethnos	Literally 'nation', or ethnic group. When the term designated a historical 'people', it often carried connotations of shared language, territory, religious rituals and customs, and so on. The term could also be used to designate any biologically related group (such as an animal species).
euhemerism	Named after Euhemerus of Messana (fourth century BCE), the term refers to the notion that the gods of ancient religion were originally humans who were deified after their deaths for their contributions to human culture or general greatness.
eusebeia	Usually translated as 'piety', the term often combined notions of filial devotion, allegiance to one's fatherland and commitment to ancestral religious beliefs, rituals and sacred sites.
Galerius' palinode	A document issued by the emperor Galerius that reversed his original policy of persecuting Christians. It was thus a 'palinode' or 'recantation' of his earlier forceful approach to Christianity.
Great Persecution, the	The general label given to the period of persecution under the Tetrarchs beginning in 303 (following initial purges of Christians from the army and imperial administration) and usually considered to end with the death of Maximinus Daia in 313, though Licinius seems later to have adopted some policy of hostility toward Christians after his peace with Constantine had begun to deteriorate.
Hexapla, the	The 'six-fold' work of Origen, which placed in parallel columns the Hebrew text of the Old Testament, followed by a transliteration into Greek, and then various Greek translations (the Septuagint, and those of Aquila, Symmachus and Theodotion, as well as any others that Origen may have had at his disposal).
homoousios	Literally, of the 'same substance', this phrase was adopted at the Council of Nicaea to describe the relationship of the Father and the Son in the Trinity. It was considered inappropriate by Arius and his supporters. Eusebius explained his reasons for agreeing to the term's inclusion in the Nicene Creed in his *Epistle to the Caesareans*.

hypostasis   Literally, 'subsistence', this term was applied by Eusebius to the individual identity and existence of each member of the Trinity (in particular that of the Son) in opposition to Marcellus' denial of such a notion as applicable to the Son. Earlier the term had been applied by Porphyry to Plotinus' three levels of Being (the One, Intellect and the World Soul).

inscripturation   A term used to designate the process by which early Christians began to describe contemporary events, people, nations or their world generally through the language, concepts or stories of their Scriptures (for instance, identifying Constantine as a new Moses).

Intellect, the   The name for the second ontological level in Plotinus' tripartite model of reality. The Intellect arose by 'procession' from the One and was considered to possess the Forms (as elicited by Plato) used for the creation of the cosmos. See 'the One' and 'the World Soul'.

logos   Literally a 'word', whether vocalized, written or internal, and hence also 'reason'; among Stoics and Platonists the term could also be applied to rational principles by which the physical world was ordered.

Logos, the   Literally, the 'Word' (that is, of God) spoken at the creation of the world. The term is applied to the Son in the Trinity following its application to the one who 'became flesh and dwelt among us' (according to the prologue of the Gospel of John).

Middle Platonism   A broad and sometimes ambiguous label for the scattered Platonist authors who followed temporally the so-called New Academy in the first century BCE; they are often identified as emphasizing theological concerns, prizing the *Timaeus* and positing a First and Second God at the highest levels of an ontological hierarchy. The 'school' is represented by Philo of Alexandria, Plutarch, Celsus, Albinus, Numenius and others. See 'Neoplatonism'.

monad   The first principle in a Neopythagorean or Platonic ontological framework.

Neoplatonism   A modern label for the Platonism following Plotinus, which emphasized a tripartite model of reality (the One, Intellect and the World Soul) and aimed for the philosopher's union with the One. See 'Middle Platonism'.

Nicaea, Council of

An ecumenical gathering hosted by Constantine in May of 325 to deal with the debate between Alexander of Alexandria and Arius, who had already been declared a heretic by a synod in Alexandria. The council of roughly 300 bishops opted for the inclusion in its declaration (the Nicene Creed) of a clause that the Father and Son were of the 'same substance' (*homoousios*), thereby denying the position of Arius, who rejected the idea of consubstantiality. At the council Arius and a small number of supporters were exiled. The council also rejected the Jewish computation in favour of a Roman one for setting the date of Easter in order to follow the spring equinox. The council's canons also cover other areas of ecclesiastical procedure and discipline.

Nicene Creed, the

The declaration of Christian beliefs established by the Council of Nicaea in 325, which stated the Father and Son of the Trinity to be of the 'same substance' (*homoousios*). Eusebius assented to the Creed, though with his own particular understanding of its key elements.

One, the

An appellation for the highest level of reality in Plotinus' system, drawing on Plato's *Parmenides*. The One was thought to be beyond verbal description or even discursive thought, and ultimately to be 'beyond being' (a phrase from Plato's *Republic*). See 'Intellect' and 'the World Soul'.

Origenism

A label used (often by opponents in a polemic manner) to refer to the beliefs of various authors or groups at different points in Late Antiquity who were deemed to propagate alleged or actual features distinctive of Origen's thought, such as a commitment to a final restoration of all creation, even the Devil, an undue denial of bodily goodness, a belief in the pre-existence of souls, the privileging of an allegorical approach to biblical interpretation, and so on. Eusebius is often seen as a proponent of an early phase of 'Origenism'.

paideia

The common term for 'education', which was used frequently to denote the high 'culture' attained through rigorous education in the Greek language, as well as Greek literature and thought.

pneumatology   Any account of the identity, nature and role of the Holy Spirit (*pneuma*), the third person of the Trinity.

pros lexin   Literally 'to the letter', often used to designate the 'literal', rather than 'allegorical', figural or symbolic, exegesis of a biblical passage.

second God   A term for the divine creator (or 'Demiurge') of the cosmos, existing below the highest First God, whose absolute transcendence precluded any involvement in the lower work of creation. The concept has been seen as typical of Middle Platonic thinking.

Septuagint, the   Literally, the 'Seventy' (*Septuaginta* in Latin), hence abbreviated 'LXX', this term refers to the most common Greek translation of the Hebrew Bible (the Old Testament) used in early Christianity, which, according to tradition, was made by 70 (or 72) Jews in Alexandria in the third century BCE.

Tetrarchy, the   The 'rule of four' emperors, established by Diocletian in 293 as a means of stabilizing the disorder of the 'Third Century Crisis'. It lasted in various forms until Licinius and Constantine defeated their rivals (*c.*313).

Third Century Crisis   A label applied to the period 235–84, in which the Roman Empire experienced instability in the economy, foreign relations and the regime. It was ended by Diocletian and his establishment of the Tetrarchy.

World Soul, the   The third level in Plotinus' tripartite ontological system. The World Soul was considered to contain the demiurgic agent, creating and ordering the cosmos, as well as to possess the hypostatic location of the individuation of particular souls who would descend into matter. See 'the One' and 'Intellect'.

Abbreviations

IN THE MAIN TEXT I have used English translations of the titles of Eusebius' works, while in the notes I have opted for the common abbreviations based on the Latinized forms of the titles. Note that quotations from texts for which no English version is listed below are my own translations.

ad Marin.   *Epistula ad Marinum (or Quaestiones evangelicae ad Marinum)*
[Letter to Marinus or Gospel Questions to Marinus]

Greek text: Claudio Zamagni, *Les Questions et réponses sur les évangiles d'Eusèbe de Césarée*, Ph.D. dissertation (University of Lausanne, 2003), pp. 56–63.

English translation: Roger Pearse, ed., *Eusebius of Caesarea: Gospel Problems and Solutions* (Ipswich: Chieftain Publishing, 2010), pp. 181–253.

ad Steph.   *Epistula ad Stephanum (or Quaestiones evangelicae ad Stephanum)*
[Letter to Stephanus or Gospel Questions to Stephanus]

Greek text: Claudio Zamagni, *Les Questions et réponses sur les évangiles d'Eusèbe de Césarée*, Ph.D. dissertation (University of Lausanne, 2003), pp. 32–55.

English translation: Roger Pearse, ed., *Eusebius of Caesarea: Gospel Problems and Solutions* (Ipswich: Chieftain Publishing, 2010), pp. 7–175.

c.Marc.	*contra Marcellum [Against Marcellus]*
	Greek text: Erich Klostermann, ed., *Eusebius Werke*, vol. 4, *Gegen Marcell, Über die kirchliche Theologie*, Die griechischen christlichen Schriftsteller 14 (Leipzig: J.C. Hinrichs'sche Buchhandlung, 1906), pp. 1–58.
Comm.Isa.	*Commentaria in Isaiam [Commentary on Isaiah]*
	Greek text: Joseph Ziegler, ed., *Eusebius Werke*, vol. 9, *Der Jesajakommentar*, Die griechischen christlichen Schriftsteller 56 (Berlin: Akademie-Verlag, 1975) [page references in the notes are to this edition].
Comm.Psalm.	*Commentaria in Psalmos [Commentary on the Psalms]*
	Greek text: Jean-Paul Migne, ed., Patrologiae cursus completus, Series Graecae, vol. 23 (Paris, 1857) [PG 23].
DE	*Demonstratio evangelica [Proof of the Gospel]*
	Greek text: Ivar A. Heikel, ed., *Eusebius Werke*, vol. 6, *Die Demonstratio Evangelica*, Die griechischen christlichen Schriftsteller 23 (Berlin: Akademie-Verlag, 1913).
	English translation: W.J. Ferrar, ed. and trans., *The Proof of the Gospel* (Grand Rapids, MI: Baker Book House, 1981).
Eccl.Theol	*De ecclesiastica theologia [Ecclesiastical Theology]*
	Greek text: Erich Klostermann, ed., *Eusebius Werke*, vol. 4, *Gegen Marcell, Über die kirchliche Theologie*, Die griechischen christlichen Schriftsteller 14 (Leipzig: J.C. Hinrichs'sche Buchhandlung, 1906), pp. 60–182.
Ecl.Proph.	*Eclogae propheticae [Prophetic Selections]*
	See *GEI*.
GEI	*Generalis elementaria introductio [General Elementary Introduction]*
	Greek text: Jean-Paul Migne, ed., Patrologiae cursus completus, Series Graecae, vol. 22 (Paris, 1857) [PG 22; containing the extant Books 6–9 under the subtitle *Eclogae propheticae*].
HE	*Historia ecclesiastica [Ecclesiastical History]*
	Greek text: Eduard Schwartz, ed., *Eusebius Werke*, vol. 2 (parts 1–3), *Die Kirchengeschichte*, Die griechischen christlichen Schriftsteller 9.1–3 (Leipzig: J.C. Hinrichs'sche Buchhandlung, 1903, 1908, 1909).

English translations: Kirsopp Lake, trans., *Eusebius: Ecclesiastical History, Books 1–5,* Loeb Classical Library 153 (Cambridge, MA: Harvard University Press, 1980); J.E.L. Oulton, trans., *Eusebius: Ecclesiastical History, Books 6–10,* Loeb Classical Library 265 (Cambridge, MA: Harvard University Press, 1980).

LC *Laus Constantini [In Praise of Constantine; referred to in the text as Tricennial Oration].*

Greek text: Ivar A. Heikel, ed., *Eusebius Werke,* vol. 1, *Über das Leben Constantins, Constantins Rede an die heilige Versammlung, Tricennatsrede an Constantin,* Die griechischen christlichen Schriftsteller 7 (Leipzig: J.C. Hinrichs'sche Buchhandlung, 1902), pp. 195–223.

English translation: H.A. Drake, *In Praise of Constantine: A Historical Study and New Translation of Eusebius' Tricennial Orations* (Berkeley, CA: University of California Press, 1975), pp. 83–102.

M.Pal. *De martyribus Palestinae [Martyrs of Palestine]*

Greek text: Eduard Schwartz, ed., *Eusebius Werke,* vol. 2 (parts 1–3), *Die Kirchengeschichte,* Die griechischen christlichen Schriftsteller 9.1–3 (Leipzig: J.C. Hinrichs'sche Buchhandlung, 1908), pp. 907–50.

Syriac text: William Cureton, trans., *History of the Martyrs of Palestine by Eusebius Bishop of Caesarea, Discovered in a Very Ancient Syriac Manuscript* (London: Williams & Norgate, 1861).

English translation: Hugh Jackson Lawlor and J.E.L. Oulton, eds and trans., *Eusebius Bishop of Caesarea: The Ecclesiastical History and Martyrs of Palestine,* vol. 2 (London: SPCK, 1954), pp. 327–400.

Onom. *Onomasticon*

English translation: R. Steven Notley and Ze'ev Safrai, eds and trans., *Eusebius, Onomasticon: A Triglott Edition with Notes and Commentary* (Leiden: Brill, 2005).

PE *Praeparatio evangelica [Preparation for the Gospel]*

Greek text: Karl Mras, ed., *Eusebius Werke,* vol. 8, *Die Praeparatio Evangelica,* Die griechischen christlichen Schriftsteller 43.1–2 (Berlin: Akademie-Verlag, 1954, 1956).

English translation: E.H. Gifford, trans., *Preparation for the Gospel,* 2 vols (Grand Rapids, MI: Baker Book House, 1981).

SC   *De sepulchro Christi [Oration on Christ's Sepulchre]*

Greek text: Ivar A. Heikel, ed., *Eusebius Werke*, vol. 1, *Über das Leben Constantins, Constantins Rede an die heilige Versammlung, Tricennatsrede an Constantin*, Die griechischen christlichen Schriftsteller 7 (Leipzig: J.C. Hinrichs'sche Buchhandlung, 1902), pp. 223–59.

English translation: H.A. Drake, *In Praise of Constantine: A Historical Study and New Translation of Eusebius' Tricennial Orations* (Berkeley, CA: University of California Press, 1975), pp. 103–27.

Theoph.   *Theophania [Theophany]*

Greek text: Hugo Gressman, ed., *Eusebius Werke*, vol. 3, *Die Theophanie*, Die griechischen christlichen Schriftsteller 11.2 (Leipzig: J.C. Hinrichs'sche Buchhandlung, 1904).

Syriac text: Samuel Lee, ed., *Eusebius, Bishop of Caesarea, on the Theophania, or Divine Manifestation of Our Lord and Saviour Jesus Christ. A Syriac Version. Edited from an Ancient Manuscript Recently Discovered by S. Lee* (London: Society for the Publication of Oriental Texts, 1842).

English translation: Samuel Lee, trans., *Eusebius, Bishop of Caesarea on the Theophania* (Cambridge: Cambridge University Press, 1843).

VC   *De vita Constantini [Life of Constantine]*

Greek text: Ivar A. Heikel, ed., *Eusebius Werke*, vol. 1, *Über das Leben Constantins, Constantins Rede an die heilige Versammlung, Tricennatsrede an Constantin*, Die griechischen christlichen Schriftsteller 7 (Leipzig: J.C. Hinrichs'sche Buchhandlung, 1902), pp. 3–148.

English translation: Averil Cameron and Stuart G. Hall, trans. *Eusebius: Life of Constantine* (Oxford: Clarendon Press, 1999).

Notes

I. CONTEXTS, LIFE AND WORKS

1   See especially: J. Patrich, 'Caesarea in the time of Eusebius', in Sabrina Inowlocki and Claudio Zamagni, eds, *Reconsidering Eusebius* (Leiden: Brill, 2011), pp. 1–24; Terence Donaldson, ed., *Religious Rivalries and the Struggle for Success in Caesarea Maritima* (Waterloo: Wilfrid Laurier University Press, 2000); Avner Raban and Kenneth Holum, eds, *Caesarea Maritima: A Retrospective after Two Millennia* (Leiden: Brill, 1996).

2   See Lorenzo Perrone, 'Eusebius of Caesarea as a Christian writer', in Avner Raban and Kenneth Holum, eds, *Caesarea Maritima: A Retrospective after Two Millennia* (Leiden: Brill, 1996), pp. 515–30.

3   See the relevant studies in Simon Swain and M.J. Edwards, eds, *Approaching Late Antiquity* (Oxford: Oxford University Press, 2004).

4   *Scriptores historiae Augustae*, Gallienus 4.7–8; 5.6–7; 6.1–8; 11.6–9.

5   Porphyry, *Life of Plotinus* 12. See also Lukas de Blois, 'Emperorship in a period of crises: Changes in emperor worship, imperial ideology and perceptions of imperial authority in the Roman Empire in the third century A D', in Lukas de Blois, et al., eds, *The Impact of Imperial Rome on Religions, Ritual and Religious Life in the Roman Empire* (Leiden: Brill, 2006), pp. 268–78.

6   See: Dionysius of Alexandria, quoted in *HE* 7.23.4; Fergus Millar, *The Emperor in the Roman World* (London: Duckworth, 1977), pp. 571–2. It is uncertain whether Gallienus was intentionally attempting to revoke his father's persecuting policy with a formal edict of toleration or that he even had Christians in mind at all (as stated by Timothy Barnes, *Early Christian Hagiography and Roman History* (Tübingen: Mohr Siebeck, 2010), pp. 97–105) in the letter to Egyptian bishops quoted by Eusebius at *HE* 7.13; instead, it seems that he was merely responding to a petition by the bishops, which had attempted to use a recent ruling that aimed at a more general decision regarding the private property of priestly personnel (based on our limited

evidence, we cannot be certain if Gallienus even knew that his addressees were Christian bishops and not merely 'overseers' of some Egyptian cult). For the nature of imperial legislative responses to such petitions and the limits of such evidence in determining an emperor's precise religious position, see Jill Harries, 'Superfluous verbiage? Rhetoric and law in the age of Constantine and Julian', *Journal of Early Christian Studies* xix (2011), pp. 345–74 (though Harries' assertion of the lack of Constantine's and Eusebius' knowledge of Platonic legal thought is misleading).

7   See Richard Stoneman, *Palmyra and Its Empire* (Ann Arbor, MI: University of Michigan Press, 1995).

8   *Scriptores historiae Augustae*, Aurelian 26.3. Generally, see 22–30.

9   *VC* 1.19.

10   James Rives, 'The decree of Decius and the religion of empire', *Journal of Roman Studies* lxxxix (1999), pp. 135–54.

11   See, respectively: Lactantius, *On the Deaths of the Persecutors* 10 (also *VC* 2.50–1); *VC* 2.50; Lactantius, *Divine Institutes* 5.2. See also Elizabeth Depalma Digeser, 'An oracle of Apollo at Daphne and the Great Persecution', *Classical Philology* xcix (2004), pp. 55–7.

12   The Manichees, a religious minority with roots in Persia, were also persecuted by Diocletian. On the 'minimalist' view, see Kate Cooper, 'Christianity, private power, and the law from Decius to Constantine: The minimalist view', *Journal of Early Christian Studies* xix (2011), pp. 327–43.

13   *HE* 8.2.4–5.

14   See the differing evidence of *HE* 8.13.12–13 and Lactantius, *On the Deaths of the Persecutors* 15.6–7; 16.1.

15   *VC* 1.15–16. See *HE* 8.13.13.

16   On Maxentius' policy towards Christians, see Millar, *Emperor*. For the claim that Maxentius was not a usurper but a Tetrarchic heir presumptive, see Timothy Barnes, *Constantine: Dynasty, Religion and Power in the Later Roman Empire* (Oxford: Wiley-Blackwell, 2011), p. 48.

17   Lactantius, *On the Deaths of the Persecutors* 11.

18   A translation of Peter's letter by James Hawkins is found in Arthur Cleveland Coxe, ed., *Ante-Nicene Fathers*, vol. 6 (New York, NY: The Christian Literature Company, 1890), pp. 269–79. See also the first canon of the Synod of Ancyra (314).

19   For 'Galerius' palinode' see *HE* 8.17. The label 'Galerius' palinode' is something of a misnomer, since the names of Constantine and Licinius also head the document.

20   *M.Pal.* 1.1–2 (Greek). The words are from *Iliad* 2.204–5.

21   Even if the speech put into the mouth of Licinius at *VC* 2.5 is a literary invention, there is no reason to doubt that his anti-Christian measures in the East were integrally tied to his anti-Constantinian position. Indeed, his persecution of Christians probably had more to do with his suspicions of their political alliances towards his Western rival than their religious propensities.

22   For a solid treatment of the reign of Constantine, see Noel Lenski, 'The reign of Constantine', in Noel Lenski, ed., *The Cambridge Companion to the Age of Constantine* (Cambridge: Cambridge University Press, 2006), pp. 59–90.

23 For a critique of the common understanding that the Tetrarchic principle was opposed in its very conception to the dynastic principle, see Barnes, *Constantine*, pp. 46–51. Although intriguing, Barnes' argument rests on evidence that may prove insufficiently persuasive to many historians. More soundly, see Bill Leadbetter, 'The illegitimacy of Constantine and the birth of the Tetrarchy', in S.N.C. Lieu and Dominic Montserrat, eds, *Constantine: History, Historiography and Legend* (London and New York, NY: Routledge, 1998), pp. 74–85.

24 Timothy Barnes, in *Early Christian Hagiography*, p. 98, with n. 4, and *Constantine and Eusebius*, pp. 93–7, has registered a rather extreme reaction to the continued use of the modern label 'Edict of Milan' for Licinius' letter of 312, in spite of widespread recognition among those who use it that it was not an edict and it was not issued from Milan. Since imperial letters carried the force of law and since Licinius seems to have issued it as a result of his conference with Constantine at Milan, the label (when presented with scare quotes) is less deceptive than Barnes makes out. For the significant difference between this declaration of freedom and other edicts of 'toleration', see Noel Lenski, '*Libertas* and the fusion of Roman and Christian values', in G. Crifò, ed., *Atti dell'Accademia romanistica costantiniana XVIII 2007* (Perugia and Naples: Edizioni scientifiche italiana, 2011), pp. 242–3.

25 Jacob Burckhardt, *The Age of Constantine the Great*, trans. Moses Hadas (Berkeley, CA: University of California Press, 1949), p. 283. See also: p. 260: 'Constantine's historical memory has suffered the greatest misfortune conceivable [...] He has fallen into the hands of the most objectionable of all eulogists, who has utterly falsified his likeness. The man is Eusebius of Caesarea'; p. 293: 'Eusebius [...] has been proven guilty of so many distortions, dissimulations, and inventions that he has forfeited all claim to figure as a decisive source'; p. 313: 'He presents an account of the [Arian] conflict which is unique in its kind for dishonesty and intentional meagerness.' I have cited all of these quotations elsewhere. See 'Introduction', in Aaron P. Johnson and Jeremy Schott, eds, *Eusebius of Caesarea: Tradition and Innovations* (Washington DC: Center for Hellenic Studies Press, 2013), p. 2.

26 One of the most erudite and comprehensive studies that has challenged the dismissal of Eusebius is Barnes, *Constantine and Eusebius*. See also Barnes, *Constantine*, pp. 16–17.

27 See variously: H.A. Drake, *Constantine and the Bishops* (Baltimore, MD: Johns Hopkins University Press, 2000); Lenski, 'Reign of Constantine', pp. 59–90; Barnes, *Constantine*, pp. 74–80; Raymond Van Dam, *Remembering Constantine at the Milvian Bridge* (Cambridge: Cambridge University Press, 2011), the last of which should be used with caution.

28 See: Clifford Ando, 'Pagan apologetics and Christian intolerance in the ages of Themistius and Augustine', *Journal of Early Christian Studies* iv (1996), pp. 171–207; John Vanderspoel, 'The background to Augustine's denial of religious plurality', in H.A. Meynell, ed., *Grace, Politics and Desire: Essays on Augustine* (Calgary: University of Calgary Press, 1990), pp. 179–93.

29 See: Frank Trombley, *Hellenic Religion and Christianization*, 2 vols (Leiden: Brill, 2001); John Dillon, 'The religion of the last Hellenes', in John Scheid, ed., *Rites et croyances dans les religions du monde romain*, Entretiens sur l'antiquité classique 53 (Geneva: Fondation Hardt, 2007), pp. 117–38.

30 See especially Drake, *Constantine and the Bishops*.

31 See: Barnes, *Constantine and Eusebius*, pp. 261–3; Richard Burgess, 'The summer of blood: The "Great Massacre" of 337 and the promotion of the sons of Constantine', *Dumbarton Oaks Papers* lxii (2008), pp. 5–51.

32 See Ammianus, *Res Gestae* 14.11, though the picture of Gallus' behaviour is far from flattering. See also 14.1, 7, 9.

33 See Julian, *Letter to the Athenians* 272a, 277b.

34 William Adler, 'Sextus Julius Africanus and the Roman Near East in the third century', *Journal of Theological Studies* lv/2 (2004), pp. 520–50.

35 On Bardaisan, see Ilaria Ramelli, *Bardaisan of Edessa: A Reassessment of the Evidence and a New Interpretation* (Piscataway, NJ: Gorgias Press, 2009). On Julius Africanus, see Martin Wallraff and Laura Mecella, eds, *Die Kestoi des Julius Africanus und ihre Überlieferung* (Berlin and New York, NY: Walter de Gruyter, 2009).

36 See: Scott F. Johnson, 'Travel, cartography, and cosmology', in Scott F. Johnson, ed., *The Oxford Handbook of Late Antiquity* (Oxford: Oxford University Press, 2012), pp. 562–94; Annette Yoshiko Reed, 'Beyond the land of Nod: Syriac images of Asia and the historiography of "the West"', *History of Religions* xlix (2009), pp. 48–87; John Matthews, 'Hostages, philosophers, pilgrims, and the diffusion of ideas in the late Roman Mediterranean and Near East', in F.M. Clover and R.S. Humphreys, eds, *Tradition and Innovation in Late Antiquity* (Madison, WI: University of Wisconsin Press, 1989), pp. 29–49.

37 Peter Brown, 'Approaches to the religious crisis of the third century AD', *English Historical Review* lxxxiii (1968), p. 555.

38 See *HE* 6.21.3.

39 For more than one Origen and Ammonius, see: Richard Goulet, 'Porphyre, Ammonius, les deux Origène et les autres', in Richard Goulet, *Études sur les vies de philosophes de l'antiquité tardive* (Paris: Vrin, 2001), pp. 267–90; Mark Edwards, 'Ammonius, teacher of Origen', *Journal of Ecclesiastical History* xliv (1993), pp. 169–81. For a single Origen, see Elizabeth DePalma Digeser, 'Origen on the *Limes*: Rhetoric and the polarization of identity in the late third century', in Elizabeth DePalma Digeser and Robert M. Frakes, eds, *The Rhetoric of Power in Late Antiquity* (London: I.B.Tauris, 2010), pp. 197–218. See also Marco Zambon, 'Porfirio e Origene uno status quaestionis', in Sébastien Morlet, ed., *Le Traité de Porphyre contre les chrétiens* (Paris: Études augustiniennes, 2011), pp. 107–64.

40 See Mark Edwards, *Culture and Philosophy in the Age of Plotinus* (London: Duckworth, 2006).

41 See Porphyry, *Life of Plotinus* 19.

42 See *Scriptores historiae Augustae*, Aurelian 30.3.

43 Paul Kalligas, 'Traces of Longinus' library in Eusebius' *Praeparatio evangelica*', *Classical Quarterly* li (2001), pp. 584–98. See also Chapter 2.

44 See Luc Brisson, 'Longinus Platonicus Philosophus et Philologus: I. Longinus Philosophus', *Aufstieg und Niedergang der römischen Welt* ii/36.7 (1994), pp. 5214–99.

45 See Sébastien Morlet, 'Que savons-nous du *Contre Porphyre* d'Eusèbe?', *Revue d'études Grecques* cxxv (2012), pp. 473–514, whose collection of 'fragments' contain no verbatim quotations of the work.

46 See Socrates, *Ecclesiastical History* 3.23.37–9. See also Nicephorus Callistus, *Ecclesiastical History* 10.36 (PG 146.561a).

47 See Jeremy Schott, *Christianity, Empire, and the Making of Religion in Late Antiquity* (Philadelphia, PA: University of Pennsylvania Press, 2008), pp. 177–85. A good deal of misunderstanding surrounds Porphyry's *Against the Christians*; some of the most helpful recent treatments are: Richard Goulet, 'Hypothèses récentes sur le traité de Porphyre Contre les chrétiens', in Michel Narcy and Éric Rebillard, eds, *Hellénisme et Christianisme* (Villeneuve-d'Ascq: Presses Universitaires du Septentrion, 2004), pp. 61–109; Christoph Riedweg, 'Porphyrios über Christus und die Christen: De philosophia ex oraculis haurienda und Adversus Christianos im Vergleich', in *L'Apologétique chrétienne gréco-latine à l'époque prénicénienne*, Entretiens sur l'antiquité classique, t. LI (Geneva: Fondation Hardt, 2005), pp. 151–203; Sébastien Morlet, ed., *Le Traité de Porphyre contre les chrétiens* (Paris: Études augustiniennes, 2011).

48 See Aaron P. Johnson, *Religion and Identity in Porphyry of Tyre* (Cambridge: Cambridge University Press, 2013).

49 See Porphyry, *Life of Plotinus* 17 (Greek critics), 12 (Platonopolis), 8 (poor writing), 2 (lonely death).

50 Porphyry, *Life of Plotinus* 23.

51 Iamblichus, *On the Mysteries* 3.13; 7.4–5.

52 See: Gregory Shaw, 'Theurgy: Rituals of unification in the Neoplatonism of Iamblichus', *Traditio* xli (1995), pp. 1–28; Elizabeth DePalma Digeser, 'The power of religious rituals: A philosophical quarrel on the eve of the Great Persecution', in Andrew Cain and Noel Lenski, eds, *The Power of Religion in Late Antiquity* (Burlington, VT: Ashgate, 2009), pp. 81–92; Sergio Knipe, 'Subjugating the divine: Iamblichus on the theurgic evocation', in Andrew Cain and Noel Lenski, eds, *The Power of Religion in Late Antiquity* (Burlington, VT: Ashgate, 2009), pp. 93–102.

53 *HE* 6.16. See also: Barnes, *Constantine and Eusebius*, pp. 91–2; Anthony Grafton and Megan Williams, *Christianity and the Transformation of the Book* (Cambridge, MA: Harvard University Press, 2006).

54 See variously: Eberhard Nestle, 'Alttestamentliches aus Eusebius', *Zeitschrift für die alttestamentliche Wissenschaft* xxix (1909), pp. 57–8; Michael Hollerich, *Eusebius of Caesarea's Commentary on Isaiah: Christian Exegesis in the Age of Constantine* (Oxford: Clarendon Press, 1999), pp. 81–5; Jörg Ulrich, *Euseb von Caesarea und die Juden. Studien zur Rolle der Juden in der Theologie des Eusebius von Caesarea* (Berlin and New York, NY: Walter de Gruyter, 1999), pp. 192–201; Aaron P. Johnson, 'The blackness of Ethiopians: Classical ethnography and Eusebius' commentary on the Psalms', *Harvard Theological Review* xcic/2 (2006), pp. 179–200.

55 See: Sébastien Morlet, 'Origen as an exegetical source in Eusebius' *Prophetical Extracts'*, in Aaron P. Johnson and Jeremy Schott, eds, *Eusebius of Caesarea: Tradition and Innovations* (Washington DC: Center for Hellenic Studies Press, 2013), pp. 207–37; Ilaria Ramelli, 'Origen, Eusebius, the doctrine of apokatastasis, and its relation to Christology', in Aaron P. Johnson and Jeremy Schott, eds, *Eusebius of Caesarea: Tradition and Innovations* (Washington DC: Center for Hellenic Studies Press, 2013), pp. 307–23.

56 Barnes, *Constantine and Eusebius*, pp. 153–4.

57 *HE* 8.9.4.

58 Richard Burgess, 'The dates and editions of Eusebius' *Chronici canones* and *Historia ecclesiastica'*, *Journal of Theological Studies* xlviii (1997), pp. 471–504.

59 For the date of *c.*310, see Eduard Schwartz, 'Eusebios von Caesarea', *Realencyclopädie der classischen Altertumswissenschaft*, vol. 11 (Stuttgart: J.B. Metzlersche Buchhandlung, 1909), col. 1387.

60 See his glancing reference to his presbyterate in the *Epistle to the Caesareans*, quoted in Athanasius, *On the Decrees of the Council of Nicaea* 33. See Hans-Georg Opitz, ed., *Athanasius Werke*, vol. 3 (part 1), *Urkunden zur Geschichte des arianischen Streites* (Berlin: Walter de Gruyter, 1934), no. 3.

61 *PE* 4.2.11. See also Jean Sirinelli and Édouard des Places, *Eusèbe de Césarée. La Préparation évangélique, Livre I*, Sources Chrétiennes 206 (Paris: Les Éditions du Cerf, 1974), pp. 8–14.

62 Indeed, Constantine himself used the phrase 'second God' in his *Oration to the Saints*; but there is scholarly disagreement as to the *Oration's* date. See variously: Barnes, *Constantine*, pp. 113–20; Mark Edwards, 'The Arian heresy and the oration to the saints', *Vigiliae Christianae* xlix (1995), pp. 379–87; and, more compellingly, H.A. Drake, 'Suggestions of date in Constantine's *Oration to the Saints'*, *American Journal of Philology* cvi (1985), pp. 335–49.

63 See Sébastien Morlet, *La Démonstration évangélique d'Eusèbe de Césarée. Étude sur l'apologétique chrétienne à l'époque de Constantin* (Paris: Études augustiniennes, 2009), pp. 80–93, which therefore suggests that its only firm *terminus ante quem* is 333, the death of Theodotus, the addressee of both works.

64 See *DE* 4.16, 182d.

65 See: *VC* 3.58; *SC* 13.7. For the cult at Baalbek, see *Theoph.* 2.14.

66 *Theoph.* 3.61.

67 The reference to the recent end of war and discord at *Theoph.* 2.76 is too vague to be of much use for dating purposes.

68 *Pace* Samuel Lee, trans., *Eusebius, Bishop of Caesarea on the Theophania* (Cambridge: Cambridge University Press, 1843), pp. xxi–xxii.

69 *HE* 1.1.7.

70 The foremost defender of such a thesis is Timothy Barnes, in 'The editions of Eusebius' Ecclesiastical History', *Greek, Roman and Byzantine Studies* xxi (1980), pp. 191–201, and *Constantine and Eusebius*, pp. 148–63.

71 *HE* 10.4.10 and 16, respectively.

72 See Barnes, *Early Christian Hagiography*, pp. 40–54.

73 For the earlier date, see Hans-Georg Opitz, 'Die Zeitfolge des arianischen Streites von den Anfängen bis zum Jahre 328', *Zeitschrift für die Neutestamentliche Wissenschaft* xxxiii (1934), pp. 131–59. For the later date, see: Rowan Williams, *Arius: Heresy and Tradition* (London: SCM Press, 2001), pp. 48–61; Sara Parvis, *Marcellus of Ancyra and the Lost Years of the Arian Controversy, 325–345* (Oxford: Oxford University Press, 2006), pp. 68–72; David Gwynn, *The Eusebians: The Polemic of Athanasius of Alexandria and the Construction of the Arian Controversy* (Oxford: Oxford University Press, 2007), pp. 59–69.

74 See Eusebius' letters to Euphration and Alexander of Alexandria, Opitz, *Urkunden*, nos 3 and 7. The only evidence for the synod is a letter in Syriac translation (contained in three different manuscripts) addressed to Alexander of Byzantium (or Thessaloníki) by Ossius (or a certain Eusebius), which is not without its problems. For the Syriac text and Eduard Schwartz's Greek translation, see Opitz, *Urkunden*, no. 18. For an English translation, see F.L. Cross, 'The Council of Antioch in 325 A D', *Church Quarterly Review* cxxviii (1939), pp. 49–76.

75 Eusebius, *Letter to the Caesareans*, quoted in Athanasius, *On the Decrees of the Council of Nicaea* 33. See Opitz, *Urkunden*, no. 22.

76 For Arius' rejection of *homoousios*, see his *Letter to Alexander of Alexandria*, in Opitz, *Urkunden*, no. 6.5.

77 See Parvis, *Marcellus of Ancyra*, pp. 101–7.

78 *Comm.Isa.* 2.36, p. 316.9–25, citing Isaiah 49:23; 1.28, pp. 20.29–21.5, citing Isaiah 2:18–21.

79 *Comm.Psalm.* 67:23, 25–6 (PG 23:705d, 709b).

80 There is disagreement on the audiences of these two speeches. See: H.A. Drake, *In Praise of Constantine: A Historical Study and New Translation of Eusebius' Tricennial Orations* (Berkeley, CA: University of California Press, 1975); Barnes, *Constantine and Eusebius*, p. 253.

81 For the dubious nature of the protocol followed in these synods, see Parvis, *Marcellus of Ancyra*, pp. 123–9 (though the precise degree to which Eusebius was responsible for orchestrating their bad form or whether he merely allowed other figures to manipulate them remains uncertain).

82 The fact that Athanasius refused to attend a synod slated for Caesarea and only submitted himself when it was moved to Tyre, however, provides a hint of his perception of how Eusebius might feel towards him. See: Athanasius, *Apology against the Arians* 77; Sozomen, *Ecclesiastical History* 2.25; Theodoret, *Ecclesiastical History* 1.26.

83 The argument of Frederick Cornwallis Conybeare, that Eusebius of Emesa, not our Eusebius, was the author of the two works, *c.*341, was aptly refuted by Erich Klostermann in *Eusebius Werke*, vol. 4, *Gegen Marcell, Über die kirchliche Theologie*, Die griechischen christlichen Schriftsteller 14 (Leipzig: J.C. Hinrichs'sche Buchhandlung, 1906), pp. ix–xvi.

84 *c.Marc.* 2.4.29–30.

85 *Eccl.Theol.* 1.praef.1–2. On Flacillus, see Barnes, *Constantine and Eusebius*, pp. 228–9.

86 Barnes, *Constantine and Eusebius*, pp. 264–5, supposes both anti-Marcellan

works to have been written after Marcellus' return from exile in 337; it seems doubtful, however, that Eusebius would not have mentioned this turn of events when remarking only vaguely that some think he was wronged when deposed at Constantinople in 336.

87 *Pace* Timothy Barnes, who claims that a later editor stitched together blocks of material composed by Eusebius after his death. Of Barnes' work, see: 'Panegyric, history and hagiography in Eusebius' *Life of Constantine*', in Rowan Williams, ed., *The Making of Orthodoxy: Essays in Honour of Henry Chadwick* (Cambridge: Cambridge University Press, 2002), pp. 94–114; 'The two drafts of Eusebius' *Life of Constantine*', in Timothy Barnes, *From Eusebius to Augustine* (Aldershot: Ashgate, 1994), Chapter 12; *Constantine*, p. 11. For an illuminating response, see Averil Cameron, 'Eusebius' *Vita Constantini* and the construction of Constantine', in Simon Swain and M.J. Edwards, eds, *Portraits: Biographical Representation in the Greek and Latin Literature of the Roman Empire* (Oxford: Oxford University Press, 1997), pp. 145–74. On the date of Eusebius' death, see Barnes, *Constantine and Eusebius*, p. 263.

88 See Barnes, *Constantine and Eusebius*, pp. 261–3.

89 See A.P. Johnson, 'Introduction'.

II. DEFENDING THE FAITH

1 Though the manuscripts attribute the *Against Hierocles* to 'Eusebius Pamphilou', I have serious reservations regarding its attribution to our Eusebius. *Pace*: Salvatore Borzì, 'Sull'autenticità del *Contra Hieroclem* di Eusebio di Cesarea', *Augustinianum* xliii (2003), pp. 397–416; Christopher Jones, 'Apollonius of Tyana in Late Antiquity', in Scott F. Johnson, ed., *Greek Literature in Late Antiquity: Dynamism, Didacticism, Classicism* (Aldershot: Ashgate, 2006), pp. 49–64; *Philostratus: Apollonius of Tyana*, Loeb Classical Library 458 (Cambridge, MA: Harvard University Press, 2006), p. 152. Thomas Hägg's argument against Eusebian authorship remains persuasive: see Thomas Hägg, 'Hierocles the lover of truth and Eusebius the sophist', *Symbolae Osloenses* lxvii (1992), pp. 138–50. See also Aaron P. Johnson, 'The author of the *Against Hierocles*: A response to Borzì and Jones', *Journal of Theological Studies* lxiv (2014), pp. 574–94.

2 F.J. Foakes-Jackson, *Eusebius Pamphili, Bishop of Caesarea in Palestine and First Christian Historian: A Study of the Man and His Writings* (Cambridge: Heffers, 1933), p. 128.

3 See 'Introduction', in Aaron P. Johnson and Jeremy Schott, eds, *Eusebius of Caesarea: Tradition and Innovations* (Washington DC: Center for Hellenic Studies Press, 2013).

4 *PE* 1.1.12, 4b–c.

5 See Aaron P. Johnson, 'Eusebius' *Praeparatio evangelica* as literary experiment', in Scott F. Johnson, ed., *Greek Literature in Late Antiquity: Dynamism, Didacticism, Classicism* (Aldershot: Ashgate, 2006), pp. 67–89.

6   For the range of polemical issues, see Aryeh Kofsky, *Eusebius of Caesarea against the Pagans* (Leiden: Brill, 2000).

7   *PE* 1.2.2–4, 5a–c.

8   The most comprehensive treatment of this issue is Sébastien Morlet, 'Eusebius' polemic against Porphyry: A reassessment', in Sabrina Inowlocki and Claudio Zamagni, eds, *Reconsidering Eusebius* (Leiden: Brill, 2011), pp. 119–50.

9   See Aaron P. Johnson, 'Rethinking the authenticity of Porphyry, *Contra Christianos*, fr. 1', *Studia Patristica* xlvi (2010), pp. 53–8.

10   See: Aaron P. Johnson, *Religion and Identity in Porphyry of Tyre: The Limits of Hellenism in Late Antiquity* (Cambridge: Cambridge University Press, 2013), Chapter 7; 'Philosophy, Hellenicity, law: Porphyry on Origen, again', *Journal of Hellenic Studies* cxxxii (2012), pp. 55–69.

11   See: Daniel Richter, 'Plutarch on Isis and Osiris: Text, cult, and cultural appropriation', *Transactions of the American Philological Association* cxxxi (2001), pp. 191–216; Jeremy Schott, *Christianity, Empire, and the Making of Religion in Late Antiquity* (Philadelphia, PA: University of Pennsylvania Press, 2008).

12   See: George Boys-Stones, *Post-Hellenistic Philosophy* (Oxford: Oxford University Press, 2001); Arthur Droge, *Homer or Moses? Early Christian Interpretations of the History of Culture* (Tübingen: Mohr Siebeck, 1989).

13   Aaron P. Johnson, *Ethnicity and Argument in Eusebius' Praeparatio evangelica* (Oxford: Oxford University Press, 2006).

14   *PE* 1.9.13–18, 29d–30c.

15   *PE* 7.3–5.

16   The theory that Greek religion worshipped deified humans has been attached to the name of Euhemerus – euhemerism – an author whose sole surviving verbatim fragment expressing this notion is none other than Eusebius' *Preparation* (2.2.52–62, citing the lost sixth book of Diodorus' *Bibliothēkē* as an intermediary).

17   *PE* 2.1.53–6, 52a–c.

18   *PE* 10.9–14.

19   *PE* 2.6.19, 74c.

20   *PE* 4–5.

21   *PE* 6. For discussion see Richard Stoneman, *The Ancient Oracles: Making the Gods Speak* (New Haven, CT: Yale University Press, 2011), pp. 205–9.

22   *PE* 11–13.

23   *PE* 13.13–21.

24   *PE* 12.11.1, 584c; 12.13.1, 586a.

25   See Clement of Alexandria, *Stromateis* 1.15, 360; repeated in *PE* 9.6.9, 411a.

26   See A.P. Johnson, *Religion and Identity*.

27   *PE* 12.51–2. See A.P. Johnson, 'Introduction'.

28   On Gellius' use of excerpts, see William A. Johnson, *Readers and Reading Culture in the High Roman Empire* (Oxford: Oxford University Press, 2010), pp. 118–36, especially p. 132.

29   *PE* 4.1.1–2, 129d–130b.

30   *PE* 2.6.13–20, 73b–74c.

31 *PE* 5.1.9, 179d; 6.praef.3, 236c. See also 4.6.2, 142d. On Porphyry's *Philosophy from Oracles*, see: Aaron P. Johnson, 'Arbiter of the oracular: Reading religion in Porphyry of Tyre', in Andrew Cain and Noel Lenski, eds, *The Power of Religion in Late Antiquity* (Burlington, VT: Ashgate, 2009), pp. 103–15; Richard Stoneman, *The Ancient Oracles: Making the Gods Speak* (New Haven, CT: Yale University Press, 2011), pp. 171–89, especially pp. 184–9.

32 *PE* 4.5.1–2, 141a–d.

33 *PE* 1.6.5–6, 18a–b.

34 See Paul Kalligas, 'Traces of Longinus' library in Eusebius' *Praeparatio evangelica*', *Classical Quarterly* li (2001), pp. 584–98.

35 Porphyry, *Life of Plotinus* 19.

36 These executions are reported at *PE* 4.2.10–11, 135c–d.

37 Plotinus is quoted at *PE* 11.17 and 15.10 and 22.

38 Eustochius' edition: Paul Henry, *Recherches sur la Préparation évangélique d'Eusèbe et l'édition perdue des oeuvres de Plotin publiée par Eustochius* (Paris: E. Leroux, 1935); Porphyry's edition: Marie-Odile Goulet-Cazé, 'Deux traités plotiniens chez Eusèbe de Césarée', in Cristina D'Ancona, ed., *The Libraries of the Neoplatonists* (Leiden: Brill: 2007), pp. 63–97; Marco Zambon, 'Edizione e prima circolazione degli scritti di Plotino: Porfirio ed Eusebio di Cesarea', in Walter Beierwaltes and Matteo Bianchetti, eds, *Plotino e l'ontologia* (Milan: Albo versorio, 2006), pp. 55–78; Amelius' edition: John Rist, 'Basil's Neoplatonism', in Paul J. Fedwick, ed., *Basil of Caesarea: Christian, Humanist, Ascetic* (Toronto: PIMS, 1981), pp. 135–220.

39 Porphyry, *Life of Plotinus* 19.26.

40 In spite of strong recommendations that we posit a pagan named Origen (whom we find in Platonic philosophical sources, such as Porphyry and Proclus) separate from the well-known Christian Origen, the latter may well be the same person mentioned by the Platonists. See: Marco Zambon, 'Porfirio e Origene uno status quaestionis', in Sébastien Morlet, ed., *Le Traité de Porphyre contre les chrétiens* (Paris: Études augustiniennes, 2011), pp. 107–64; Elizabeth DePalma Digeser, 'Origen on the *Limes*: Rhetoric and the polarization of identity in the late third century', in Elizabeth DePalma Digeser and Robert M. Frakes, eds, *The Rhetoric of Power in Late Antiquity* (London: I.B.Tauris, 2010), pp. 197–218.

41 *PE* 1.6.5–6, 18a–b.

42 *PE* 6.10.49, 280d. See also the programmatic statements at 1.1.11–13. For discussion, see: Aryeh Kofsky, *Eusebius of Caesarea*, pp. 74–85; Timothy Barnes, *Constantine and Eusebius* (Cambridge, MA: Harvard University Press, 1981), p. 182.

43 See Daniel Boyarin, 'The Christian invention of Judaism: The Theodosian empire and the rabbinic refusal of religion', in Hent de Vries, ed., *Religion: Beyond a Concept* (New York, NY: Fordham University Press, 2008), pp. 150–77.

44 *DE* 1.2.1–2, 12a.

45 *DE* 1.2.10, 14a.

46 See: 1 Corinthians 1:22; Galatians 3:28; Colossians 3:11.

47 See: A.P. Johnson, *Religion and Identity*; Schott, *Christianity, Empire*; Valerio Neri,

'Romani, greci, barbari: identità etniche ed universalismi nell'opera di Eusebio di Cesarea', *Adamantius* xvi (2010), pp. 63–87.

48 See: Alan Cameron, *The Last Pagans of Rome* (Oxford: Oxford University Press, 2011), pp. 14–32; Carine Van Liefferinge, '"Ethniques" et "Hellènes". Quelques réflexions sur la portée nationale du paganisme', in Edouard Delruelle and Vinciane Pirenne-Delforge, eds, *Kèpoi: de la religion à la philosophie: mélanges offerts à André Motte, Kernos Supplément 11* (Liège: Centre international d'étude de la religion grecque antique, 2001), pp. 247–55.

49 I register here my discontent at the way translators of the *PE* and *DE* almost invariably translate the Greek terms *eusebeia* and *theosebeia* as 'religion'. For further discussion of the nature of ethnicity and religion in early Christian texts, see, of my own work: 'Hellenism and its discontents', in Scott F. Johnson, ed., *Oxford Handbook of Late Antiquity* (Oxford: Oxford University Press, 2012), pp. 437–66; 'Ethnicity: Greeks, Jews and Christians', in Jeremy McInerney, ed., *Blackwell Guide to Ethnicity in the Ancient Mediterranean* (Oxford: Wiley-Blackwell), forthcoming; *Ethnicity and Argument*.

50 See Barnes, *Constantine and Eusebius* (Cambridge, MA: Harvard University Press, 1981), pp. 186–7. Samuel Lee, the English translator, on the contrary, considered the *Theophany* to pre-date the *Preparation* and *Proof*. See Samuel Lee, trans., *Eusebius, Bishop of Caesarea on the Theophania* (Cambridge: Cambridge University Press, 1843), pp. xxi–xxii.

51 *Theoph.* 1.47 (Syriac, p. 39).

52 See *Theoph.* 4.8,11 and 4.3–5.

53 *Eccl.Theol.* 2.22.3.

III. WRITING THE CURRICULUM

1 See: Pierre Hadot, 'Théologie, exégèse, révélation, écriture dans la philosophie grecque', in Michel Tardieu, ed., *Les Règles de l'interprétation* (Paris: Les Éditions du Cerf, 1987), pp. 13–34; David Sedley, 'Plato's *Auctoritas* and the rebirth of the commentary tradition', in Jonathan Barnes and Miriam Griffin, eds, *Philosophia Togata II: Plato and Aristotle at Rome* (Oxford: Clarendon Press, 1997), pp. 112–16.

2 See: Pierre Hadot, *Philosophy as a Way of Life*, trans. Michael Chase (Oxford: Blackwell, 1995); Philippe Hoffmann, 'What was commentary in Late Antiquity? The example of the Neoplatonic commentators', in Mary Louise Gill and Pierre Pellegrin, eds, *Companion to Ancient Philosophy* (Oxford: Wiley-Blackwell, 2009), pp. 597–622.

3 See Albinus, *Prologus* 5.

4 See L.G. Westerink, *Anonymous Prolegomena to Platonic Philosophy* (Amsterdam: North-Holland Publishing Co., 1962), pp. xxxvii–xxxviii.

5 See: Jaap Mansfeld, *Prolegomena: Questions to Be Settled before the Study of an Author, or a Text* (Leiden: Brill, 1994); Ilsetraut Hadot, 'Le commentaire philosophique continu dans l'antiquité', *L'Antiquité tardive* v (1997), pp. 169–76; Frances Young, *Biblical Exegesis and the Formation of Christian Culture* (Peabody, MA:

Hendrickson, 2002), pp. 76–81; Pierluigi Dorandi, 'Testi e commenti, manuali e insegnamento: la forma sistematica e i metodi della filosofia in età postellenistica', *Aufstieg und Niedergang der römischen Welt* ii/36.7 (1994), pp. 5027–100.

6   Porphyry, *Life of Plotinus* 14.11–18. See: John Dillon, 'Philosophy as a profession in Late Antiquity', in Simon Swain and M.J. Edwards, eds, *Approaching Late Antiquity* (Oxford: Oxford University Press, 2004), pp. 401–18; Aaron P. Johnson, *Religion and Identity in Porphyry of Tyre: The Limits of Hellenism in Late Antiquity* (Cambridge: Cambridge University Press, 2013), Chapter 4.

7   Marinus, *Vita Procli* 38.

8   See: H. Gregory Snyder, *Teachers and Texts in the Ancient World* (London and New York, NY: Routledge, 2000); Robert Lamberton, 'The Neoplatonists and their books', in Margalit Finkelberg and Guy G. Stroumsa, eds, *Homer, the Bible, and Beyond* (Leiden: Brill, 2003), pp. 195–212.

9   See: Aaron P. Johnson, 'Eusebius the educator', in Sabrina Inowlocki and Claudio Zamagni, eds, *Reconsidering Eusebius* (Leiden: Brill, 2011), pp. 99–118; 'The tenth book of Eusebius' *General Elementary Introduction*: A critique of the Wallace-Hadrill thesis', *Journal of Theological Studies* lxii/1 (2011), pp. 144–60.

10   *GEI* 6 (= *Ecl.Proph.* 1).1 (PG 22.1021a).

11   This marks a shift from my earlier assessment in 'Eusebius the educator', in Sabrina Inowlocki and Claudio Zamagni, eds, *Reconsidering Eusebius* (Leiden: Brill, 2011), pp. 107–8.

12   See John G. Cook, *The Interpretation of the Old Testament in Greco-Roman Paganism* (Tübingen: Mohr Siebeck, 2004), pp. 36–41, 167–73.

13   See Hadot, *Philosophy*.

14   *GEI* 9 (= *Ecl.Proph.* 4).praef. (PG 22.1193a–c).

15   *GEI* 3 (= *Ecl.Proph.* 3).7 (PG 22.1168a).

16   *GEI* 6 (= *Ecl.Proph.* 1).1 (PG 22.1024b–c).

17   1 Kings 8:26–7.

18   Eusebius quotes this passage at *GEI* 6 (= *Ecl.Proph.* 1).24 (PG 22.1085a).

19   *GEI* 6 (= *Ecl.Proph.* 1).22 (PG 22.1084c).

20   The current 18 chapters are thus a truncation of the 45 chapters listed in the fortunately extant table of contents for this book. On the so-called 'great lacuna', see: G. Mercati, 'La grande lacuna delle Ecloghe profetiche di Eusebio di Cesarea', in *Mémorial L. Petit* (Bucharest: Institut français d'études byzantines, 1948), pp. 1–3; G. Dorival, 'Remarques sur les *Eklogai prophétiques* d'Eusèbe de Césarée', in Bart Janssens, Bram Roosen and Peter Van Deun, eds, *Philomathestatos: Studies in Greek Patristic and Byzantine Texts Presented to Jacques Noret for his Sixty-Fifth Birthday* (Leuven: Peeters Publishers, 2004), pp. 203–24.

21   *GEI* 8 (= *Ecl.Proph.* 3).10 (PG 22.1136a–c). See Ernst Bammel, 'Der Jude des Celsus', in Ernst Bammel, *Judaica* (Tübingen: Mohr Siebeck, 1986), pp. 265–83.

22   *GEI* 8 (= *Ecl.Proph.* 3).46 (PG 22.1176a–1192a).

23   *GEI* 8 (= *Ecl.Proph.* 3).46 (PG 22.1180a). See William Adler, 'Eusebius' critique of Africanus', in Martin Wallraff, ed., *Julius Africanus und die christliche Weltchronistik* (Berlin: Walter de Gruyter, 2006), pp. 147–60.

24 *GEI* 9 (= *Ecl.Proph.* 4).4–5 (PG 22. 1204c–1208a). See more vaguely 1209b: 'we shall send the lover of learning to the commentaries on this passage.' See also: *GEI* 9 (= *Ecl.Proph.* 4).24 (PG 22.1237b); *GEI* 9 (= *Ecl.Proph.* 4).31 (PG 22.1253d).

25 For the use of cross-references in earlier exegetical literature, see Young, *Biblical Exegesis*, pp. 130–7.

26 *GEI* 9 (= *Ecl.Proph.* 4).8 (PG 22.1212c–d).

27 *GEI* 9 (= *Ecl.Proph.* 4).4 (PG 22.1204a–b and 22.1217a). See Sébastien Morlet, 'Origen as an exegetical source in Eusebius' *Prophetical Extracts*', in Aaron P. Johnson and Jeremy Schott, eds, *Eusebius of Caesarea: Tradition and Innovations* (Washington DC: Center for Hellenic Studies Press, 2013), pp. 207–37. The PG editor has noted that Eusebius wrongly identifies the cross-reference as Leviticus; the correct passage is Deuteronomy 22:27.

28 *GEI* 9 (= *Ecl.Proph.* 4).2 (PG 22.1200c–d); Isaiah 3:10 and Wisdom 2:12.

29 Isaiah 2:3 and 65:1.

30 See Michael Hollerich, *Eusebius of Caesarea's Commentary on Isaiah: Christian Exegesis in the Age of Constantine* (Oxford: Clarendon Press, 1999), pp. 37–40, for a brief and useful discussion of the distinctive features of the three portions of prophetic material comprised in the book of Isaiah.

31 See Robert Lamberton, *Homer the Theologian* (Berkeley, CA: University of California Press, 1986).

32 For the few short fragments that survive from Books 1–5 of *GEI*, see PG 22.1271–1274.

33 See Aaron P. Johnson, 'Eusebius' *Praeparatio evangelica* as literary experiment', in Scott F. Johnson, ed., *Greek Literature in Late Antiquity: Dynamism, Didacticism, Classicism* (Aldershot: Ashgate, 2006), pp. 67–89.

34 The best and most exhaustive treatment is Sébastien Morlet, *La Démonstration évangélique d'Eusèbe de Césarée. Étude sur l'apologétique chrétienne à l'époque de Constantin* (Paris: Études augustiniennes, 2009).

35 See Morlet, *Démonstration évangélique*, pp. 332–57, 439–47.

36 An instance of such an accusation of Christian incoherence occurs in Porphyry, *Against the Christians*, fr. 39 (= *HE* 6.19). See Aaron P. Johnson, 'Philosophy, Hellenicity, law: Porphyry on Origen, again', *Journal of Hellenic Studies* cxxxii (2012), pp. 55–69.

37 *DE* 1.3.

38 Deuteronomy 18:15, quoted at *DE* 1.3.43, 6c. Note that W.J. Ferrar's version, which I have used in this chapter, is often more of a paraphrase than a strict or accurate translation. Furthermore, it is not based on the critical edition of Ivar A. Heikel. The marginal notation (based on Fabricius' edition) is given in the references following the book and chapter numeration for ease of reference to the precise location in Ferrar's translation, Heikel's critical edition or the outdated edition of Jean-Paul Migne, ed., Patrologiae cursus completus, Series Graecae, vol. 22 (Paris, 1857) – which nonetheless seems to be more accessible in libraries than that of Heikel.

39 Numbers 24:5–7, quoted at *DE* 1.3.44, 6c–d.

40 *DE* 1.3.46, 6d–7a.

41 *PE* 7.6.

42 See variously: Eugene Gallagher, 'Piety and polity: Eusebius' defense of the Gospel', in J. Neusner, E.S. Frerichs and A.J. Levine, eds, *Religious Writings and Religious Systems*, vol. 2 (Atlanta, GA: Scholars Press, 1989), pp. 139–55; 'Eusebius the apologist: The evidence of the preparation and the proof', *Studia Patristica* xxvi (1993), pp. 251–60; Aryeh Kofsky, 'Eusebius of Caesarea and the Christian–Jewish polemic', in Ora Limor and Guy G. Stroumsa, eds, *Contra Iudaeos: Ancient and Medieval Polemics between Christians and Jews* (Tübingen: Mohr Siebeck, 1996), pp. 59–83; Jörg Ulrich, *Euseb von Caesarea und die Juden. Studien zur Rolle der Juden in der Theologie des Eusebius von Caesarea* (Berlin and New York, NY: Walter de Gruyter, 1999).

43 *DE* 1.5.1–2, 9c–d (translation adapted).

44 *DE* 2.1.1, 44b (translation adapted).

45 See *DE* 4.16.3, 182d, for an allusion to Licinius.

46 *DE* 4.2–9; 4.10–14.

47 And preliminarily in *DE* 4.15–17.

48 *DE* 4.15.15, 173c.

49 *DE* 4.16.16, 173c, 185b–c.

50 Numbers 13:16 LXX. The LXX gives the form Ausē. It should be noted that the editor of the *Patrologiae cursus completus, Series Graecae* edition of the *DE* misidentifies the reference as Numbers 13:17.

51 *DE* 4.17.1–3, 195b–d; 4.17.4–5, 195d–6a; 4.17.5, 196a. See the parallel passage at *GEI* 6 (= *Ecl.Proph.* 1).11 (PG 22.1057c–d).

52 *DE* 4.17.15, 198b. For the reference to Jesus as a high priest see *DE* 4.17.5, 196a. See also the parallel passage at *GEI* 6 (= *Ecl.Proph.* 1).11 (PG 22.1057c–d).

53 *DE* 4.17.19, 199a; 4.17.21, 199b.

54 See *GEI* 6 (= *Ecl.Proph.* 1).5 (PG 22.1037b–c), discussed above. See also: *DE* 4.7.2, 156c; *DE* 5.3; *DE* 5.6; *Comm.Psalm.* 67:23 (PG 23.705d–708a); *Comm. Psalm.* 67:25, 26 (PG 23.709b); *HE* 1.2.9; *HE* 1.2.3, 5, 11. There is no use of the dual-Lord approach in the *Comm.Isa.*, on which see below.

55 *DE* 5.8.2–3, 232d–233a (translation adapted).

56 Lienhard helpfully identifies this 'two-hypostasis' (or 'dyohypostatic') approach as one of the twin poles of fourth-century theological discourse, the other being a 'one-hypostasis' (or 'miahypostatic') approach. See Joseph Lienhard, *Contra Marcellum: Marcellus of Ancyra and Fourth-Century Theology* (Washington DC: Catholic University of America Press, 1999), pp. 28–46.

57 See Morlet, *Démonstration évangélique*, pp. 497–506, for a thorough analysis of this terminology.

58 *DE* 9.1.11–12, 419d.

59 *DE* 9.1.14, 420a–b.

60 See Young, *Biblical Exegesis*, pp. 161–213.

61 See: Claudio Zamagni, 'Eusebius' exegesis between Alexandria and Antioch', in Sabrina Inowlocki and Claudio Zamagni, eds, *Reconsidering Eusebius* (Leiden: Brill, 2011), pp. 151–76; Morlet, 'Origen as an exegetical source', pp. 207–37.

62 For this view, see Carmelo Curti, 'L'esegesi di Eusebio di Cesarea: caratteri e sviluppo', in Carmelo Curti, *Eusebiana, I: Commentarii in Psalmos* (Catania: Centro di studi sull'antico cristianesimo, 1987), pp. 195–213.

63 *GEI* 9 (= *Ecl.Proph.* 4).7 (PG 22.1209b).

64 See *HE* 6.32.1. For discussion of Origen's exegetical work on Isaiah, see Michael Hollerich, *Eusebius of Caesarea's Commentary on Isaiah: Christian Exegesis in the Age of Constantine* (Oxford: Clarendon Press, 1999), pp. 46–57.

65 See *HE* 6.24.2.

66 This conclusion is drawn from Joseph Ziegler's reconstruction, which bases itself primarily on the single, belatedly discovered copy of it in the margins of a Florentine manuscript, in addition to the sifted remains of excerpts in the medieval catenae (that is, the 'chains' of quotations from patristic commentaries on particular biblical books). See Joseph Ziegler, ed., *Eusebius Werke*, vol. 9, *Der Jesajakommentar*, Die griechischen christlichen Schriftsteller 56 (Berlin: Akademie-Verlag, 1975).

67 On the anonymous *Commentary on the Parmenides*, see: Pierre Hadot, *Porphyre et Victorinus* (Paris: Études augustiniennes, 1968); Gerald Bechtle, *The Anonymous Commentary on Plato's Parmenides* (Stuttgart: Verlag Paul Haupt, 1999).

68 Cordula Bandt and others have commenced work on an edition for the Griechischen christlichen Schriftsteller series.

69 See: M.-J. Rondeau, 'Eusèbe de Césarée. Le Commentaire sur les psaumes', in M.-J. Rondeau and J. Kirchmeyer, eds, *Dictionnaire de spiritualité* (Paris: Beauchesne, 1961), cols 1688–90; Michael Hollerich, 'Eusebius's *Commentary on the Psalms* and its place in the origins of Christian biblical scholarship', in Aaron P. Johnson and Jeremy Schott, eds, *Eusebius of Caesarea: Tradition and Innovations* (Washington DC: Center for Hellenic Studies Press, 2013), pp. 151–67. For thematic analysis, see: Carmelo Curti, *Eusebiana, I: Commentarii in Psalmos* (Catania: Centro di studi sull'antico cristianesimo, 1987); M.-J. Rondeau, *Les Commentaires patristiques du Psautier*, Orientalia Christiana Analecta 220 (Rome: Pontificium Institutum Studiorum Orientalium, 1985), pp. 169–95; Aaron P. Johnson, 'The blackness of Ethiopians: Classical ethnography and Eusebius' commentary on the Psalms', *Harvard Theological Review* xcic/2 (2006), pp. 179–200.

70 See *Comm.Isa.* 2.36, p. 316.19–20.

71 *Comm.Isa.* 1.80, p. 142.4–21.

72 Eusebius seems to allude here to Genesis 36:8, though this is not noted in Ziegler's notes. See also Jeremy Schott, 'Textuality and territorialization: Eusebius' exegeses of Isaiah, and empire', in Aaron P. Johnson and Jeremy Schott, eds, *Eusebius of Caesarea: Tradition and Innovations* (Washington DC: Center for Hellenic Studies Press, 2013), pp. 169–88.

73 *Comm.Isa.* 1.80, p. 143.14.

74 Young, *Biblical Exegesis*, pp. 130–7.

75 *Comm.Isa.* 1.72, pp. 112.34–113.10.

76 *Comm.Isa.* 1.72, p. 113.23–25.

77 See *GEI* 8.11 (PG 22.1136d).

78 See: *GEI* 6.13 (PG 22.1109d); 7.5 (PG 22.1100a); 7.13 (PG 22.1109d–1112a); 8.3 (PG 22.1125c).

79 *Comm.Isa.* 1.72, p. 113.17–18.

80 For a date of 327, see Timothy Barnes, *Constantine and Eusebius* (Cambridge, MA: Harvard University Press, 1981), p. 228. For a date of 331, see David Sutherland Wallace-Hadrill, *Eusebius of Caesarea* (London: A.R. Mowbray & Co., Ltd., 1960), p. 56, n. 9. It is not entirely certain from the Greek text of the work's preface whether it comprised four books or only four sections, since Eusebius states, 'in the one before this I rendered the promised subjects,' and then he names the three sections/books; if they were all 'in the [work] before this [point]', then they could certainly be deemed books; otherwise, they might only be sections of 'the [book] before this one'. The translation of the preface by Notley and Safrai is inadequate and misleading.

81 Timothy Barnes, in *Constantine and Eusebius*, pp. 110–11, has argued for a much earlier date of *c*.293. Andrew Louth, in 'The date of Eusebius' *Historia ecclesiastica*', *Journal of Theological Studies* xli (1990), pp. 111–23, has defended the traditional later dating. See Erich Klostermann, eds., *Eusebius Werke*, vol. 4, *Gegen Marcell, Über die kirchliche Theologie*, Die griechischen christlichen Schriftsteller 14 (Leipzig: J.C. Hinrichs'sche Buchhandlung, 1906), pp. xi–xii.

82 *Onom.* praef. This third part of the original work may have been a map: '*ōs en graphē tupōi* [...] *tēn eikona diacharaxas*' ('I sketched out the image as if in the figured relief of a painting'). *Pace* Benjamin Isaac, 'Eusebius and the geography of Roman provinces', in D.L. Kennedy, ed., *The Roman Army in the East, Journal of Roman Archaeology Supplement 18* (Ann Arbor, MI: Journal of Roman Archaeology, 1996), pp. 153–67.

83 For the *Onomasticon* as a pilgrimage handbook, see Wallace-Hadrill, *Eusebius of Caesarea*, pp. 201–5.

84 See *Onom.*, 'Zeib', 'Kariathaeim', 'Chōba', respectively.

85 On Eusebius' sources, see R. Steven Notley and Ze'ev Safrai, *Eusebius, Onomasticon: A Triglott Edition with Notes and Commentary* (Leiden: Brill, 2005), pp. xi–xxxvii (though I am hesitant to accept fully their claim that Eusebius' own compositional work was limited to the entries of names from the Gospels).

86 See *Onom.*, 'Bēthaabara', 'Bēthphagē', 'Gergesa', 'Gethsimanē', 'Ōr', respectively. For the tombs, see: 'Gaas' and 'Thamnathsara' (Joshua); 'Ephratha' (Rachel); 'Eltheke' (Amos); 'Keeila' (Habakkuk, or 'Ambakoum'); 'Suchem' (Joseph).

87 The *Gospel Canons* are usefully printed in the Nestle–Aland Greek New Testament, the standard critical edition. See *Novum Testamentum Graece* (Stuttgart: Deutsche Bibelgesellschaft, 1898–1993), pp. 84–9 (of the preliminary section).

88 See the *Epistle to Carpianus* 3–14. For a discussion and translation, see Harold Oliver, 'The epistle of Eusebius to Carpianus: Textual tradition and translation', *Novum Testamentum* iii (1959), pp. 138–45.

89 See Cook, *Interpretation*, pp. 136–8, 147, 289, 300.

90 *ad Steph.* 1.1. This initially hostile tone would seem at first to place it in a similar category as Porphyry's *Letter to Anebo*, which furnished a series of questions critical of

traditional Egyptian religion and theological conceptions. See A.P. Johnson, *Religion and Identity*, Chapter 1. The apparently hostile tone of the *ad Steph.* quickly gives way, however, to a more irenic attitude, and so the parallel cannot be pushed too far.
91   *ad Steph.* 16.5; *ad Marin.* praef.
92   See: Claudio Zamagni, *Les Questions et réponses sur les évangiles d'Eusèbe de Césarée*, Ph.D. dissertation (University of Lausanne, 2003); 'New perspectives on Eusebius' *Questions and Answers on the Gospels*: The manuscripts', in Aaron P. Johnson and Jeremy Schott, eds, *Eusebius of Caesarea: Tradition and Innovations* (Washington DC: Center for Hellenic Studies Press, 2013), pp. 239–61.
93   *ad Steph.* 7.5.
94   *ad Steph.* 8.
95   *ad Steph.* 7.4–5.
96   *ad Steph.* 7.1–2; 9.1.
97   Morlet, *Démonstration évangélique*, pp. 477–8.

IV. WRITING PAST AND PEOPLEHOOD

1   Most recently, see: Erica Carotenuto, *Tradizione e innovazione nella Historia ecclesiastica di Eusebio di Cesarea* (Naples: Istituto Italiano per gli Studi Storici, 2001); Marie Verdoner, *Narrated Reality: The Historia Ecclesiastica of Eusebius of Caesarea* (Frankfurt am Main: Peter Lang, 2011); Sébastien Morlet, 'Écrire l'histoire selon Eusèbe de Césarée', *L'Information littéraire* lvii (2005), pp. 3–15; 'Entre histoire et exégèse. Réflexions sur la logique narrative du livre I de l'*Histoire ecclésiastique* d'Eusèbe', *Adamantius* xiv (2008), pp. 191–8; Sébastien Morlet and Lorenzo Perrone, eds, *Eusèbe de Césarée. Histoire ecclésiastique. Commentaire, Tome 1: Études d'introduction. Anagôgê* (Paris: Les Belles Lettres; Les Éditions du Cerf, 2012). See also the relevant essays in Aaron P. Johnson and Jeremy Schott, eds, *Eusebius of Caesarea: Tradition and Innovations* (Washington DC: Center for Hellenic Studies Press, 2013).
2   *HE* 1.1.3. On the importance of approaching the work in terms of a *diēgēsis*, see Christoph Markschies, 'Eusebius als Schriftsteller: Beobachtungen zum sechsten Buch der Kirchengeschichte', in A.M. Castagno, ed., *La biografia di Origene fra storia e agiografia* (Villa Verucchio: Pazzini Stampatore Editore, 2005), pp. 33–50; repr. in Christoph Markschies, *Origenes und sein Erbe: Gesammelte Studien* (Berlin: Walter de Gruyter, 2007).
3   *HE* 1.1.4 (translation adapted).
4   See David DeVore, 'Genre and Eusebius' *Ecclesiastical History*: Toward a focused debate', in Aaron P. Johnson and Jeremy Schott, eds, *Eusebius of Caesarea: Tradition and Innovations* (Washington DC: Center for Hellenic Studies Press, 2013), pp. 19–49.
5   See Jean Sirinelli, *Les Vues historiques d'Eusèbe de Césarée durant la période prénicéene* (Dakar: Université de Dakar, 1961), for the ways in which the historiographical visions of these two works were part of a larger project.

6   On Eusebius' use and divergence from earlier chronographers see: Alden A. Mosshammer, *The Chronicle of Eusebius and the Greek Chronographic Tradition* (Lewisburg, PA: Bucknell University Press, 1979); Adler, 'Eusebius' *Chronicle*', pp. 467–91.

7   I do not mean to deny that apologetic motives may have provided a stimulus for composing the *Chronicon* (on which, see: Richard Burgess, 'The dates and editions of Eusebius' *Chronici canones* and *Historia ecclesiastica*', *Journal of Theological Studies* xlviii (1997), pp. 488–97; William Adler, 'Eusebius' *Chronicle* and its legacy', in Harold W. Attridge and Gohei Hata, eds, *Eusebius, Christianity, and Judaism* (Detroit, MI: Wayne State University Press, 1992), pp. 467–91); only that Eusebius allowed other nations to have figures who had chronological precedence over Abraham.

8   Interestingly, Rome receives a column for the period from Aeneas to the end of the monarchy (years of Abraham 839–1504), but then is missing until the time of Julius Caesar (year of Abraham 1969). However, notes of historical events at Rome are periodically given in the margins.

9   Brian Croke, 'The originality of Eusebius' *Chronicle*', *American Journal of Philology* ciii (1982), p. 195.

10   For an assessment of what can be known of Eusebius' sources and where they might have originated, see Andrew Carriker, *The Library of Eusebius of Caesarea* (Leiden: Brill, 2003).

11   For a more nuanced account, see DeVore, 'Genre and Eusebius' *Ecclesiastical History*', pp. 19–49.

12   *HE* 1.5.2. See Luke 2:2.

13   Sébastien Morlet, 'Entre histoire et exégèse. Réflexions sur la logique narrative du livre I de l'*Histoire ecclésiastique* d'Eusèbe', *Adamantius* xiv (2008), pp. 191–8.

14   The influence of Josephus as a model should not be carried too far, however. See David DeVore, 'Eusebius' un-Josephan history: Two portraits of Philo of Alexandria and the sources of ecclesiastical historiography', *Studia Patristica*, forthcoming.

15   See for example: Michael Hollerich, 'Religion and politics in the writings of Eusebius: Reassessing the first "court theologian"', *Church History* lix (1990), pp. 309–25; Aaron P. Johnson, *Ethnicity and Argument in Eusebius' Praeparatio evangelica* (Oxford: Oxford University Press, 2006), pp. 174–92. Recent work in general may be moving away from the 'court theologian' model even when not directly targeting it as such. See for example: Teresa Morgan, 'Eusebius of Caesarea and Christian historiography', *Athenaeum* xciii (2005), pp. 193–208; Valerio Neri, 'Romani, greci, barbari: identità etniche ed universalismi nell'opera di Eusebio di Cesarea', *Adamantius* xvi (2010), pp. 63–87, especially pp. 74–85.

16   See Erica Carotenuto, *Tradizione e innovazione nella Historia ecclesiastica di Eusebio di Cesarea* (Naples: Istituto Italiano per gli Studi Storici, 2001).

17   On the visual impression (the *mise en page*) of the *Chronicon*, see Anthony Grafton and Megan Williams, *Christianity and the Transformation of the Book* (Cambridge, MA: Harvard University Press, 2006).

18   See: Arthur Droge, 'The apologetic dimensions of the *Ecclesiastical History*', in

Harold W. Attridge and Gohei Hata, eds, *Eusebius, Christianity, and Judaism* (Detroit, MI: Wayne State University Press, 1992), pp. 492–509; Marie Verdoner, 'Transgeneric crosses. Apologetics in the Church history of Eusebius', in Anders-Christian Jacobsen and Jörg Ulrich, eds, *Three Greek Apologists. Drei griechische Apologeten* (Frankfurt am Main: Peter Lang, 2007), pp. 75–92.

19   The fullest account of Eusebius' use of quotations in the *HE* is Carotenuto, *Tradizione e innovazione*.

20   *HE* 2.10; 2.12; 2.25; 3.36; 4.8; 6.19.

21   *HE* 4.18; 5.16–17; 5.24; 5.28; 6.11; 6.19.

22   See Morgan, 'Eusebius of Caesarea and Christian historiography'.

23   *HE* 2.13; 2.15; 2.23; 3.36; 3.10; 4.23; 4.25; 5.19.

24   *HE* 6.12, where Serapion attacks the Gospel of Peter.

25   *HE* 3.7.9; 3.32.2; 4.15.1.

26   See for example *HE* 3.23.

27   *HE* 5.1; though see *HE* 5.2 on the profit to be derived from later quotations.

28   See *HE* 1.13.5 and 6.20.1, respectively.

29   For reading as a kind of walking, see Michel de Certeau, *The Practice of Everyday Life* (Berkeley, CA: University of California Press, 1984), pp. 169, 174. For reading as a tour of the Caesarean library, see Sabrina Inowlocki, 'Eusebius' construction of a Christian culture in an apologetic context: Reading the *Praeparatio evangelica* as a library', in Sabrina Inowlocki and Claudio Zamagni, eds, *Reconsidering Eusebius* (Leiden: Brill, 2011), pp. 199–223.

30   *HE* 3.6.1; 3.23.5; 5.19.3.

31   *HE* 5.20.3.

32   An example of the latter is the so-called *Testimonium Flavianum*. While I am not entirely convinced, the best argument in favour of the *Testimonium*'s being a Eusebian forgery is Ken Olson, 'A Eusebian reading of the *Testimonium Flavianum*', in Aaron P. Johnson and Jeremy Schott, eds, *Eusebius of Caesarea: Tradition and Innovations* (Washington DC: Center for Hellenic Studies Press, 2013), pp. 97–114.

33   See Andrew Louth, 'Introduction', in G.A. Williamson, trans., *Eusebius: History of the Church* (London: Penguin, 1990), p. xxiii.

34   See especially Robert Grant, *Eusebius as Church Historian* (Oxford: Clarendon Press, 1980). For sound criticism of Grant, see Thomas Heyne, 'The devious Eusebius? An evaluation of the *Ecclesiastical History* and its critics', *Studia Patristica* xlvi (2010), pp. 325–31.

35   See: Burgess, 'Dates and editions', pp. 471–97; William Adler, *Time Immemorial: Archaic History and its Sources in Christian Chronography from Julius Africanus to George Syncellus* (Washington DC: Dumbarton Oaks, 1989), pp. 69–70.

36   See Verdoner, 'Transgeneric crosses'.

37   *HE* 1.1.1–2.

38   Josephus, *Antiquities*, 20.11.2.

39   *HE* 1.4.2.

40   *HE* 1.3.10. As Eusebius himself notes at *HE* 1.2.27 – although the allusion is missed in Kirsopp Lake's translation – his discussion here draws on his earlier

work, the *Prophetic Selections* (which is the surviving portion of the *Introduction*). See Chapter 3.

41 *HE* 1.2.1; 1.2.3. On Eusebius' theology of Christ as the Word (Logos), see Chapter 5.

42 *HE* 1.4.4–6.

43 See: *HE* 2.praef.1; DeVore, 'Genre and Eusebius' *Ecclesiastical History*'.

44 Two seemingly anomalous writers are included along with the many Christian writers: Josephus (see *HE* 3.9) and Philo (see *HE* 2.18). Their inclusion is due primarily to their usefulness in elucidating the other themes of Eusebius' work, especially the destruction of the Jews of Judea – see Michael Hardwick, *Josephus as an Historical Source in Patristic Literature through Eusebius* (Atlanta, GA: Scholars Press, 1989), pp. 69–102, 119–25. In addition, as one of the greatest allegorical exegetes of the Hebrew Scriptures, Philo received a prominent place both in the *History* and in the *Preparation*. See Sabrina Inowlocki, 'Eusebius of Caesarea's *Interpretatio Christiana* of Philo's *De vita contemplativa*', *Harvard Theological Review* xcvii (2004), pp. 305–28.

45 Until the very recent examination of David DeVore, *Roman Society, Greek Historiographies, and Christian Brilliance in the Ecclesiastical History of Eusebius of Caesarea*, Ph.D. dissertation (University of California, Berkeley, 2013). See also the limited discussions of: Arnaldo Momigliano, 'Pagan and Christian historiography in the fourth century', in Arnaldo Momigliano, ed., *The Conflict Between Paganism and Christianity in the Fourth Century* (Oxford: Clarendon Press, 1963), pp. 79–99; David Dungan, *Constantine's Bible* (Minneapolis, MN: Fortress Press, 2006), pp. 38–42 (which is otherwise frequently misleading and inaccurate).

46 See Robert Grant, 'Eusebius and his lives of Origen', in *Forma futuri. Studi in onore del Cardinale Michele Pellegrino* (Turin: Bottega d'Erasmo, 1975), pp. 635–49; Patricia Cox, *Biography in Late Antiquity* (Berkeley, CA: University of California Press, 1983).

47 *HE* 6.2.2.

48 For a perceptive literary analysis of this theme, see James Corke-Webster, 'Mothers and martyrdom: Familial piety and the model of the Maccabees in Eusebius of Caesarea's *Ecclesiastical History*', in Aaron P. Johnson and Jeremy Schott, eds, *Eusebius of Caesarea: Tradition and Innovations* (Washington DC: Center for Hellenic Studies Press, 2013), pp. 51–82.

49 Eusebius admits his later death under Gallus. See *HE* 7.1.1.

50 *HE* 6.39.5 (translation adapted).

51 *HE* 5.praef.3–4.

52 On the development of the notion of heresy, see Alain Le Boulluec, *La Notion d'hérésie* (Paris: Études augustiniennes, 1985); in Eusebius, see Meike Willing, *Eusebius von Cäsarea als Häreseograph* (Berlin: Walter de Gruyter, 2008).

53 See *HE* 5.16.12–13. For important exceptions, see *HE* 4.15.46; 5.16.22; 7.12.

54 See Markschies, 'Eusebius als Schriftsteller'.

55 This same argument recurs in Eusebius' *On the Feast of Pascha*; for discussion and translation of this short treatise, see Mark DelCogliano, 'The promotion of the Constantinian agenda in Eusebius of Caesarea's *On the Feast of Pascha*', in Sabrina

Inowlocki and Claudio Zamagni, eds, *Reconsidering Eusebius* (Leiden: Brill, 2011), pp. 39–68.

56   See *HE* 3.6; 3.8.

57   *HE* 4.6.4. See also *HE* 2.12.3; 6.20.1; 7.5.1. For the continued use of 'Jerusalem', see for example: 3.22.1; 3.32.1; 3.35; 4.5.1.

58   *HE* 4.6.4 (my translation).

59   See Andrew Clay, *A Commentary on Eusebius of Caesarea, Ecclesiastical History, Book VIII*, Ph.D. dissertation (University of Colorado, 2012).

60   See: Eduard Schwartz, ed., *Eusebius Werke*, vol. 2 (parts 1–3), *Die Kirchengeschichte*, Die griechischen christlichen Schriftsteller 9.1–3 (Leipzig: J.C. Hinrichs'sche Buchhandlung, 1909); Timothy Barnes, *Constantine and Eusebius* (Cambridge, MA: Harvard University Press, 1981), pp. 148–63; *Early Christian Hagiography and Roman History* (Tübingen: Mohr Siebeck, 2010), pp. 12, 43 (n. 1); *Constantine: Dynasty, Religion and Power in the Later Roman Empire* (Oxford: Wiley-Blackwell, 2011), pp. 11–12 (where Barnes cites his earlier *Constantine and Eusebius* without clarifying the ways in which he has softened his position in light of more recent scholarship, especially by Andrew Louth and Richard Burgess; see next note); Grant, *Eusebius as Church Historian*; William Tabernee, 'Eusebius' "Theology of Persecution": As seen in the various editions of his Church history', *Journal of Early Christian Studies* v (1997), pp. 319–34.

61   Andrew Louth, 'The date of Eusebius' *Historia ecclesiastica*', *Journal of Theological Studies* xli (1990), pp. 111–23; Burgess, 'Dates and editions'.

62   Purported changes in Eusebius' theology of persecution are made the basis for determining multiple editions in Tabernee, 'Eusebius' "Theology of Persecution"'.

63   *GEI* 6 (= *Ecl.Proph.* 1).8 (PG 22.1048c).

64   The work is, nonetheless, mentioned at *HE* 4.15.47.

65   The Greek fragments were published in the lower register of Eduard Schwartz's edition. For discussion, see Schwartz, *Kirchengeschichte*, pp. xlix–l, lix–lx. The Syriac text and an English translation were published in William Cureton, *History of the Martyrs of Palestine by Eusebius Bishop of Caesarea, Discovered in a Very Ancient Syriac Manuscript* (London: Williams & Norgate, 1861).

66   *M.Pal.* 13.14 (Greek). See: Schwartz, *Kirchengeschichte*, pp. lix; Timothy Barnes, 'The editions of Eusebius' Ecclesiastical History', *Greek, Roman and Byzantine Studies* xxi (1980), pp. 191–201; Clay, *Commentary*, pp. 14–16.

67   The Syriac translation seems to be the most thorough in this regard, and furthermore removes the name of Crispus (Constantine's son who was executed by his father in 326).

68   See for example *HE* 9.9.1; 9.9.12; 9.9a.12; 9.10.3; 9.11.8.

69   See for example *HE* 9.9.1; 9.9.12.

70   The most thorough discussion of the manuscripts remains that of Schwartz, *Kirchengeschichte*, although this is confused by the introduction of hypothetical arguments for multiple editions based not on the manuscript witnesses but on psychological explanations. For corrections and updates, see Matthieu Cassin, 'Tradition manuscrite grecque de *L'Histoire ecclésiastique*', in Sébastien Morlet and

Lorenzo Perrone, eds, *Eusèbe de Césarée. Histoire ecclésiastique. Commentaire, Tome 1: Études d'introduction. Anagôgê* (Paris: Les Belles Lettres; Les Éditions du Cerf, 2012), pp. 209–42. The brief discussion of Kirsopp Lake (in the introduction to his translation) is useful as a preliminary introduction. See also the helpful list of differences in Barnes, 'The editions of Eusebius' *Ecclesiastical History*', pp. 196–7. For important criticisms of Schwartz, see: Satoshi Toda, 'The Syriac version of Eusebius' *Ecclesiastical History* revisited', *Studia Patristica* xlvi (2010), pp. 333–8; Hugh Jackson Lawlor, *Eusebiana* (Amsterdam: Philo Press, 1973).

71 Matthieu Cassin, Muriel Debié, Michel-Yves Perrin and Giusto Traina in 'La question des éditions de *l'Histoire ecclésiastique* et le livre X', in Sébastien Morlet and Lorenzo Perrone, eds, *Eusèbe de Césarée. Histoire ecclésiastique. Commentaire, Tome 1: Études d'introduction. Anagôgê* (Paris: Les Belles Lettres; Les Éditions du Cerf, 2012), pp. 202–6, have also recently argued for an economic approach that posits two 'states' or 'stages' of the text, which was composed over time, rather than two 'editions' of the text. I am grateful to Sébastien Morlet for kindly sending me this chapter before its publication.

72 Richard Burgess, 'The dates and editions of Eusebius' *Chronici canones* and *Historia ecclesiastica*', *Journal of Theological Studies* xlviii (1997), pp. 495–7.

73 While *HE* 8.16.1 is very similar to 1.1.2, it is not identical. There is no reason to suppose that Eusebius could not have recalled his earlier statement when writing Book 8 in a single composition, rather than positing that one or both statements are the result of a later editorial revision.

74 See Lawlor, *Eusebiana*, pp. 244–5.

75 See *VC* 1.55.1; 1.59.2 (aside from variations in the precise spelling, none of the manuscript witnesses for these passages differ in the inclusion of Licinius' name). Oblique designations of Licinius as the unnamed 'tyrant' or the 'God-hater' occur at *VC* 1.49.2; 1.51.2; 2.18. See the anonymous references to Galerius and Maximinus Daia at *VC* 1.57–8.

76 Schwartz, *Kirchengeschichte*, p. l. It should be noted that the term *damnatio memoriae* is itself a modern coinage (though the removal of names from documents was practised) and there are certain important difficulties in the ancient evidence for such a practice. See Cassin, Debié and Perrin, 'La question des éditions', pp. 194–5.

77 Themistius, *Oration* 6.83b. See earlier Julian, *Symposium* 328d–329a (though he had been named once, at 315d).

78 See Matthieu Cassin, 'Tradition manuscrite grecque de *L'Histoire ecclésiastique*', in Sébastien Morlet and Lorenzo Perrone, eds, *Eusèbe de Césarée. Histoire ecclésiastique. Commentaire, Tome 1: Études d'introduction. Anagôgê* (Paris: Les Belles Lettres; Les Éditions du Cerf, 2012), pp. 211–37, which revises Schwartz's earlier datings of the manuscripts.

79 See Toda, 'Syriac version', p. 334.

80 Lawlor, *Eusebiana*, p. 245. See also the comprehensive list of occurrences of Licinius in the *HE* in Cassin, Debié and Perrin, 'La question des éditions', pp. 193–4.

81 Lawlor, *Eusebiana*, pp. 246–8.

82 *HE* 8.13.6.

83 See Schwartz, *Kirchengeschichte*, pp. lix–lx, where it is noted that the longer version contains the addition of material about the construction of martyria and seems to have less of a sense of immediacy. Unfortunately, Timothy Barnes' argument in *Early Christian Hagiography*, pp. 389–90, for the reverse order of the two recensions does not address Schwartz's argument.

84 For the early date, see Marilena Amerise, 'Note sulla datazione del panegirico per l'inaugurazione della basilica di Tiro', *Adamantius* xiv (2008), pp. 229–34. For the later dating (based on dating the Battle of Cibalae), see: Timothy Barnes, 'Lactantius and Constantine', *Journal of Roman Studies* lxiii (1973), pp. 29–46; *Constantine and Eusebius* (Cambridge, MA: Harvard University Press, 1981), pp. 66–7; Noel Lenski, 'The reign of Constantine', in Noel Lenski, ed., *The Cambridge Companion to the Age of Constantine* (Cambridge: Cambridge University Press, 2006), pp. 73–4.

85 That the dossier of imperial documents contained in 10.5–7 would belong to the edition sent to Paulinus is confirmed by the declaration at 10.2.2, that he would include them 'at the proper place in this work'.

86 See Cassin, Debié and Perrin, 'La question des éditions', pp. 198–9. In favour of a gradual, accumulative mode of composition, see pp. 200–2.

87 Were there similar forms of address in the earlier books, or is this a belated dedication? The possibility that there were similar forms of address in the earlier books appears unlikely, since the preface to the *Onomasticon* refers to the earlier books as if they were an independent project of Eusebius, while the present book is in response to a 'proposal', *prothesis*, put forth by Paulinus, which Eusebius is now answering.

88 That is, the final sentence of Book 9 as preserved in the ATERM manuscripts.

89 For a criticism of Schwartz on the related problem of the divergent manuscript witnesses to the ending of Book 9 and the opening of Book 10, see Lawlor, *Eusebiana*, pp. 250–3.

90 See *PE* 1.10.54–5, 42b–d; 2.praef.1–4, 43d–44b.

91 Clay, *Commentary*, pp. 17–29.

92 However, see Cassin, Debié and Perrin, 'La question des éditions'.

93 Burgess, 'Dates and editions', p. 499. Lightfoot's early suggestion of two editions was otherwise not followed by subsequent twentieth-century scholarship. Even Andrew Louth, in 'The date of Eusebius' *Historia ecclesiastica*', who had performed such an admirable reassessment of much of that scholarship, allowed for three editions.

94 See especially David Olster, *Roman Defeat, Christian Response, and the Literary Construction of the Jew* (Philadelphia, PA: University of Pennsylvania Press, 1984).

V. ARTICULATING THE WORD

1 See for example: Hendrik Berkhof, *Die Theologie des Eusebius von Caesarea* (Amsterdam: Uitgeversmaatschappij Holland, 1939), p. 38 (Eusebius was unoriginal and had a 'limited intellect'); George Léonard Prestige, *God in Patristic Thought* (London: SPCK, 1936), p. xxvii (Eusebius was 'a rather confused theologian').

2   For Marcellus' position (which is arguably not Sabellian), see: Joseph Lienhard, *Contra Marcellum: Marcellus of Ancyra and Fourth-Century Theology* (Washington DC: Catholic University of America Press, 1999), pp. 47–68; Sara Parvis, *Marcellus of Ancyra and the Lost Years of the Arian Controversy, 325–345* (Oxford: Oxford University Press, 2006), pp. 30–7. On Asterius, see: Lienhard, *Contra Marcellum*, pp. 89–101; Parvis, *Marcellus of Ancyra*, pp. 111–16; Mark DelCogliano, 'Eusebius of Caesarea on Asterius of Cappadocia in the anti-Marcellan writings: A case study of mutual defense within the Eusebian alliance', in Aaron P. Johnson and Jeremy Schott, eds, *Eusebius of Caesarea: Tradition and Innovations* (Washington DC: Center for Hellenic Studies Press, 2013), pp. 263–87; Markus Vinzent, *Asterius von Kappadokien: Die theologischen Fragmente, Einleitung, kritischer Text, Übersetzung und Kommentar* (Leiden: Brill, 1993). Though Eusebius proved a powerful ally of Asterius in his anti-Marcellan works, an over-emphasis on external ecclesio-political factors should not occlude the clear ways in which those writings continued his pre-Nicene theological concerns; in any case, we cannot determine whether Eusebius would have been 'incandescent with rage' when he read Marcellus' work against Asterius. See Parvis, *Marcellus of Ancyra*, p. 123.

3   *Pace* R.P.C. Hanson, *The Search for the Christian Doctrine of God* (London: T&T Clark, 1988), p. 59. For his distance from Arius, see: Kelley Spoerl, 'Anti-Arian polemic in Eusebius of Caesarea's *Ecclesiastical Theology*', *Studia Patristica* xxxii (1997), pp. 33–8; Mark DelCogliano, 'Eusebian theologies of the Son as the image of God before 341', *Journal of Early Christian Studies* xiv/4 (2006), pp. 459–84. For problems with the very label 'Arians' or even of 'Eusebians' see: Lienhard, *Contra Marcellum*, pp. 28–46; Lewis Ayres, *Nicaea and Its Legacy* (Oxford: Oxford University Press, 2006), pp. 52–61; David Gwynn, *The Eusebians: The Polemic of Athanasius of Alexandria and the Construction of the Arian Controversy* (Oxford: Oxford University Press, 2007). This is not to deny that Arius may have been able to tap into existing socio-ecclesiastical networks. See Parvis, *Marcellus of Ancyra*, pp. 39–50.

4   For a sensitive treatment, see Colm Luibhéid, *Eusebius of Caesarea and the Arian Crisis* (Dublin: Irish Academic Press, 1981).

5   See Ilaria Ramelli, 'Origen, Eusebius, the doctrine of apokatastasis, and its relation to Christology', in Aaron P. Johnson and Jeremy Schott, eds, *Eusebius of Caesarea: Tradition and Innovations* (Washington DC: Center for Hellenic Studies Press, 2013), pp. 307–23.

6   See Timothy Barnes, *Constantine and Eusebius* (Cambridge, MA: Harvard University Press, 1981), pp. 224–44.

7   See *PE* 11.18.

8   Plato, *Epistles* 2.312d, cited by Eusebius at *PE* 11.20.2, 541c.

9   See Aaron P. Johnson, *Religion and Identity in Porphyry of Tyre: The Limits of Hellenism in Late Antiquity* (Cambridge: Cambridge University Press, 2013).

10   See *PE* 11.17. See also Marco Zambon, 'Edizione e prima circolazione degli scritti di Plotino: Porfirio ed Eusebio di Cesarea', in Walter Beierwaltes and Matteo Bianchetti, eds, *Plotino e l'ontologia* (Milan: Albo versorio, 2006), pp. 55–78. The

fact that one of these two treatises was *Enneads* 5.1 is of some significance, since it was in this treatise that Plotinus expressed, at *Enneads* 5.1.3.7, the distinction between internal *logos* (*endiathetos logos*) and uttered *logos* (*prophorikos logos*), which would play a significant role in Eusebius' polemic against Marcellus, as we shall see. For discussion of the Plotinus passage, see: John Rist, *Plotinus: Road to Reality* (Cambridge: Cambridge University Press, 1967), pp. 100–1; David Robertson, *Word and Meaning in Ancient Alexandria* (Burlington, VT: Ashgate, 2008), pp. 67–70.

11   See *PE* 11.20.

12   See: Friedo Ricken, 'Die Logoslehre des Eusebios von Caesarea und der Mittelplatonismus', *Theologie und Philosophie* xlii (1967), pp. 341–58; Holger Strutwolf, *Die Trinitätstheologie und Christologie des Euseb von Caesarea* (Göttingen: Vandenhoeck & Ruprecht, 1999).

13   See *c.Marc.* 1.2.30; 1.3.9; 1.3.12–13.

14   As rightly noted in Jon Robertson, *Christ as Mediator: A Study of the Theologies of Eusebius of Caesarea, Marcellus of Ancyra, and Athanasius of Alexandria* (Oxford: Oxford University Press, 2007), pp. 41–3. See also Rebecca Lyman, *Christology and Cosmology: Models of Divine Activity in Origen, Eusebius and Athanasius* (Oxford: Clarendon Press, 1993), pp. 99–100.

15   These verses are quoted together at *DE* 5.praef, 210d.

16   Marcellus, quoted at *c.Marc.* 2.2.38. See *Eccl.Theol.* 1.17.6–7.

17   *Eccl.Theol.* 1.17.1–3; 1.17.6–7; 2.8.1; 2.11.1; 2.24.3. For Porphyry, too, the *logos prophorikos* was 'indicative' (*sēmantikon*) of inner emotions. See *On Abstinence from Eating Meat* 3.3.1–3.

18   His rejection of *en* to identify the relation of the Son to the Father only seems to have arisen during his debate with Marcellus; earlier, Eusebius himself had declared that the Word was *with* God (see *DE* 5.4, 225c).

19   The notion of the Logos as having a distinct hypostasis goes back to Clement. See: Mark Edwards, 'Clement of Alexandria and his doctrine of the Logos', *Vigiliae Christianae* liv (2000), pp. 159–77; David Robertson, *Word and Meaning in Ancient Alexandria* (Burlington, VT: Ashgate, 2008), p. 30.

20   See: Plotinus, *Enneads* 5.1.3; Porphyry, *Against the Christians*, frag. 86.

21   Eusebius had already rejected the application of the notion of *prophorikos logos* to the Logos at *DE* 5.5.8, 230a.

22   See *DE* 4.5, 153c.

23   See Ricken, 'Die Logoslehre', pp. 349–50.

24   See R.E. Witt, 'The Plotinian Logos and its Stoic basis', *Classical Quarterly* xxv (1931), pp. 106–9.

25   See *PE* 7.3–4.

26   *Eccl.Theol.* 1.20.92–3; 1.20.95–6.

27   See *PE* 7.5.

28   *c.Marc.* 1.1.11. See *GEI* 6 (= *Ecl.Proph.* 1).9 (PG 22.1052c).

29   In this, Eusebius stands pointedly against Arius' collapsing of the begotten/made distinction. Later, Eusebius will be at special pains to explain that the language of

being made in Proverbs 8 still applies to the Son (= Wisdom) without, however, classifying the Son with any other made things.

30 Significantly, Basil of Caesarea's later identification of Marcellus as a Sabellian seems to follow closely that of Eusebius. See Joseph Lienhard, 'Basil of Caesarea, Marcellus of Ancyra, and "Sabellius"', *Church History* lviii (1989), pp. 157–67.

31 *Eccl.Theol.* 2.7.1–2. It may not necessitate positing two Gods, but Eusebius had himself posited a 'second God' in earlier works – see for example *GEI* 6 (= *Ecl. Proph.* 1).12 (PG 22.1068c). His works do, however, attempt to maintain a general consistency in speaking of the Son as God without the article (anarthrous) and the Father as God with the article (articular). In the quotations in the present chapter I have noted whether each usage of the title God is anarthrous or articular.

32 *c.Marc.* 1.4.26–7.

33 There is little evidence that Porphyry would have warmed to the identification. See A.P. Johnson, *Religion and Identity*. On Porphyry's thought compared to Atticus, see Marco Zambon, *Porphyre et le moyen-platonisme* (Paris: Vrin, 2002).

34 *Eccl.Theol.* 2.6.1.

35 See Porphyry, *Commentary on the Timaeus*, fr. 51.

36 Plotinus, *Enneads* 6.8.13.4. See: Rist, *Plotinus*, especially p. 79, on the problems associated with the necessity of emanation (or procession) and the divine will in Plotinus' thought; more briefly, Rebecca Lyman, *Christology and Cosmology: Models of Divine Activity in Origen, Eusebius and Athanasius* (Oxford: Clarendon Press, 1993), pp. 13–15.

37 *Eccl.Theol.* 2.6.2–3.

38 For the distinctiveness of Eusebius' account of divine will, see Lyman, *Christology and Cosmology*, pp. 94–8 (especially p. 95), 109–11.

39 See Marcellus at *c.Marc.* 2.3.29, where he also asserts that the 'form of a slave' mentioned by Paul in Philippians 2:7 was likewise a reference to Christ's body.

40 Marcellus at *c.Marc.* 2.3.24, 27–8.

41 See DelCogliano, 'Eusebian theologies of the Son'.

42 *c.Marc.* 2.3.25.

43 See *PE* 7.10.9–13, 316a–d.

44 Jeremy Schott, 'Quotations from Origen and the theologies of textuality in Eusebius' *Apology for Origen, Against Marcellus*, and *On Ecclesiastical Theology*' (unpublished paper delivered at the Society of Biblical Literature annual conference, Atlanta, GA, 2010).

45 See Plato, *Republic* 10.602c–d and 7.533d.

46 *Eccl.Theol.* 2.7.17.

47 *Eccl.Theol.* 2.17.3.

48 A.H. Armstrong, trans., *Plotinus: Ennead III*, Loeb Classical Library 442 (Cambridge, MA: Harvard University Press, 1967), 3.2.1.

49 *Eccl.Theol.* 2.21.8.

50 *Eccl.Theol.* 2.23.2.

51 *Eccl.Theol.* 2.23.3.

52 *Eccl.Theol.* 2.7.12–15. It may be significant that the term *theïkē* seems to occur first in Greek literature in the writings of Porphyry.

53 *Eccl.Theol.* 2.7.16.

54 For the text, which was earlier printed in Jean-Paul Migne, ed., Patrologiae cursus completus, Series Graecae, vol. 23 (Paris, 1857), see Torsten Krannich, Christoph Schubert and Claudia Sode, eds, *Die ikonoklastische Synode von Hiereia 754* (Tübingen: Mohr Siebeck, 2002). For the English translation, see Daniel Sahas, *Icon and Logos* (Toronto: University of Toronto Press, 1986). For a moderate defence of its attribution to our Eusebius, see Timothy Barnes, 'Notes on the letter of Eusebius to Constantia', *Studia Patristica* xlvi (2010), pp. 313–17. On its importance in constructions of Eusebius as an 'Arian' heretic, see the excellent study of David Gwynn, 'From iconoclasm to Arianism: The construction of Christian tradition in the Iconoclast Controversy', *Greek, Roman and Byzantine Studies* xlvii (2007), pp. 225–51.

55 *Eccl.Theol.* 3.2.27.

56 *Eccl.Theol.* 3.2.29.

57 Marcellus at *Eccl.Theol.* 3.2.28.

58 There is some uncertainty about how the various features presented by Eusebius here actually cohered in Marcellus' thought. See Parvis, *Marcellus of Ancyra*, pp. 34–7. For general discussion, see Lienhard, *Contra Marcellum*, pp. 58–61.

59 See Mark DelCogliano, 'Basil of Caesarea on Proverbs 8:22 and the sources of Pro-Nicene theology', *Journal of Theological Studies* lix (2008), pp. 183–90.

60 The following is translated from the LXX, which was Eusebius' base text.

61 *PE* 11.14.8–9, 532d.

62 *PE* 11.14, 533a.

63 Wisdom of Solomon at *PE* 11.14.10, 532d. See Ricken, 'Die Logoslehre', pp. 349–50 on Middle Platonist comparanda.

64 *Eccl.Theol.* 3.2.1.

65 *Eccl.Theol.* 3.2.3.

66 *Eccl.Theol.* 3.2.4. Eusebius' quotation here is from Proverbs 7:4: he has here moved beyond his focus on the passage from Proverbs 8. The 'your' is a reference to the human reader.

67 Though Eusebius had referred to the Son as a 'product' (*dēmiourgēma*) at *DE* 4.2.1, 146b, he otherwise avoided identifying the Son as a 'creature' (*ktisma*). See: James Stevenson, *Studies in Eusebius* (Cambridge: Cambridge University Press, 1929), p. 83; David Sutherland Wallace-Hadrill, *Eusebius of Caesarea* (London: A.R. Mowbray & Co., Ltd., 1960), pp. 129–30. The assertion that Eusebius calls the Son a *ktisma* at *DE* 4.5.13 and 5.1.8–9 are incorrect: see Gwynn, *The Eusebians*, p. 218. Even when he defends what he thought were Arius' views in the face of what he thought was Alexander of Alexandria's misrepresentations and refers to the Arian claim that the Son was 'the perfect creation [*ktisma*]' – which would seem to parallel directly Eusebius' phrase of the Son being 'the perfect product [*dēmiourgēma*]' at *DE* 4.2 – Eusebius emphasizes that Arius did not mean that the Son was like 'one of the created things [*ktismata*]' (*Epistle to Alexander* = Hans-Georg Opitz, ed.,

Athanasius Werke, vol. 3 (part 1), *Urkunden zur Geschichte des arianischen Streites* (Berlin: Walter de Gruyter, 1934), no. 7.2–3).

68   *Eccl.Theol.* 3.3.39; 3.3.46; 3.3.38.

69   *Eccl.Theol.* 3.3.49.

70   *Eccl.Theol.* 3.3.50. The language here is certainly Platonic: see Plato, *Timaeus* 28a. See also Strutwolf, *Die Trinitätstheologie*, pp. 190–1.

71   *Eccl.Theol.* 3.3.53.

72   Quoted at *Eccl.Theol.* 3.3.54. Most modern translations of this verse render the verb *poiein* as 'do' rather than 'make'. However, both meanings are equally possible; Eusebius clearly understands it in the latter sense here.

73   *Eccl.Theol.* 3.3.56, quoting John 5:20.

74   Ricken, 'Die Logoslehre', p. 349.

75   Plato, *Timaeus* 28a–29b.

76   See Philo and Clement of Alexandria, quoted at *PE* 11.24, 547a, and 11.25, 549b.

77   *Eccl.Theol.* 3.15.8. The quotation here comes from a discussion of the final state of humanity at the fulfilment of time, but remains appropriate for understanding the Word's/Wisdom's representational relationship to humanity in creation as well.

78   On Eusebius' notion of the Holy Spirit (pneumatology), see Volker Drecoll, 'How Binitarian/Trinitarian was Eusebius?', in Aaron P. Johnson and Jeremy Schott, eds, *Eusebius of Caesarea: Tradition and Innovations* (Washington DC: Center for Hellenic Studies Press, 2013), pp. 289–305.

79   Marcellus at *Eccl.Theol.* 3.4.2. It is possible that Eusebius offered a preliminary counter-description of the relation of monad-triad in his *Oration on Christ's Sepulchre*, delivered before Constantine at Constantinople in the heat of the debate with Marcellus. See *LC* 6.11–13.

80   *Eccl.Theol.* 3.4.3–5.

81   *Eccl.Theol.* 3.4.6–7; 3.5.10; 3.5.1–3.

82   *Eccl.Theol.* 3.5.12.

83   *Eccl.Theol.* 3.5.14. See also 3.5.16.

84   *Eccl.Theol.* 3.5.17. See Origen, *On First Principles* 1.3.5.

85   *Eccl.Theol.* 3.5.19.

86   *Eccl.Theol.* 3.5.19–21.

87   *Eccl.Theol.* 3.6.1.

88   *Eccl.Theol.* 3.5.22, drawing on 1 Corinthians 12:8–9.

89   *Eccl.Theol.* 3.6.1.

90   *Eccl.Theol.* 3.6.3, citing John 1:3.

VI. SPEAKING, TRUTH AND POWER

1   See: *PE* 1.4.4; *DE* 3.7, 139d–141a; 6.20, 299c–d; 7.2, 345a–b; *SC* 16.4–5; *Comm. Isa.* 1.26, pp. 14.26–15.10; 1.75, pp. 126.31–127.13. See also Aaron P. Johnson, *Ethnicity and Argument in Eusebius' Praeparatio evangelica* (Oxford: Oxford University Press, 2006), pp. 174–92.

2   See: *HE* 3.5.1; 3.7.4; 3.8.10–11; 4.6.1–4; *Comm.Isa.* 1.35, pp. 31.35–32.3; 1.42, pp. 42.32–43.2, 43.16–19. For the emperor Titus, see *Comm.Psalm.* 79 (PG 23.829d); 73:1 (PG 23.853b); 89:4 (PG 23.1133d).

3   See: *HE* 9.9.10–11; *VC* 1.28–31, 40; 2.7–9.

4   *GEI* 6. (= *Ecl.Proph.* 1).8 (PG 22.1048c).

5   *HE* 10.4.16.

6   *DE* 4.16, 182d.

7   For favourable mention of Crispus (who was later executed by his father on conspiracy charges), see *HE* 10.9.4.

8   *Comm.Isa.* 2.36, p. 316.9–25, citing Isaiah 49:23.

9   *Comm.Isa.* 1.28, pp. 20.29–21.5, citing Isaiah 2:18–21.

10 Constantine, the 'truly God-beloved and thrice-blessed emperor', called a synod to deal with Marcellus' dubious ideas (*c.Marc.* 2.4.29–31); on images of emperors as an example of the Son being an image of the Father, see *Eccl.Theol.* 2.23.3; 3.21.1. See: A.H. Armstrong, 'Some comments on the development of the theology of images', *Studia Patristica* ix/3 (1966), pp. 117–26; Ernst Kitzinger, 'The cult of images in the age before iconoclasm', *Dumbarton Oaks Papers* viii (1954), pp. 83–150.

11 See Michael Hollerich, 'Religion and politics in the writings of Eusebius: Reassessing the first "court theologian"', *Church History* lix (1990), pp. 309–25.

12 See Timothy Barnes, 'Panegyric, history and hagiography in Eusebius' *Life of Constantine*', in Rowan Williams, ed., *The Making of Orthodoxy: Essays in Honour of Henry Chadwick* (Cambridge: Cambridge University Press, 2002), pp. 94–114.

13 *VC* 4.64.2. See Averil Cameron, 'Eusebius of Caesarea and the rethinking of history', in E. Gabba, ed., *Tria corda: Scritti in onore di Arnaldo Momigliano* (Como: Biblioteca di Athenaeum, 1983), pp. 71–88.

14 See Averil Cameron, 'Eusebius' *Vita Constantini* and the construction of Constantine', in Simon Swain and M.J. Edwards, eds, *Portraits: Biographical Representation in the Greek and Latin Literature of the Roman Empire* (Oxford: Oxford University Press, 1997), pp. 145–74.

15 *VC* 1.1; 4.33, 46.

16 Ivar A. Heikel, ed., *Eusebius Werke*, vol. 1, *Über das Leben Constantins, Constantins Rede an die heilige Versammlung, Tricennatsrede an Constantin*, Die griechischen christlichen Schriftsteller 7 (Leipzig: J.C. Hinrichs'sche Buchhandlung, 1902), pp. civ–cvi, 223.

17 H.A. Drake, *In Praise of Constantine: A Historical Study and New Translation of Eusebius' Tricennial Orations* (Berkeley, CA: University of California Press, 1975), pp. 30–45.

18 *LC* praef.4.

19 *LC* 1.1 (translation adapted).

20 I use scare quotes here since this is a modern label that does not align with Eusebius' own use of the term, which is limited to pagan civic (*polis*) theology. See A.P. Johnson, *Ethnicity and Argument*, pp. 156–8.

21 *LC* 1.5.

22 *LC* 2.1–5.

23 See: E.R. Goodenough, 'The political philosophy of Hellenistic kingship', *Yale Classical Studies* i (1928), pp. 55–102; Glenn Chesnut, 'The ruler and the Logos in Neopythagorean, Middle Platonic, and Late Stoic political philosophy', *Aufstieg und Niedergang der römischen Welt* ii/16.2 (1978), pp. 1310–32.

24 See Drake, *In Praise of Constantine*, pp. 37–8.

25 *LC* 4.4.

26 *LC* 4.2–3.

27 *Latin Panegyrics* IV (X).7.3–4; 13.5.

28 *Latin Panegyrics* IV (X).14.

29 The battle is mentioned obliquely only at *LC* 9.8 and 13.

30 See *PE* 7.2.

31 *LC* 7.3–4, 6, 8, 10.

32 *LC* 7.13 (translation adapted).

33 *LC* 8.1–9.8.

34 See: Norman Baynes, 'Eusebius and the Christian empire', *Mélanges Bidez: Annuaire de l'Institut de philologie et d'histoire orientales et slaves* ii (1934), pp. 13–18; repr. in Norman Baynes, *Byzantine Studies and Other Essays* (London: University of London, 1955), pp. 168–72; J.-M. Sansterre, 'Eusèbe de Césarée et la naissance de la théorie "césaropapiste"', *Byzantion* xlii (1972), pp. 131–95, 532–94.

35 *LC* 4.2.

36 *LC* 5.5. See also *LC* 5.8; 6.9, 18–21.

37 *LC* 3.5.

38 *LC* 7.7.

39 *LC* 2.4; 10.4.

40 *LC* 4. See also *SC* 12.3.

41 *LC* 4.2.

42 *LC* 6.11–13.

43 *LC* 1.1; 3.4.

44 See *SC* 11.3–7. *Pace* Heikel, *Über das Leben Constantins*, p. cvi, who claims that the prologue to the *Tricennial Oration* applies to the entire combined speech of the *Tricennial Oration* proper (that is, Chapters 1–10) and the *Oration on Christ's Sepulchre* (that is, Chapters 11–18).

45 *SC* 11.3, 4.

46 *SC* 11.8–12, 16.

47 *SC* 16.7.

48 *LC* 7.3–4.

49 *SC* 13.6–8.

50 *SC* 14, 15.

51 *SC* 16.3; 15.8; 15.9; 15.13.

52 *VC* 1.1.3.

53 *VC* 1.2.3.

54 *VC* 1.3.2–4.

55 *VC* 1.9.2–3.

56 *VC* 1.10.4.

57 See Anna Wilson, 'Biographical models: The Constantinian period and beyond', in S.N.C. Lieu and Dominic Montserrat, eds, *Constantine: History, Historiography and Legend* (London and New York, NY: Routledge, 1998), pp. 112–21.

58 See Arnaldo Momigliano, *The Development of Greek Biography* (Cambridge, MA: Harvard University Press, 1993).

59 Isocrates, *Evagoras* 73. See Aaron P. Johnson, 'Ancestors as icons: The lives of Hebrew saints in Eusebius' *Praeparatio evangelica*', *Greek, Roman and Byzantine Studies* xliv (2004), pp. 245–64.

60 Plutarch, *Life of Alexander* 1.3 (my translation).

61 *VC* 1.10.1.

62 *VC* 3.10.3–4. See also *VC* 1.19; 4.53.

63 See Peter Van Nuffelen, 'Eusebius and images of truth in the *Life of Constantine*', in Aaron P. Johnson and Jeremy Schott, eds, *Eusebius of Caesarea: Tradition and Innovations* (Washington DC: Center for Hellenic Studies Press, 2013), pp. 133–49.

64 *VC* 3.3.1–2.

65 *VC* 4.15.1.

66 See Evelyn B. Harrison, 'The Constantinian portrait', *Dumbarton Oaks Papers* xxi (1967), pp. 79–96.

67 *VC* 1.11.1; 1.27–38; 2.6.2–2.8.3.

68 See Paul Stephenson, *Constantine: Roman Emperor, Christian Victor* (New York, NY: Overlook Press, 2009), pp. 182–7.

69 Michael S. Williams, *Authorised Lives in Early Christian Biography: Between Eusebius and Augustine* (Cambridge: Cambridge University Press, 2008).

70 See: *VC* 3.7–8, which quotes Acts 2:5, 9–11; *VC* 3.3, which quotes Isaiah 27:1.

71 See: Claudia Rapp, 'Imperial ideology in the making: Eusebius of Caesarea on Constantine as "Bishop"', *Journal of Theological Studies* xlix (1998), pp. 685–95; Anna Wilson, 'Biographical models: The Constantinian period and beyond', in S.N.C. Lieu and Dominic Montserrat, eds, *Constantine: History, Historiography and Legend* (London and New York, NY: Routledge, 1998), pp. 112–21; Finn Damgaard, 'Propaganda against propaganda: Revisiting Eusebius' use of the figure of Moses in the *Life of Constantine*', in Aaron P. Johnson and Jeremy Schott, eds, *Eusebius of Caesarea: Tradition and Innovations* (Washington DC: Center for Hellenic Studies Press, 2013).

72 See, respectively: Exodus 2:11–15 (*VC* 1.12; 1.20.2); Exodus 15 (*VC* 1.38.2–5); Exodus 9:12 (*VC* 2.11.2); Exodus 33:7–11 (*VC* 2.12.1).

73 *VC* 1.20.2.

74 See, respectively: Exodus 3 (*VC* 1.32); Noel Lenski, '*Libertas* and the fusion of Roman and Christian values', in G. Crifò, ed., *Atti dell'Accademia romanistica costantiniana XVIII 2007* (Perugia and Naples: Edizioni scientifiche italiana, 2011), pp. 245–6; Numbers 21:9 and John 3:14 (*VC* 2.6.2–2.9.3).

75 See: Exodus 17:8–13 (*VC* 4.5.2); Exodus 25–7 (*VC* 1.31). This possible parallel is suggested by Averil Cameron and Stuart G. Hall in *Eusebius: Life of Constantine* (Oxford: Clarendon Press, 1999), p. 205.

76 See, respectively: Exodus 18:13–26 (*VC* 1.44; 2.63; 3.6); *VC* 2.20–1; 2.45; 4.34, 36–7; 3.10.3; 4.25; 3.5.1–2.

77 *VC* 4.58–60. See Exodus 25–7. The association is not as close as it could be. See Eusebius' oration at Tyre for a sustained and explicit parallel between the tabernacle and a church building (*HE* 10.4); for discussion of that oration, see Jeremy Schott, 'Eusebius' *Panegyric on the Building of Churches* (*HE* 10.4.2–72): Aesthetics and the politics of Christian architecture', in Sabrina Inowlocki and Claudio Zamagni, eds, *Reconsidering Eusebius* (Leiden: Brill, 2011), pp. 177–98.

78 *VC* 4.18–20.

79 *VC* 4.62.2.

80 *VC* 4.36.2; 4.37.

81 *VC* 4.33.

82 *VC* 4.35.2; 4.35.3.

83 See, respectively, *VC* 1.19.1; 1.28.1; 2.8.2; 1.30.

84 *VC* 2.47.2.

85 Timothy Barnes, *Constantine: Dynasty, Religion and Power in the Later Roman Empire* (Oxford: Wiley-Blackwell, 2011), p. 76.

86 For the four letters, see *VC* 2.46; 3.61; 4.35; 4.36.

87 See Porphyry, *Life of Plotinus* 19.19–23; 10.33–9. See also John Finamore, 'Biography as self-promotion: Porphyry's *Vita Plotini*', *Dionysius* xxiii (2005), pp. 49–61.

88 Hans-Georg Opitz, ed., *Athanasius Werke*, vol. 3 (part 1), *Urkunden zur Geschichte des arianischen Streites* (Berlin: Walter de Gruyter, 1934), no. 22.

89 In the priority given to consensus, Eusebius was similar to Constantine himself. See the admirable study of H.A. Drake, *Constantine and the Bishops* (Baltimore, MD: Johns Hopkins University Press, 2000).

90 *VC* 2.63; 3.12.2.

91 *VC* 3.13.1.

92 *VC* 4.52.1.

93 *VC* 4.52.2.

94 For the textual relationship between the *HE* and *VC*, see the excellent commentary of Cameron and Hall, *Eusebius: Life of Constantine*.

95 *VC* 1.26.

96 *VC* 1.27.1; 1.36.1; 1.37.2; 1.27.2–1.32.3.

97 *VC* 1.33–5.

98 *VC* 1.51–4; 2.5; 1.49–50; 1.54–5; 1.57–8.

99 *VC* 1.5.1; 1.55.2; 3.1.7.

100 *VC* 3.1.2–7.

101 *VC* 2.19.2.

102 *VC* 1.26; 2.3; 2.11; 2.13; 1.45; 3.13.1; 3.23; 2.14.

103 See Richard Burgess, 'The summer of blood: The "Great Massacre" of 337 and the promotion of the sons of Constantine', *Dumbarton Oaks Papers* lxii (2008), pp. 5–51.

104 *VC* 4.62.3.

105 *VC* 4.67.3.

BIBLIOGRAPHY

Adler, William, *Time Immemorial: Archaic History and its Sources in Christian Chronography from Julius Africanus to George Syncellus* (Washington DC: Dumbarton Oaks, 1989).

—— 'Eusebius' *Chronicle* and its legacy', in Harold W. Attridge and Gohei Hata, eds, *Eusebius, Christianity, and Judaism* (Detroit, MI: Wayne State University Press, 1992), pp. 467–91.

—— 'Sextus Julius Africanus and the Roman Near East in the third century', *Journal of Theological Studies* lv/2 (2004), pp. 520–50.

—— 'Eusebius' critique of Africanus', in Martin Wallraff, ed., *Julius Africanus und die christliche Weltchronistik* (Berlin: Walter de Gruyter, 2006), pp. 147–60.

Amerise, Marilena, 'Note sulla datazione del panegirico per l'inaugurazione della basilica di Tiro', *Adamantius* xiv (2008), pp. 229–34.

Ando, Clifford, 'Pagan apologetics and Christian intolerance in the ages of Themistius and Augustine', *Journal of Early Christian Studies* iv (1996), pp. 171–207.

Armstrong, A.H., 'Some comments on the development of the theology of images', *Studia Patristica* ix/3 (1966), pp. 117–26.

Ayres, Lewis, *Nicaea and Its Legacy* (Oxford: Oxford University Press, 2006).

Bammel, Ernst, 'Der Jude des Celsus', in Ernst Bammel, *Judaica* (Tübingen: Mohr Siebeck, 1986), pp. 265–83.

Barnes, Timothy, 'Lactantius and Constantine', *Journal of Roman Studies* lxiii (1973), pp. 29–46.

—— 'Sossianus Hierocles and the antecedents of the "Great Persecution"', *Harvard Studies in Classical Philology* lxxx (1976), pp. 239–52.

—— 'The editions of Eusebius' *Ecclesiastical History*', *Greek, Roman and Byzantine Studies* xxi (1980), pp. 191–201.

—— *Constantine and Eusebius* (Cambridge, MA: Harvard University Press, 1981).

—— 'The two drafts of Eusebius' *Life of Constantine*', in Timothy Barnes, *From Eusebius to Augustine* (Aldershot: Ashgate, 1994), Chapter Twelve.

—— 'Panegyric, history and hagiography in Eusebius' *Life of Constantine*', in Rowan Williams, ed., *The Making of Orthodoxy: Essays in Honour of Henry Chadwick* (Cambridge: Cambridge University Press, 2002), pp. 94–114.

—— *Early Christian Hagiography and Roman History* (Tübingen: Mohr Siebeck, 2010).

—— 'Notes on the letter of Eusebius to Constantia', *Studia Patristica* xlvi (2010), pp. 313–17.

—— *Constantine: Dynasty, Religion and Power in the Later Roman Empire* (Oxford: Wiley-Blackwell, 2011).

Baynes, Norman, 'Eusebius and the Christian empire', *Mélanges Bidez: Annuaire de l'Institut de philologie et d'histoire orientales et slaves* ii (1934), pp. 13–18; repr. in Norman Baynes, *Byzantine Studies and Other Essays* (London: University of London, 1955), pp. 168–72.

Bechtle, Gerald, *The Anonymous Commentary on Plato's Parmenides* (Stuttgart: Verlag Paul Haupt, 1999).

Berkhof, Hendrik, *Die Theologie des Eusebius von Caesarea* (Amsterdam: Uitgeversmaatschappij Holland, 1939).

Blois, Lukas de, 'Emperorship in a period of crises: Changes in emperor worship, imperial ideology and perceptions of imperial authority in the Roman Empire in the third century A D', in Lukas de Blois, et al., eds, *The Impact of Imperial Rome on Religions, Ritual and Religious Life in the Roman Empire* (Leiden: Brill, 2006), pp. 268–78.

Borzì, Salvatore, 'Sull'autenticità del *Contra Hieroclem* di Eusebio di Cesarea', *Augustinianum* xliii (2003), pp. 397–416.

Boyarin, Daniel, 'The Christian invention of Judaism: The Theodosian empire and the rabbinic refusal of religion', in Hent de Vries, ed., *Religion: Beyond a Concept* (New York, NY: Fordham University Press, 2008), pp. 150–77.

Boys-Stones, George, *Post-Hellenistic Philosophy* (Oxford: Oxford University Press, 2001).

Brisson, Luc, 'Longinus Platonicus Philosophus et Philologus: I. Longinus Philosophus', *Aufstieg und Niedergang der römischen Welt* ii/36.7 (1994), pp. 5214–99.

Brock, Sebastian, 'Aspects of translation technique in antiquity', in Sebastian Brock, *Syriac Perspectives on Late Antiquity* (London: Variorum, 1984), Chapter Three.

Brown, Peter, 'Approaches to the religious crisis of the third century A D', *English Historical Review* lxxxiii (1968), pp. 542–58.

Burckhardt, Jacob, *The Age of Constantine the Great*, trans. Moses Hadas (Berkeley, CA: University of California Press, 1949).

Burgess, Richard, 'The dates and editions of Eusebius' *Chronici canones* and *Historia ecclesiastica*', *Journal of Theological Studies* xlviii (1997), pp. 471–504.

—— 'The summer of blood: The "Great Massacre" of 337 and the promotion of the sons of Constantine', *Dumbarton Oaks Papers* lxii (2008), pp. 5–51.

Cameron, Alan, *The Last Pagans of Rome* (Oxford: Oxford University Press, 2011).

Cameron, Averil, 'Eusebius of Caesarea and the rethinking of history', in E. Gabba, ed., *Tria corda: Scritti in onore di Arnaldo Momigliano* (Como: Biblioteca di Athenaeum, 1983), pp. 71–88.

—— 'Eusebius' *Vita Constantini* and the construction of Constantine', in Simon Swain and M.J. Edwards, eds, *Portraits: Biographical Representation in the Greek and Latin Literature of the Roman Empire* (Oxford: Oxford University Press, 1997), pp. 145–74.

Cameron, Averil and Stuart G. Hall, trans., *Eusebius: Life of Constantine* (Oxford: Clarendon Press, 1999).

Carotenuto, Erica, *Tradizione e innovazione nella Historia ecclesiastica di Eusebio di Cesarea* (Naples: Istituto Italiano per gli Studi Storici, 2001).

Carriker, Andrew, *The Library of Eusebius of Caesarea* (Leiden: Brill, 2003).

Cassin, Matthieu, 'Tradition manuscrite grecque de *L'Histoire ecclésiastique*', in Sébastien Morlet and Lorenzo Perrone, eds, *Eusèbe de Césarée. Histoire ecclésiastique. Commentaire, Tome 1: Études d'introduction. Anagôgê* (Paris: Les Belles Lettres; Les Éditions du Cerf, 2012), pp. 209–42.

Cassin, Matthieu, Muriel Debié and Michel-Yves Perrin, with Giusto Traina, 'La question des éditions de *l'Histoire ecclésiastique* et le livre X', in Sébastien Morlet and Lorenzo Perrone, eds, *Eusèbe de Césarée. Histoire ecclésiastique. Commentaire, Tome 1: Études d'introduction. Anagôgê* (Paris: Les Belles Lettres; Les Éditions du Cerf, 2012), pp. 185–207.

Certeau, Michel de, *The Practice of Everyday Life* (Berkeley, CA: University of California Press, 1984).

Chadwick, Henry, 'Ossius of Cordova and the presidency of the Council of Antioch, 325', *Journal of Theological Studies* ix (1958), pp. 292–304.

Chesnut, Glenn, 'The ruler and the Logos in Neopythagorean, Middle Platonic, and Late Stoic political philosophy', *Aufstieg und Niedergang der römischen Welt* ii/16.2 (1978), pp. 1310–32.

—— *The First Christian Histories* (Macon, GA: Mercer University Press, 1986).

Clay, Andrew, *A Commentary on Eusebius of Caesarea, Ecclesiastical History, Book VIII*, Ph.D. dissertation (University of Colorado, 2012).

Cleveland Coxe, Arthur, ed., *Ante-Nicene Fathers*, vol. 6 (New York, NY: The Christian Literature Company, 1890).

Cook, John G., *The Interpretation of the New Testament in Greco-Roman Paganism* (Tübingen: Mohr Siebeck, 2000).

Cooper, Kate, 'Christianity, private power, and the law from Decius to Constantine: The minimalist view', *Journal of Early Christian Studies* xix (2011), pp. 327–43.

Corke-Webster, James, 'Mothers and martyrdom: Familial piety and the model of the Maccabees in Eusebius of Caesarea's *Ecclesiastical History*', in Aaron P. Johnson and Jeremy Schott, eds, *Eusebius of Caesarea: Tradition and Innovations* (Washington DC: Center for Hellenic Studies Press, 2013), pp. 51–82.

Cox, Patricia, *Biography in Late Antiquity* (Berkeley, CA: University of California Press, 1983).

Croke, Brian, 'The originality of Eusebius' *Chronicle*', *American Journal of Philology* ciii (1982), pp. 195–200.

Cross, F.L., 'The Council of Antioch in 325 AD', *Church Quarterly Review* cxxviii (1939), pp. 49–76.

Cureton, William, trans., *History of the Martyrs of Palestine by Eusebius Bishop of Caesarea, Discovered in a Very Ancient Syriac Manuscript* (London: Williams & Norgate, 1861).

Curti, Carmelo, 'L'esegesi di Eusebio di Cesarea: caratteri e sviluppo', in Carmelo Curti, *Eusebiana, I: Commentarii in Psalmos* (Catania: Centro di studi sull'antico cristianesimo, 1987), pp. 195–213.

—— *Eusebiana, I: Commentarii in Psalmos* (Catania: Centro di studi sull'antico cristianesimo, 1987).

Damgaard, Finn, 'Propaganda against propaganda: Revisiting Eusebius' use of the figure of Moses in the *Life of Constantine*', in Aaron P. Johnson and Jeremy Schott, eds, *Eusebius of Caesarea: Tradition and Innovations* (Washington DC: Center for Hellenic Studies Press, 2013).

DelCogliano, Mark, 'Eusebian theologies of the Son as the image of God before 341', *Journal of Early Christian Studies* xiv/4 (2006), pp. 459–84.

—— 'Basil of Caesarea on Proverbs 8:22 and the sources of Pro-Nicene theology', *Journal of Theological Studies* lix (2008), pp. 183–90.

—— 'The promotion of the Constantinian agenda in Eusebius of Caesarea's *On the Feast of Pascha*', in Sabrina Inowlocki and Claudio Zamagni, eds, *Reconsidering Eusebius* (Leiden: Brill, 2011), pp. 39–68.

—— 'Eusebius of Caesarea on Asterius of Cappadocia in the anti-Marcellan writings: A case study of mutual defense within the Eusebian alliance', in Aaron P. Johnson and Jeremy Schott, eds, *Eusebius of Caesarea: Tradition and Innovations* (Washington DC: Center for Hellenic Studies Press, 2013), pp. 263–87.

DeVore, David, 'Genre and Eusebius' *Ecclesiastical History*: Toward a focused debate', in Aaron P. Johnson and Jeremy Schott, eds, *Eusebius of Caesarea: Tradition and Innovations* (Washington DC: Center for Hellenic Studies Press, 2013), pp. 19–49.

—— *Roman Society, Greek Historiographies, and Christian Brilliance in the Ecclesiastical History of Eusebius of Caesarea*, Ph.D. dissertation (University of California, Berkeley, 2013).

—— 'Eusebius' un-Josephan history: Two portraits of Philo of Alexandria and the sources of ecclesiastical historiography', *Studia Patristica*, forthcoming.

Digeser, Elizabeth Depalma, 'An oracle of Apollo at Daphne and the Great Persecution', *Classical Philology* xcix (2004), pp. 55–7.

—— 'The power of religious rituals: A philosophical quarrel on the eve of the Great Persecution', in Andrew Cain and Noel Lenski, eds, *The Power of Religion in Late Antiquity* (Burlington, VT: Ashgate, 2009), pp. 81–92.

—— 'Origen on the *Limes*: Rhetoric and the polarization of identity in the late third century', in Elizabeth DePalma Digeser and Robert M. Frakes, eds, *The Rhetoric of Power in Late Antiquity* (London: I.B.Tauris, 2010), pp. 197–218.

Dillon, John, 'Philosophy as a profession in Late Antiquity', in Simon Swain and M.J. Edwards, eds, *Approaching Late Antiquity* (Oxford: Oxford University Press, 2004), pp. 401–18.

———— 'The religion of the last Hellenes', in John Scheid, ed., *Rites et croyances dans les religions du monde romain*, Entretiens sur l'antiquité classique 53 (Geneva: Fondation Hardt, 2007), pp. 117–38.

Donaldson, Terence, ed., *Religious Rivalries and the Struggle for Success in Caesarea Maritima* (Waterloo: Wilfrid Laurier University Press, 2000).

Dorandi, Pierluigi, 'Testi e commenti, manuali e insegnamento: la forma sistematica e i metodi della filosofia in età postellenistica', *Aufstieg und Niedergang der römischen Welt* ii/36.7 (1994), pp. 5027–100.

Dorival, G., 'Remarques sur les *Eklogai prophétiques* d'Eusèbe de Césarée', in Bart Janssens, Bram Roosen and Peter Van Deun, eds, *Philomathestatos: Studies in Greek Patristic and Byzantine Texts Presented to Jacques Noret for his Sixty-Fifth Birthday* (Leuven: Peeters Publishers, 2004), pp. 203–24.

Drake, H.A., *In Praise of Constantine: A Historical Study and New Translation of Eusebius' Tricennial Orations* (Berkeley, CA: University of California Press, 1975).

———— 'Suggestions of date in Constantine's *Oration to the Saints*', *American Journal of Philology* cvi (1985), pp. 335–49.

———— *Constantine and the Bishops* (Baltimore, MD: Johns Hopkins University Press, 2000).

Drecoll, Volker, 'How Binitarian/Trinitarian was Eusebius?', in Aaron P. Johnson and Jeremy Schott, eds, *Eusebius of Caesarea: Tradition and Innovations* (Washington DC: Center for Hellenic Studies Press, 2013), pp. 289–305.

Droge, Arthur, *Homer or Moses? Early Christian Interpretations of the History of Culture* (Tübingen: Mohr Siebeck, 1989).

———— 'The apologetic dimensions of the *Ecclesiastical History*', in Harold W. Attridge and Gohei Hata, eds, *Eusebius, Christianity, and Judaism* (Detroit, MI: Wayne State University Press, 1992), pp. 492–509.

Dungan, David, *Constantine's Bible* (Minneapolis, MN: Fortress Press, 2006).

Edwards, Mark, 'Ammonius, teacher of Origen', *Journal of Ecclesiastical History* xliv (1993), pp. 169–81.

———— 'The Arian heresy and the oration to the saints', *Vigiliae Christianae* xlix (1995), pp. 379–87.

———— 'Clement of Alexandria and his doctrine of the Logos', *Vigiliae Christianae* liv (2000), pp. 159–77.

———— *Culture and Philosophy in the Age of Plotinus* (London: Duckworth, 2006).

Ferrar, W.J., ed. and trans., *The Proof of the Gospel* (Grand Rapids, MI: Baker Book House, 1981).

Finamore, John, 'Biography as self-promotion: Porphyry's *Vita Plotini*', *Dionysius* xxiii (2005), pp. 49–61.

Foakes-Jackson, F.J., *Eusebius Pamphili, Bishop of Caesarea in Palestine and First Christian Historian: A Study of the Man and His Writings* (Cambridge: Heffers, 1933).

Gallagher, Eugene, 'Piety and polity: Eusebius' defense of the Gospel', in J. Neusner, E.S. Frerichs and A.J. Levine, eds, *Religious Writings and Religious Systems*, vol. 2 (Atlanta, GA: Scholars Press, 1989), pp. 139–55.

—— 'Eusebius the apologist: The evidence of the preparation and the proof', *Studia Patristica* xxvi (1993), pp. 251–60.

Gifford, E.H., trans., *Preparation for the Gospel*, 2 vols (Grand Rapids, MI: Baker Book House, 1981).

Goodenough, E.R., 'The political philosophy of Hellenistic kingship', *Yale Classical Studies* i (1928), pp. 55–102.

Goulet-Cazé, Marie-Odile, 'Deux traités plotiniens chez Eusèbe de Césarée', in Cristina D'Ancona, ed., *The Libraries of the Neoplatonists* (Leiden: Brill: 2007), pp. 63–97.

Goulet, Richard, 'Porphyre, Ammonius, les deux Origène et les autres', in Richard Goulet, *Études sur les vies de philosophes de l'antiquité tardive* (Paris: Vrin, 2001), pp. 267–90.

—— 'Hypothèses récentes sur le traité de Porphyre *Contre les chrétiens*', in Michel Narcy and Éric Rebillard, eds, *Hellénisme et Christianisme* (Villeneuve-d'Ascq: Presses Universitaires du Septentrion, 2004), pp. 61–109.

Grafton, Anthony, and Megan Williams, *Christianity and the Transformation of the Book* (Cambridge, MA: Harvard University Press, 2006).

Grant, Robert, 'Eusebius and his lives of Origen', in *Forma futuri. Studi in onore del Cardinale Michele Pellegrino* (Turin: Bottega d'Erasmo, 1975), pp. 635–49.

—— *Eusebius as Church Historian* (Oxford: Clarendon Press, 1980).

Gressman, Hugo, ed., *Eusebius Werke*, vol. 3, *Die Theophanie*, Die griechischen christlichen Schriftsteller 11.2 (Leipzig: J.C. Hinrichs'sche Buchhandlung, 1904).

Gwynn, David, *The Eusebians: The Polemic of Athanasius of Alexandria and the Construction of the Arian Controversy* (Oxford: Oxford University Press, 2007).

—— 'From iconoclasm to Arianism: The construction of Christian tradition in the Iconoclast Controversy', *Greek, Roman and Byzantine Studies* xlvii (2007), pp. 225–51.

Hadot, Ilsetraut, 'Le commentaire philosophique continu dans l'antiquité', *L'Antiquité tardive* v (1997), pp. 169–76.

Hadot, Pierre, *Porphyre et Victorinus* (Paris: Études augustiniennes, 1968).

—— 'Théologie, exégèse, révélation, écriture dans la philosophie grecque', in Michel Tardieu, ed., *Les Règles de l'interprétation* (Paris: Les Éditions du Cerf, 1987), pp. 13–34.

—— *Philosophy as a Way of Life*, trans. Michael Chase (Oxford: Blackwell, 1995).

Hägg, Thomas, 'Hierocles the lover of truth and Eusebius the sophist', *Symbolae Osloenses* lxvii (1992), pp. 138–50.

Hanson, R.P.C., *The Search for the Christian Doctrine of God* (London: T&T Clark, 1988).

Hardwick, Michael, *Josephus as an Historical Source in Patristic Literature through Eusebius* (Atlanta, GA: Scholars Press, 1989).

Harries, Jill, 'Superfluous verbiage? Rhetoric and law in the age of Constantine and Julian', *Journal of Early Christian Studies* xix (2011), pp. 345–74.

Harrison, Evelyn B., 'The Constantinian portrait', *Dumbarton Oaks Papers* xxi (1967), pp. 79–96.

Heikel, Ivar A., ed., *Eusebius Werke*, vol. 1, *Über das Leben Constantins, Constantins Rede an die heilige Versammlung, Tricennatsrede an Constantin*, Die griechischen christlichen Schriftsteller 7 (Leipzig: J.C. Hinrichs'sche Buchhandlung, 1902)

——— ed., *Eusebius Werke*, vol. 6, *Die Demonstratio Evangelica*, Die griechischen christlichen Schriftsteller 23 (Berlin: Akademie-Verlag, 1913).

Henry, Paul, *Recherches sur la Préparation évangélique d'Eusèbe et l'édition perdue des oeuvres de Plotin publiée par Eustochius* (Paris: E. Leroux, 1935).

Heyne, Thomas, 'The devious Eusebius? An evaluation of the *Ecclesiastical History* and its critics', *Studia Patristica* xlvi (2010), pp. 325–31.

Hoffmann, Philippe, 'What was commentary in Late Antiquity? The example of the Neoplatonic commentators', in Mary Louise Gill and Pierre Pellegrin, eds, *Companion to Ancient Philosophy* (Oxford: Wiley-Blackwell, 2009), pp. 597–622.

Hollerich, Michael, 'Religion and politics in the writings of Eusebius: Reassessing the first "court theologian"', *Church History* lix (1990), pp. 309–25.

——— *Eusebius of Caesarea's Commentary on Isaiah: Christian Exegesis in the Age of Constantine* (Oxford: Clarendon Press, 1999).

——— 'Eusebius's *Commentary on the Psalms* and its place in the origins of Christian biblical scholarship', in Aaron P. Johnson and Jeremy Schott, eds, *Eusebius of Caesarea: Tradition and Innovations* (Washington DC: Center for Hellenic Studies Press, 2013), pp. 151–67.

Inowlocki, Sabrina, 'Eusebius of Caesarea's *Interpretatio Christiana* of Philo's *De vita contemplativa*', *Harvard Theological Review* xcvii (2004), pp. 305–28.

——— 'Eusebius' construction of a Christian culture in an apologetic context: Reading the *Praeparatio evangelica* as a library', in Sabrina Inowlocki and Claudio Zamagni, eds, *Reconsidering Eusebius* (Leiden: Brill, 2011), pp. 199–223.

Isaac, Benjamin, 'Eusebius and the geography of Roman provinces', in D.L. Kennedy, ed., *The Roman Army in the East, Journal of Roman Archaeology Supplement 18* (Ann Arbor, MI: Journal of Roman Archaeology, 1996), pp. 153–67.

Johnson, Aaron P., 'Ancestors as icons: The lives of Hebrew saints in Eusebius' *Praeparatio evangelica*', *Greek, Roman and Byzantine Studies* xliv (2004), pp. 245–64.

——— 'The blackness of Ethiopians: Classical ethnography and Eusebius' commentary on the Psalms', *Harvard Theological Review* xcic/2 (2006), pp. 179–200.

——— *Ethnicity and Argument in Eusebius' Praeparatio evangelica* (Oxford: Oxford University Press, 2006).

——— 'Eusebius' *Praeparatio evangelica* as literary experiment', in Scott F. Johnson, ed., *Greek Literature in Late Antiquity: Dynamism, Didacticism, Classicism* (Aldershot: Ashgate, 2006), pp. 67–89.

——— 'Arbiter of the oracular: Reading religion in Porphyry of Tyre', in Andrew Cain and Noel Lenski, eds, *The Power of Religion in Late Antiquity* (Burlington, VT: Ashgate, 2009), pp. 103–15.

——— 'Rethinking the authenticity of Porphyry, *Contra Christianos*, fr. 1', *Studia Patristica* xlvi (2010), pp. 53–8.

——— 'Eusebius the educator', in Sabrina Inowlocki and Claudio Zamagni, eds, *Reconsidering Eusebius* (Leiden: Brill, 2011), pp. 99–118.

—— 'The tenth book of Eusebius' *General Elementary Introduction*: A critique of the Wallace-Hadrill thesis', *Journal of Theological Studies* lxii/1 (2011), pp. 144–60.

——'Hellenism and its discontents', in Scott F. Johnson, ed., *Oxford Handbook of Late Antiquity* (Oxford: Oxford University Press, 2012), pp. 437–66.

—— 'Philosophy, Hellenicity, law: Porphyry on Origen, again', *Journal of Hellenic Studies* cxxxii (2012), pp. 55–69.

——'Introduction', in Aaron P. Johnson and Jeremy Schott, eds, *Eusebius of Caesarea: Tradition and Innovations* (Washington DC: Center for Hellenic Studies Press, 2013).

——*Religion and Identity in Porphyry of Tyre: The Limits of Hellenism in Late Antiquity* (Cambridge: Cambridge University Press, 2013).

—— 'The author of the *Against Hierocles*: A response to Borzì and Jones', *Journal of Theological Studies* lxiv (2014), pp. 574–94.

—— 'Ethnicity: Greeks, Jews and Christians', in Jeremy McInerney, ed., *Blackwell Guide to Ethnicity in the Ancient Mediterranean* (Oxford: Wiley-Blackwell), forthcoming.

——'Words at war: Textual violence in Eusebius', in Kate Cooper and Jamie Wood, eds, *Fear and Belonging in Late Antiquity: Social Control and the Spectre of Violence in Household, School, and Monastery* (Cambridge: Cambridge University Press), forthcoming.

Johnson, Scott F., 'Travel, cartography, and cosmology', in Scott F. Johnson, ed., *The Oxford Handbook of Late Antiquity* (Oxford: Oxford University Press, 2012), pp. 562–94.

Johnson, William A., *Readers and Reading Culture in the High Roman Empire* (Oxford: Oxford University Press, 2010).

Jones, Christopher. 'Apollonius of Tyana in Late Antiquity', in Scott F. Johnson, ed., *Greek Literature in Late Antiquity: Dynamism, Didacticism, Classicism* (Aldershot: Ashgate, 2006), pp. 49–64.

——*Philostratus: Apollonius of Tyana*, Loeb Classical Library 458 (Cambridge, MA: Harvard University Press, 2006).

Kalligas, Paul, 'Traces of Longinus' library in Eusebius' *Praeparatio evangelica*', *Classical Quarterly* li (2001), pp. 584–98.

Kitzinger, Ernst, 'The cult of images in the age before iconoclasm', *Dumbarton Oaks Papers* viii (1954), pp. 83–150.

Klostermann, Erich, ed., *Eusebius Werke*, vol. 4, *Gegen Marcell, Über die kirchliche Theologie*, Die griechischen christlichen Schriftsteller 14 (Leipzig: J.C. Hinrichs'sche Buchhandlung, 1906).

Knipe, Sergio, 'Subjugating the divine: Iamblichus on the theurgic evocation', in Andrew Cain and Noel Lenski, eds, *The Power of Religion in Late Antiquity* (Burlington, VT: Ashgate, 2009), pp. 93–102.

Kofsky, Aryeh, 'Eusebius of Caesarea and the Christian–Jewish polemic', in Ora Limor and Guy G. Stroumsa, eds, *Contra Iudaeos: Ancient and Medieval Polemics between Christians and Jews* (Tübingen: Mohr Siebeck, 1996), pp. 59–83.

——*Eusebius of Caesarea against the Pagans* (Leiden: Brill, 2000).

Krannich, Torsten, Christoph Schubert and Claudia Sode, eds, *Die ikonoklastische Synode von Hiereia 754* (Tübingen: Mohr Siebeck, 2002).

Lake, Kirsopp, trans., *Eusebius: Ecclesiastical History, Books 1–5*, Loeb Classical Library 153 (Cambridge, MA: Harvard University Press, 1980).

Lamberton, Robert, *Homer the Theologian* (Berkeley, CA: University of California Press, 1986).

——'The Neoplatonists and their books', in Margalit Finkelberg and Guy G. Stroumsa, eds, *Homer, the Bible, and Beyond* (Leiden: Brill, 2003), pp. 195–212.

Lawlor, Hugh Jackson, and J.E.L. Oulton, eds and trans., *Eusebius Bishop of Caesarea: The Ecclesiastical History and Martyrs of Palestine* (London: SPCK, 1954).

Lawlor, Hugh Jackson, *Eusebiana* (Amsterdam: Philo Press, 1973).

Le Boulluec, Alain, *La Notion d'hérésie* (Paris: Études augustiniennes, 1985).

Leadbetter, Bill, 'The illegitimacy of Constantine and the birth of the Tetrarchy', in S.N.C. Lieu and Dominic Montserrat, eds, *Constantine: History, Historiography and Legend* (London and New York, NY: Routledge, 1998), pp. 74–85.

Lee, Samuel, ed., *Eusebius, Bishop of Caesarea, on the Theophania, or Divine Manifestation of Our Lord and Saviour Jesus Christ. A Syriac Version. Edited from an Ancient Manuscript Recently Discovered by S. Lee* (London: Society for the Publication of Oriental Texts, 1842).

Lee, Samuel, trans., *Eusebius, Bishop of Caesarea on the Theophania* (Cambridge: Cambridge University Press, 1843).

Lenski, Noel, 'The reign of Constantine', in Noel Lenski, ed., *The Cambridge Companion to the Age of Constantine* (Cambridge: Cambridge University Press, 2006), pp. 59–90.

——'*Libertas* and the fusion of Roman and Christian values', in G. Crifò, ed., *Atti dell'Accademia romanistica costantiniana XVIII 2007* (Perugia and Naples: Edizioni scientifiche italiana, 2011), pp. 235–60.

Lienhard, Joseph, 'Basil of Caesarea, Marcellus of Ancyra, and "Sabellius"', *Church History* lviii (1989), pp. 157–67.

——*Contra Marcellum: Marcellus of Ancyra and Fourth-Century Theology* (Washington DC: Catholic University of America Press, 1999).

Louth, Andrew, 'The date of Eusebius' *Historia ecclesiastica*', *Journal of Theological Studies* xli (1990), pp. 111–23.

——'Introduction', in G.A. Williamson, trans., *Eusebius: History of the Church* (London: Penguin, 1990).

Luibhéid, Colm, *Eusebius of Caesarea and the Arian Crisis* (Dublin: Irish Academic Press, 1981).

Lyman, Rebecca, *Christology and Cosmology: Models of Divine Activity in Origen, Eusebius and Athanasius* (Oxford: Clarendon Press, 1993).

Maas, Michael and Edward Mathews, *Exegesis and Empire in the Early Byzantine Mediterranean* (Tübingen: Mohr Siebeck, 2003).

Mansfeld, Jaap, *Prolegomena: Questions to Be Settled before the Study of an Author, or a Text* (Leiden: Brill, 1994).

Markschies, Christoph, 'Eusebius als Schriftsteller: Beobachtungen zum sechsten Buch der Kirchengeschichte', in A.M. Castagno, ed., *La biografia di Origene fra storia e agiografia* (Villa Verucchio: Pazzini Stampatore Editore, 2005), pp. 33–50; repr. in Christoph Markschies, *Origenes und sein Erbe: Gesammelte Studien* (Berlin: Walter de Gruyter, 2007).

Matthews, John, 'Hostages, philosophers, pilgrims, and the diffusion of ideas in the late Roman Mediterranean and Near East', in F.M. Clover and R.S. Humphreys, eds, *Tradition and Innovation in Late Antiquity* (Madison, WI: University of Wisconsin Press, 1989), pp. 29–49.

Mercati, G., 'La grande lacuna delle Ecloghe profetiche di Eusebio di Cesarea', in *Mémorial L. Petit* (Bucharest: Institut français d'études byzantines, 1948), pp. 1–3.

Millar, Fergus, *The Emperor in the Roman World* (London: Duckworth, 1977).

Momigliano, Arnaldo, 'Pagan and Christian historiography in the fourth century', in Arnaldo Momigliano, ed., *The Conflict Between Paganism and Christianity in the Fourth Century* (Oxford: Clarendon Press, 1963), pp. 79–99.

—— *The Development of Greek Biography* (Cambridge, MA: Harvard University Press, 1993).

Morgan, Teresa, 'Eusebius of Caesarea and Christian historiography', *Athenaeum* xciii (2005), pp. 193–208.

Morlet, Sébastien, 'Écrire l'histoire selon Eusèbe de Césarée', *L'Information littéraire* lvii (2005), pp. 3–15.

—— 'Entre histoire et exégèse. Réflexions sur la logique narrative du livre I de l'*Histoire ecclésiastique* d'Eusèbe', *Adamantius* xiv (2008), pp. 191–8.

—— *La Démonstration évangélique d'Eusèbe de Césarée. Étude sur l'apologétique chrétienne à l'époque de Constantin* (Paris: Études augustiniennes, 2009).

—— 'Eusebius' polemic against Porphyry: A reassessment', in Sabrina Inowlocki and Claudio Zamagni, eds, *Reconsidering Eusebius* (Leiden: Brill, 2011), pp. 119–50.

—— 'Que savons-nous du *Contre Porphyre* d'Eusèbe?', *Revue d'études Grecques* cxxv (2012), pp. 473–514.

—— 'Origen as an exegetical source in Eusebius' *Prophetical Extracts*', in Aaron P. Johnson and Jeremy Schott, eds, *Eusebius of Caesarea: Tradition and Innovations* (Washington DC: Center for Hellenic Studies Press, 2013), pp. 207–37.

Morlet, Sébastien, and Lorenzo Perrone, eds, *Eusèbe de Césarée. Histoire ecclésiastique. Commentaire, Tome 1: Études d'introduction. Anagôgê* (Paris: Les Belles Lettres; Les Éditions du Cerf, 2012).

Morlet, Sébastien, ed., *Le Traité de Porphyre contre les chrétiens* (Paris: Études augustiniennes, 2011).

Mosshammer, Alden A., *The Chronicle of Eusebius and the Greek Chronographic Tradition* (Lewisburg, PA: Bucknell University Press, 1979).

Mras, Karl, ed., *Eusebius Werke*, vol. 8, *Die Praeparatio Evangelica*, Die griechischen christlichen Schriftsteller 43.1–2 (Berlin: Akademie-Verlag, 1954, 1956)

Neri, Valerio, 'Romani, greci, barbari: identità etniche ed universalismi nell'opera di Eusebio di Cesarea', *Adamantius* xvi (2010), pp. 63–87.

Nestle, Eberhard and Barbara and Kurt Aland, eds, *Novum Testamentum Graece* (Stuttgart: Deutsche Bibelgesellschaft, 1898–1993).

Nestle, Eberhard, 'Alttestamentliches aus Eusebius', *Zeitschrift fur die alttestamentliche Wissenschaft* xxix (1909), pp. 57–8.

Notley, R. Steven and Ze'ev Safrai, eds and trans., *Eusebius, Onomasticon: A Triglott Edition with Notes and Commentary* (Leiden: Brill, 2005).

Oliver, Harold, 'The epistle of Eusebius to Carpianus: Textual tradition and translation', *Novum Testamentum* iii (1959), pp. 138–45.

Olson, Ken, 'A Eusebian reading of the *Testimonium Flavianum*', in Aaron P. Johnson and Jeremy Schott, eds, *Eusebius of Caesarea: Tradition and Innovations* (Washington DC: Center for Hellenic Studies Press, 2013), pp. 97–114.

Olster, David, *Roman Defeat, Christian Response, and the Literary Construction of the Jew* (Philadelphia, PA: University of Pennsylvania Press, 1984).

Opitz, Hans-Georg, 'Die Zeitfolge des arianischen Streites von den Anfängen bis zum Jahre 328', *Zeitschrift für die Neutestamentliche Wissenschaft* xxxiii (1934), pp. 131–59.

Opitz, Hans-Georg, ed., *Athanasius Werke*, vol. 3 (part 1), *Urkunden zur Geschichte des arianischen Streites* (Berlin: Walter de Gruyter, 1934).

Oulton, J.E.L., trans., *Eusebius: Ecclesiastical History, Books 6–10*, Loeb Classical Library 265 (Cambridge, MA: Harvard University Press, 1980).

Parvis, Sara, *Marcellus of Ancyra and the Lost Years of the Arian Controversy, 325–345* (Oxford: Oxford University Press, 2006).

Patrich, J., 'Caesarea in the time of Eusebius', in Sabrina Inowlocki and Claudio Zamagni, eds, *Reconsidering Eusebius* (Leiden: Brill, 2011), pp. 1–24.

Pearse, Roger, ed., *Eusebius of Caesarea: Gospel Problems and Solutions* (Ipswich: Chieftain Publishing, 2010).

Perrone, Lorenzo, 'Eusebius of Caesarea as a Christian writer', in Avner Raban and Kenneth Holum, eds, *Caesarea Maritima: A Retrospective after Two Millennia* (Leiden: Brill, 1996), pp. 515–30.

Prestige, George Léonard, '*agen[n]ētos* and *gen[n]ētos*, and kindred words in Eusebius and the early Arians', *Journal of Theological Studies* xxiv (1923), pp. 486–96.

—— *God in Patristic Thought* (London: SPCK, 1936).

Raban, Avner, and Kenneth Holum, eds, *Caesarea Maritima: A Retrospective after Two Millennia* (Leiden: Brill, 1996).

Ramelli, Ilaria, *Bardaisan of Edessa: A Reassessment of the Evidence and a New Interpretation* (Piscataway, NJ: Gorgias Press, 2009).

—— 'Origen, Eusebius, the doctrine of apokatastasis, and its relation to Christology', in Aaron P. Johnson and Jeremy Schott, eds, *Eusebius of Caesarea: Tradition and Innovations* (Washington DC: Center for Hellenic Studies Press, 2013), pp. 307–23.

Rapp, Claudia, 'Imperial ideology in the making: Eusebius of Caesarea on Constantine as "Bishop"', *Journal of Theological Studies* xlix (1998), pp. 685–95.

Richter, Daniel, 'Plutarch on Isis and Osiris: Text, cult, and cultural appropriation', *Transactions of the American Philological Association* cxxxi (2001), pp. 191–216.

Ricken, Friedo, 'Die Logoslehre des Eusebios von Caesarea und der Mittelplatonismus', *Theologie und Philosophie* xlii (1967), pp. 341–58.

Riedweg, Christoph, 'Porphyrios über Christus und die Christen: De philosophia ex oraculis haurienda und Adversus Christianos im Vergleich', in *L'Aplogétique chrétienne gréco-latine à l'époque prénicénienne*, Entretiens sur l'antiquité classique, t. LI (Geneva: Fondation Hardt, 2005), pp. 151–203.

Rist, John, *Plotinus: Road to Reality* (Cambridge: Cambridge University Press, 1967).

—— 'Basil's Neoplatonism', in Paul J. Fedwick, ed., *Basil of Caesarea: Christian, Humanist, Ascetic* (Toronto: PIMS, 1981), pp. 135–220.

Rives, James, 'The decree of Decius and the religion of empire', *Journal of Roman Studies* lxxxix (1999), pp. 135–54.

Robertson, David, *Word and Meaning in Ancient Alexandria* (Burlington, VT: Ashgate, 2008).

Robertson, Jon, *Christ as Mediator: A Study of the Theologies of Eusebius of Caesarea, Marcellus of Ancyra, and Athanasius of Alexandria* (Oxford: Oxford University Press, 2007).

Rondeau, M.-J., 'Eusèbe de Césarée. Le Commentaire sur les psaumes', in M.-J. Rondeau and J. Kirchmeyer, eds, *Dictionnaire de spiritualité* (Paris: Beauchesne, 1961), cols 1688–90.

—— *Les Commentaires patristiques du Psautier*, Orientalia Christiana Analecta 220 (Rome: Pontificium Institutum Studiorum Orientalium, 1985).

Sahas, Daniel, *Icon and Logos* (Toronto: University of Toronto Press, 1986).

Sansterre, J.-M., 'Eusèbe de Césarée et la naissance de la théorie cesaropapiste', *Byzantion* xlii (1972), pp. 131–95, 532–94.

Schott, Jeremy, *Christianity, Empire, and the Making of Religion in Late Antiquity* (Philadelphia, PA: University of Pennsylvania Press, 2008).

—— 'Quotations from Origen and the theologies of textuality in Eusebius' *Apology for Origen*, *Against Marcellus*, and *On Ecclesiastical Theology*' (unpublished paper delivered at the Society of Biblical Literature annual conference, Atlanta, GA, 2010).

—— 'Eusebius' *Panegyric on the Building of Churches* (*HE* 10.4.2–72): Aesthetics and the politics of Christian architecture', in Sabrina Inowlocki and Claudio Zamagni, eds, *Reconsidering Eusebius* (Leiden: Brill, 2011), pp. 177–98.

—— 'Textuality and territorialization: Eusebius' exegeses of Isaiah, and empire', in Aaron P. Johnson and Jeremy Schott, eds, *Eusebius of Caesarea: Tradition and Innovations* (Washington DC: Center for Hellenic Studies Press, 2013), pp. 169–88.

Schwartz, Eduard, 'Eusebios von Caesarea', *Realencyclopädie der classischen Altertumswissenschaft*, vol. 11 (Stuttgart: J.B. Metzlersche Buchhandlung, 1909), cols 1370–439.

Schwartz, Eduard, ed., *Eusebius Werke*, vol. 2 (parts 1–3), *Die Kirchengeschichte*, Die griechischen christlichen Schriftsteller 9.1–3 (Leipzig: J.C. Hinrichs'sche Buchhandlung, 1903, 1908, 1909).

Sedley, David, 'Plato's *Auctoritas* and the rebirth of the commentary tradition', in Jonathan

Barnes and Miriam Griffin, eds, *Philosophia Togata II: Plato and Aristotle at Rome* (Oxford: Clarendon Press, 1997), pp. 110–29.

Shaw, Gregory, 'Theurgy: Rituals of unification in the Neoplatonism of Iamblichus', *Traditio* xli (1995), pp. 1–28.

Sirinelli, Jean, and Édouard des Places, *Eusèbe de Césarée. La Préparation évangélique, Livre I*, Sources Chrétiennes 206 (Paris: Les Éditions du Cerf, 1974).

Sirinelli, Jean, *Les Vues historiques d'Eusèbe de Césarée durant la période prénicéene* (Dakar: Université de Dakar, 1961).

Snyder, H. Gregory, *Teachers and Texts in the Ancient World* (London and New York, NY: Routledge, 2000).

Spoerl, Kelley, 'Anti-Arian polemic in Eusebius of Caesarea's *Ecclesiastical Theology*', *Studia Patristica* xxxii (1997), pp. 33–8.

Stephenson, Paul, *Constantine: Roman Emperor, Christian Victor* (New York, NY: Overlook Press, 2009).

Stevenson, James, ed., *A New Eusebius* (London: SPCK, 1957).

Stevenson, James, *Studies in Eusebius* (Cambridge: Cambridge University Press, 1929).

Stoneman, Richard, *Palmyra and Its Empire* (Ann Arbor, MI: University of Michigan Press, 1995).

—— *The Ancient Oracles: Making the Gods Speak* (New Haven, CT: Yale University Press, 2011).

Strutwolf, Holger, *Die Trinitätstheologie und Christologie des Euseb von Caesarea* (Göttingen: Vandenhoeck & Ruprecht, 1999).

Swain, Simon, 'Defending Hellenism: Philostratus, *In Honour of Apollonius*', in M. Edwards, M. Goodman and S. Price, eds, *Apologetics in the Roman Empire* (Oxford: Oxford University Press, 1999), pp. 157–96.

Swain, Simon, and M.J. Edwards, eds, *Approaching Late Antiquity* (Oxford: Oxford University Press, 2004).

Tabernee, William, 'Eusebius' "Theology of Persecution": As seen in the various editions of his Church history', *Journal of Early Christian Studies* v (1997), pp. 319–34.

Toda, Satoshi, 'The Syriac version of Eusebius' *Ecclesiastical History* revisited', *Studia Patristica* xlvi (2010), pp. 333–8.

Trombley, Frank, *Hellenic Religion and Christianization*, 2 vols (Leiden: Brill, 2001).

Ulrich, Jörg, *Euseb von Caesarea und die Juden. Studien zur Rolle der Juden in der Theologie des Eusebius von Caesarea* (Berlin and New York, NY: Walter de Gruyter, 1999).

Van Dam, Raymond, *Remembering Constantine at the Milvian Bridge* (Cambridge: Cambridge University Press, 2011).

Van Liefferinge, Carine, '"Ethniques" et "Hellènes". Quelques réflexions sur la portée nationale du paganisme', in Edouard Delruelle and Vinciane Pirenne-Delforge, eds, *Kêpoi: de la religion à la philosophie: mélanges offerts à André Motte, Kernos Supplément 11* (Liège: Centre international d'étude de la religion grecque antique, 2001), pp. 247–55.

Van Nuffelen, Peter, 'Eusebius and images of truth in the *Life of Constantine*', in Aaron P. Johnson and Jeremy Schott, eds, *Eusebius of Caesarea: Tradition and Innovations* (Washington DC: Center for Hellenic Studies Press, 2013), pp. 133–49.

Vanderspoel, John, 'The background to Augustine's denial of religious plurality', in H.A. Meynell, ed., *Grace, Politics and Desire: Essays on Augustine* (Calgary: University of Calgary Press, 1990), pp. 179–93.

Verdoner, Marie, 'Transgeneric crosses. Apologetics in the Church history of Eusebius', in Anders-Christian Jacobsen and Jörg Ulrich, eds, *Three Greek Apologists. Drei griechische Apologeten* (Frankfurt am Main: Peter Lang, 2007), pp. 75–92.

—— *Narrated Reality: The Historia Ecclesiastica of Eusebius of Caesarea* (Frankfurt am Main: Peter Lang, 2011).

Vinzent, Markus, *Asterius von Kappadokien: Die theologischen Fragmente, Einleitung, kritischer Text, Übersetzung und Kommentar* (Leiden: Brill, 1993).

Vinzent, Markus, ed., *Markell von Ankyra: Die Fragmente. Der Brief an Julius von Rom* (Leiden: Brill, 1996).

Wallace-Hadrill, David Sutherland, *Eusebius of Caesarea* (London: A.R. Mowbray & Co., Ltd., 1960).

Wallraff, Martin, and Laura Mecella, eds, *Die Kestoi des Julius Africanus und ihre Überlieferung* (Berlin and New York, NY: Walter de Gruyter, 2009).

Westerink, L.G., *Anonymous Prolegomena to Platonic Philosophy* (Amsterdam: North-Holland Publishing Co., 1962).

Williams, Michael S., *Authorised Lives in Early Christian Biography: Between Eusebius and Augustine* (Cambridge: Cambridge University Press, 2008).

Williams, Robert, *Bishop Lists: Formation of Apostolic Succession in Ecclesiastical Crises* (Piscataway, NJ: Gorgias Press, 2005).

Williams, Rowan, *Arius: Heresy and Tradition* (London: SCM Press, 2001).

Williamson, G.A., trans., *Eusebius: History of the Church* (London: Penguin, 1990).

Willing, Meike, *Eusebius von Cäsarea als Häreseograph* (Berlin: Walter de Gruyter, 2008).

Wilson, Anna, 'Biographical models: The Constantinian period and beyond', in S.N.C. Lieu and Dominic Montserrat, eds, *Constantine: History, Historiography and Legend* (London and New York, NY: Routledge, 1998), pp. 112–21.

Witt, R.E., 'The Plotinian Logos and its Stoic basis', *Classical Quarterly* xxv (1931), pp. 103–11.

Yoshiko Reed, Annette, 'Beyond the land of Nod: Syriac images of Asia and the historiography of "the West"', *History of Religions* xlix (2009), pp. 48–87.

Young, Frances, *Biblical Exegesis and the Formation of Christian Culture* (Peabody, MA: Hendrickson, 2002).

Zamagni, Claudio, *Les Questions et réponses sur les évangiles d'Eusèbe de Césarée*, Ph.D. dissertation (University of Lausanne, 2003).

—— 'Eusebius' exegesis between Alexandria and Antioch', in Sabrina Inowlocki and Claudio Zamagni, eds, *Reconsidering Eusebius* (Leiden: Brill, 2011), pp. 151–76.

—— 'New perspectives on Eusebius' *Questions and Answers on the Gospels*: The manuscripts', in Aaron P. Johnson and Jeremy Schott, eds, *Eusebius of Caesarea: Tradition and Innovations* (Washington DC: Center for Hellenic Studies Press, 2013), pp. 239–61.

Zambon, Marco, *Porphyre et le moyen-platonisme* (Paris: Vrin, 2002).

—— 'Edizione e prima circolazione degli scritti di Plotino: Porfirio ed Eusebio di Cesarea', in Walter Beierwaltes and Matteo Bianchetti, eds, *Plotino e l'ontologia* (Milan: Albo versorio, 2006), pp. 55–78.

—— 'Porfirio e Origene uno status quaestionis', in Sébastien Morlet, ed., *Le Traité de Porphyre contre les chrétiens* (Paris: Études augustiniennes, 2011), pp. 107–64.

Ziegler, Joseph, ed., *Eusebius Werke*, vol. 9, *Der Jesajakommentar*, Die griechischen christlichen Schriftsteller 56 (Berlin: Akademie-Verlag, 1975).

INDEX